Study Guide

for

American Government: Continuity and Change

2008 Edition

to accompany

Comprehensive, Alternate, and Texas Edition versions

prepared by

John Ben Sutter

Houston Community College

New York Boston San Francisco
London Toronto Sydney Tokyo Singapore Madrid
Mexico City Munich Paris Cape Town Hong Kong Montreal

Study Guide for American Government: Continuity and Change, 2008 Edition

Copyright ©2008 Pearson Education, Inc.

ISBN: 0-321-47995-5

1 2 3 4 5 6 7 8 9 10–OPM–10 09 08 07

TABLE OF CONTENTS

Note: Chapters 20-26 accompany *American Government, Texas Edition*

SECTION I

STUDY SKILLS

This section is designed to give you a number of ideas about how you can learn better study skills. Studying is an individual thing—what works for you might not work for others. So please use these hints to think about what tips you can use to improve your own skills.

If a suggestion doesn't work for you, try something else. But consciously think about how you study best, what kinds of settings work for you, what times of day help you to recall facts, and so on. Often, your study skills improve when you simply think consciously about how to study. If you need more help, see your professor, consult the suggested Web pages at the end of this section, and or find out what kind of help is available on campus. Most campuses today offer tutoring and counseling, often including classes on studying.

An overview of this section:

- **Note-taking**

- **Reading**

- **Taking Tests**
    - **Essay Tests**
    - **Objective Tests**

- **"The Ten Traps of Studying"**

- **Web sites of Interest**

NOTE-TAKING

Good notes often make the difference between good and superior students. Bad note-taking often serves only to confuse. No one system works for everyone, but here are a number of rules of thumb that should be helpful as you devise your own system.

The main rule of note-taking is to do what you find helpful and comfortable. Often comparing your notes to those of your colleagues or asking you professor to look at one day's notes will help you determine how well you perform this task.

1) **GO TO CLASS!!!** The single easiest way—actually, the only way—to figure out what the professor will emphasize on a test, is to attend class daily. Missing class and getting the notes from someone else is a poor substitute for attendance. Besides, "repetition is the mother of learning," as the saying goes. And if you hear it AND write it, you will be more likely to remember it.

2) **Think about taking notes BEFORE you start.** In other words, have a plan. A common way of doing this is to draw a vertical line down the paper dividing it into two parts. Take notes to the right of the line. Save the left to add information that is given to you later, for your own thoughts on the subject and for notes about the information, as you study for tests later. An alternative is to use a spiral notebook (or similar style) and use the right-hand page for notes and the left-hand page for comments, etc. Or, use a loose leaf binder so you can sort your notes and add handouts. There are many ways to organize your notes.

3) **Sit up front!** This will help you concentrate (particularly in subjects that you do not find fascinating). You will also appear interested and excited to the professor; never a bad thing!

4) **Read and prepare for class IN ADVANCE!** It will be much easier to discern the important points in a lecture if you are already familiar with the material. You will also be able to answer questions asked in class. Plus, repetition is an excellent way to remember material. It also helps to review your notes from previous classes prior to each session. This will help you at exam time, and help you to reconnect with the material and see links among topics.

5) **Arrive early and stay for the whole class.** The first sentence or two uttered by the professor often tell you what the lecture will be about; the lecture will make less sense without the context. Also, a large amount of information is often given out in the last ten minutes of class as a professor strives to cover the material. If you are putting your stuff away and zipping your book bag, not only are you being rude and making obnoxious levels of noise, but you are missing important material.

6) **LISTEN closely to the lecture or discussion.** In particular try to pick out the following:

> •ideas and concepts
> •signal words: " in contrast," "on the other hand," "What I mean here is," "The important idea is," and so on.
> •If something is unclear, <u>ask a question</u>!

7) **Take Notes, not Dictation!** Your job is not to take down every word but to summarize the points and note the facts. Use indentation, underlining, highlighting, and/or outlining to get the important information down.

> •Be brief, get main ideas down
> •Use your own words
> •Use symbols to emphasize important points, such as * or !
> •Leave spaces for words and ideas you missed or that are covered out of sequence

8) **You should always write down:**

> •names
> •dates and significant events
> •concepts, ideas, or phrases that are repeated
> •formulas, charts, drawings, etc. put on the board
> •examples given by the professor
> •professor's biases, if identifiable

9) **Find a way to make the subject interesting!** You won't remember what you consider boring and useless. You can make anything interesting with a positive attitude and a little creativity.

10) **Do not abbreviate unless** you will know later what the abbreviation stands for. Writing SC throughout your notes could mean social contract, Supreme Court, or South Carolina. Be consistent, whatever you choose. Standard abbreviations that might save you time include the following:

w/	=	with	Const	=	Constitution
w/o	=	without	dem	=	democracy
#	=	number	K	=	contract
vs	=	versus	pres	=	president
=	=	equals	nat'l	=	national
fed'l	=	federal			

11)   **Review early and often!** Skim your lectures notes before each session of class. It is a good idea to review your notes immediately after class, while the information is still fresh, so you can correct mistakes and spell out problematic abbreviations, etc. Add to your notes. Jot down ideas you have had since class, how the information in one chapter relates to that of another chapter, compare your notes from class with your reading notes and integrate them. It is helpful to outline your notes and keep a list of definitions as you go. Both will make studying for tests easier.

READING

Yes, you are in college, so you know how to read. But how do you attack and comprehend boring or difficult material? Many students simply "get through" the reading assignment and then cannot answer questions in class and do not really understand the material. In order to read critically and analytically, you must be careful, thoughtful, and have a plan of attack before you dive in.

It is probably best that you do NOT use a highlighter. At least not in the way most students use them. Many students often color huge passages thoughtlessly as they read. This is not helpful in the long run. Don't highlight material in a chapter when you first open your textbook. In your first pass through the material, how do you know what's important and what's not? If you plunge right into the material, it, at first, might all seem important, and each page ends up entirely yellow from your highlighter! Set the highlighter down. Take time to consider what you're reading. Employ a style of **active reading.** This takes more time initially, but in the long run will save you time, because you will understand the material better, remember it longer, and be able to analyze what you have read.

Rules of Reading

- **Skim the chapter, book, or article first before you try to read it.** This provides you with a road map to the contents of the piece.

- **Use the guides provided by the author and publisher.** Tables of contents, appendices, tables of charts and graphs, glossaries, indices, etc., are there for you to use. They should help you get a handle on the material.

    - **Scan the table of contents.** Often textbooks provide more than one table of contents—an abbreviated one and a complete one.
    - **Read the preface!** In the preface, the author (or some other expert) tells you what they want you to get out of their book or why they wrote it.
    - **Examine the material in BOLD in the chapter:** Look at the chapter subheadings, the terms in the outside margins; examine the pictures and what's printed underneath them
    - **Use the end pieces:** appendices, indices, glossaries, etc.

•**Decide what you think you will learn from the work.** Think about what you are about to read. What questions do you have? Do you think the author has a bias? If so, what bias and why do you think there is one? Why did the professor assign this reading? What does he/she expect you to get out of it? Here, it is often helpful to look at your syllabus; the topic may give you some understanding of why this piece was assigned.

•**Read the piece fairly quickly** to get more information about main ideas and intent. Mark any passages that look particularly difficult. Circle unfamiliar words and phrases.

•**Now you are ready to really read the piece.**

   •**Take a notebook and a pen** and keep notes as you read. Write an outline on paper and use marginal notes in the book to argue with (or sometimes agree with) the author.
   •Never read for more than an hour without a break; if your eyes glaze over and you start to fall asleep, stop and **take a break**. (This means you cannot do your reading immediately prior to class—you need to plan ahead.)
   •At the end of each section or subsection, **stop and ask yourself what you just read.** Does it make sense? What were the main ideas? Any definitions you may need to know on a test? If you can't answer those questions, you need to reread the passages with more concentration.
   •At the end of the whole piece, you should be able to **identify the author's main points**. If not, you need to reread the piece or, if you took good reading notes, reviewing your notes should be sufficient.
   •Keep a good collegiate dictionary handy whenever you're reading. If you come across a word you don't understand, **look it up!** If you don't know what that word means, you might miss the meaning of the entire sentence, or even the entire section. (And never pass up a chance to broaden your vocabulary; words are your tools in your effort to communicate your ideas effectively to others.)

•Most texts offer **summaries and questions** at the end of a chapter or in a study guide such as this one. Use them to ensure your understanding of the material. You should be able to answer the questions posed and be able to flesh out the information provided in a summary. If not, again that is a signal that you need to review the material again.

•The best way to know you have mastered the material is to try to explain it to someone else. Think of this as a self-test. Discuss the material with your classmates, tell your roommate or spouse or friend about it, or make your family listen to your summaries.

TAKING TESTS

ALWAYS:

- **Read or go over the entire test** before beginning to answer questions. You could quickly read through the whole essay exam, but don't try to read over an entire ten-page multiple-choice exam. You should go over it so you know what to expect. If it is a multi-page exam and is mostly multiple-choice questions but has an essay buried at the end, you're in trouble if you find that out 5 minutes before the end of class!

- **Make choices** if they are offered. In a multi-choice exam, eliminate the answers you know are right so that you can make a choice between fewer options.

- **Allot your time** carefully and **be aware of time during the** test, but do not set watch alarms; they will disturb others. If a question is worth 20 percent, you should spend only 20 percent of your time on it.

- Depending on your style and level of test anxiety, **choose the order** in which you will address the questions. Answer the easiest question first if you need a confidence builder, or answer the most difficult if you need to get it out of the way while you are fresh.

- **Be neat and legible.** If you are answering an objective-style exam on a Scantron, be sure to use a number two pencil and have a good, clean eraser. If you make an error, erase the incorrect mark cleanly and completely or you might lose points because of a mechanical grading error!

- **Ask questions** if you are unclear about content or procedure.

- Save time to **proofread and double check** your answers at the end.

HINTS for Essay Exams

1)   **TIME**

The most challenging part of taking essay exams is often the management of time during the exam. This is extremely important, especially for those of you who often have trouble finishing an exam. Exams are more than just tests of knowledge. They teach and reinforce important lessons about discipline, organization, and your ability to communicate what you know. Exams place a premium on your ability to make up your mind about issues and concepts, as well as to organize your thoughts and write <u>concisely</u> and <u>lucidly</u> (clearly) about topics within a given time period.

> *Hint 1*: Start with the questions that are ***worth the most points***. Then if you run out of time, you can quickly jot down identifications and short answers. You cannot write an essay in five minutes!
>
> *Hint 2*: ***Organize and think before you start to write***, preferably before you come to class to take the exam. You should study by thinking of possible questions so that you are half-way there while still studying. This will save you time during the exam period.

2) CLARITY

Clarity is essential to earning a good grade on an essay. It is not enough to simply jot down all of the facts you have studied. You must address the question as asked. For example, if the question says to address the impact of the Anti-Federalists on the U.S. government, do not include a discussion of Congressional committees. You don't get points for writing a great essay if it doesn't answer the question your professor asks!

A competent exam answer will be clear and well organized. You must have a point or an argument, as well as convey the facts.

> *Hint 3*: Be sure you ***know what the question means*** before you start writing!
>
> *Hint 4*: Use an outline to ***organize*** your thoughts before writing.
>
> *Hint 5*: Pay attention to ***keywords*** within the question and use them to understand the question and formulate the answer. For example:
>> Analyze
>> Compare and contrast
>> Discuss
>
> *Hint 6*: Keep your ***focus;*** don't wander off the subject.
>
> *Hint 7*: Read and respond to ***all parts*** of the question. Often students neglect to answer part of a question.

3) LANGUAGE

A good exam must be legible and readable in terms of grammar, punctuation and style as well as content. If your grammar and syntax are too convoluted, your meaning will be hopelessly obscured.

> *Hint 8*: Do not use words you can not define, and be sure to define all concepts you use. For example, if the question asks you to discuss the nature of federalism, ALWAYS begin with a **definition** and discussion of what that word means.
>
> *Hint 9*: Keep your sentences simple and your ideas will come through more clearly.
>
> *Hint 10*: Avoid symbols and abbreviations. The professor may not be able to

decipher them.

Hint 11: Do not use slang or colloquialisms. Do not write as you speak. An essay or essay exam is a **formal** means of conveying information.

Hint 12: **Organize**! Use paragraphs and essay format to make your essay clear and understandable. Start at the beginning and end at the end; do not jump around. If you are confused, your answer will be confused, and your grade will reflect that confusion!

4)   **CONTENT**

The single most important part of any exam is the content. You must have facts, theories, and a basic understanding of the material to do well.

Hint 13: Always choose to answer the questions you know best if a choice is given on an exam. Do not just answer the questions in order!

Hint 14: **Be specific and precise**. For example, if you are asked to identify Lyndon Johnson, do not simply say he was a President of the U.S. There have been many presidents. What did he do that was important? Why do we study him? When did he serve and how well did he govern? What is he famous for? In other words, why is your professor asking about this particular president? Answer the question given you specifically and precisely.

Hint 15: Be concise but not too concise. In other words, clarity and brevity are good, but do not overdo it and leave out important information.

Hint 16: **Do not assume** that the professor knows anything! This is your opportunity to demonstrate that YOU know it. Too often students tell their professor, "Well, I didn't include that because you already know that." You need to show your professor that YOU know it.

Hints for Objective Tests

1)   **Reconnoiter the test**. Briefly look over the entire test. Read the directions carefully. How long is it? Are there sections worth different amounts of points? Plan your strategy and allot your time.

2)   **Read each item carefully.** Don't lose points because you didn't notice a "not" or an "except" in the question. Always read every possibility. Even if answer choice (a) seems to be the most logical response, it may not be.

3)   **Answer only the questions you know cold on your first run through**. This will help you warm up and may jar your memory on tougher questions. It will also reduce your test anxiety and build your confidence.

4)   **Do not read too much into or out-think the question.** Most professors are not trying to trick you; they simply want to find out how much you have learned.

5)   **Answer every question** unless there is a severe penalty for guessing. And when guessing, use some common sense. Things are rarely "always" or "never." If you can choose only one answer and two are virtually identical, you can probably rule out those two.

6)   Always proofread and check your work. But **be careful about changing your first response** unless you are absolutely sure. First instincts are often correct.

"THE TEN TRAPS OF STUDYING"

reproduced with the permission of the Counseling and Psychological Services of the University of North Carolina, Chapel Hill

1.   "I Don't Know Where To Begin"

Take Control. Make a list of all the things you have to do. Break your workload down into manageable chunks. Prioritize! Schedule your time realistically. Don't skip classes near an exam -- you may miss a review session. Use that hour in between classes to review notes. Interrupt study time with planned study breaks. Begin studying early, with an hour or two per day, and slowly build as the exam approaches.

2.   "I've Got So Much To Study…And So Little Time"

Preview. Survey your syllabus, reading material, and notes. Identify the most important topics emphasized and areas still not understood. Previewing saves time, especially with non-fiction reading, by helping you organize and focus on the main topics. Adapt this method to your own style and study material, but remember, previewing is not an effective substitute for reading.

3.   "This Stuff Is So Dry, I Can't Even Stay Awake Reading It"

Attack! Get actively involved with the text as you read. Ask yourself, "What is important to remember about this section?" Take notes or underline key concepts. Discuss the material with others in your class. Study together. Stay on the offensive, especially with material that you don't find interesting, rather than reading passively and missing important points.

4.   "I Read It. I Understand It. But I Just Can't Get It To Sink In"

Elaborate. We remember best the things that are most meaningful to us. As you are reading, try to elaborate upon new information with your own examples. Try to integrate what you're studying with what you already know. You will be able to remember new material better if you can link it to something that's already meaningful to you. Some techniques include:

Chunking: An effective way to simplify and make information more meaningful. For example, if you wanted to remember the colors in the visible spectrum (Red, Orange, Yellow, Green, Blue, Indigo, Violet), you would have to memorize seven "chunks" of information in order. But when you take the first letter of each color and spell the name "Roy G. Biv," you reduce the information to three "chunks."

Mnemonics: Any memory-assisting technique that helps us to associate new information with something familiar. For example, to remember a formula or equation, we may use letters of the alphabet to represent certain numbers. Then we can change an abstract formula into a more meaningful word or phrase, so we'll be able to remember it better. Sound-alike associations can be very effective, too, especially while trying to learn a new language. The key is to create your own links, so you won't forget them.

5.   "I Guess I Understand It"

Test yourself. Make up questions about key sections in notes or reading. Keep in mind what the professor has stressed in the course. Examine the relationships between concepts and sections. Often, simply by changing section headings you can generate many effective questions. For example, a section entitled "Bystander Apathy" might be changed into questions such as: "What is bystander apathy?" "What are the causes of bystander apathy?" and "What are some examples of bystander apathy?"

6.   "There's Too Much To Remember"

Organize. Information is recalled better if it is represented in an organized framework that will make retrieval more systematic. There are many techniques that can help you organize new information, including: Write chapter outlines or summaries; emphasize relationships between sections. Group information into categories or hierarchies where possible.

Information Mapping. Draw up a matrix to organize and interrelate material. For example, if you were trying to understand the causes of World War I, you could make a chart listing all the major countries involved across the top, and then list the important issues and events down the side. Next, in the boxes in between, you could describe the impact each issue had on each country to help you understand these complex historical developments.

7.   "I Knew It A Minute Ago"

Review. After reading a section, try to recall the information contained in it. Try answering the questions you made up for that section. If you cannot recall enough, re-read portions you had trouble remembering. The more time you spend studying, the more you tend to recall. Even after the point where information can be perfectly recalled, further study makes the material less likely to be forgotten entirely. In other words, you can't over-study. However, how you organize and integrate new information is still more important than how much time you spend studying.

8.   "But I Like To Study In Bed"

Context. Recall is better when study contexts (physical location, as well as mental, emotional, and physical state) are similar to the test context. The greater the similarity between the study setting and the test setting, the greater the likelihood that material studied will be recalled during the test.

9.   "Cramming Before A Test Helps Keep It Fresh In My Mind"

Spacing. Start studying now. Keep studying as you go along. Begin with an hour or two a day about one week before the exam, and then increase study time as the exam approaches. Recall increases as study time gets spread out over time.

10.   "I'm Gonna Stay Up All Night 'til I Get This"

Avoid Mental Exhaustion. Take short breaks often when studying. Before a test, have a rested mind. When you take a study break, and just before you go to sleep at night, don't think about academics. Relax and unwind, mentally and physically. Otherwise, your break won't refresh you and you'll find yourself lying awake at night. It's more important than ever to take care of yourself before an exam! Eat well, sleep, and get enough exercise.

WEB SITES OF INTEREST

These are simply starting points. There are many free and quite a few commercial sites on the Internet devoted to learning, study skills, etc. A little surfing will yield many more. And remember, the more conscious you are about your coursework and studying, the better you are likely to do.

Some College and University Web Pages on Study Skills:

Middle Tennessee State University offers strategies for success in college from note-taking to memory and learning styles.
www.mtsu.edu/~studskl

The **University of North Carolina** Web site offers "Study Habits and the Ten Traps of Studying" plus more on skills and success in college.
http://caps.unc.edu/TenTraps.html

Southern Illinois University offers study help on-line as well as numerous links to other sites with similar goals.
http://www.siu.edu/departments/cola/psycho/intro/studying.html

Virginia Tech's Division of Student Affairs offers many tips for studying, reading, taking notes, etc.
http://www.ucc.vt.edu/stdyhlp.html

Dallas County Community Colleges hosts a Web site with numerous links to study aids in a number of areas, categorized for easy reference.
http://ollie.dcccd.edu/Services/StudyHelp/StudySkills

SECTION II

CHAPTER-BY-CHAPTER GUIDE

This section of the study guide will help you study each chapter of the O'Connor/Sabato text. Each of the following 26 chapters is divided into several parts to help you understand and remember the material:

- **Chapter Goals and Learning Objectives**

- **Chapter Outlines and Key Points**

- **Research Ideas and Possible Paper Topics**

- **Web sites**

- **Practice Tests**
    - **Multiple-Choice Questions**
    - **True/False Questions**
    - **Compare and Contrast Questions**
    - **Essay and Short-Answer Questions**
    - **Answers to Multiple-Choice and True/False Questions**

CHAPTER 1
THE POLITICAL LANDSCAPE

Chapter Goals and Learning Objectives

Probably one of your questions you ask of a classmate on the first day of class is, "Where are you from?" To better know and understand a person, you want to know about his or her history and background. Similarly, to know and understand our government, you need to understand its origins, its history, and its beginnings. The government we have did not suddenly descend from the sky, *deus ex machina,* one day perfectly formed. It has deep roots in the past. To understand our present, we must understand our history, the circumstances, ideas, and people who drove our development as a nation. Where did we come from? What were and are our goals? Why does our government look, act, and function the way it does? Why *this* form of government and not another?

You may be one of the many students holding this book, looking at the first chapter at the start of the new semester thinking, "I don't like politics and I'm not interested in government!" Stated bluntly, while you might not be interested in government, government is darn sure interested in *you.* From the moment of your very conception until you're dead and buried, and every moment in between, the government is involved in all aspects of your life. How so, you ask? Ask yourself: Will abortion be legal or illegal? My Mom has Parkinson's disease—why won't they let stem cell research cure it? Why are tuition rates soaring and student loans harder to get? What kind of education will my kids get when I get married? Will I be sent to a war in Iraq or some other far-off country? Is my sexual choice legal? Are we safe from terrorists? Will my civil liberties be curtailed in the effort to combat terrorism? Will there be a decent job for me in the future? Will Social Security be there when I'm old? Should my Grandfather, who is terminally ill and suffering severely, be euthanized at his request?

Who makes these decisions? Most directly, our representatives in government: in the legislative, executive and judicial branches of both the state and national government. In our republican form of government, you and I pick the people who make those decisions—if we vote; if we involve ourselves. If we don't vote, if we don't get involved, someone else picks those people who act in our behalf in government, and the decisions they make won't reflect what you want and need. From the standpoint of self-interest alone, apathy is an unwise attitude to hold about government and politics.

Our government is, essentially, made up of the people who understand it and take part in it. Can you make a difference? Can you protect yourself from the abuses of government? Can you improve your community? Can you try to make a better life for yourself and your family through having a role in politics and government? You can better answer these questions when you have an understanding of our government, its structure, and its foundations.

1

Equipped with such understandings, you can be a better citizen and, in turn, make your life, your community, and your government better. This nation is changing. It always has. It always will. Many Americans are not satisfied with the workings of the government. Many Americans do not understand how their government works. This leads to apathy and frustration. You may be one of these people. However, a thorough understanding of the system, its history, and, structure can help you improve and reform the system. Armed with this knowledge, you can become a more active participant in the political process.

This chapter is designed to give you an overview of the subject of the text as well as a look at the theories and ideas that underpin our political and economic system. The main topic headings of the chapter are:

- The Origins of American Government: What It Is and Why We Need It
- The Roots of American Government: Where Did the Ideas Come From?
- American Political Culture and the Characteristics of American Democracy
- Changing Characteristics of the American People
- Political Ideology: Its Role in the World and in American Politics
- Current Attitudes Toward American Government

In each section, there are certain facts and ideas that you should strive to understand. Many are in boldface type and appear in both the narrative and in the glossary at the end of the book. Other ideas, dates, facts, events, people, etc. are more difficult to pull out of the narrative. (Keep in mind that studying for objective tests [multiple choice, T/F] is different than studying for essay tests. See the Study Guide section on test taking for hints on study skills.)

In general, after you finish reading and studying this chapter, you should understand the following:

- the origins of American government: what it is and why we need it (essentially, the functions and structure of American government)
- the roots of American government and the philosophies that guided its development
- American political culture and the characteristics of American democracy (the enduring values that have long defined American democracy)
- the changing characteristics of the American people (such as age, racial make-up and ethnic composition)
- political ideologies of Americans and how they affect government policy
- how Americans view their government and the role it plays in their lives

In this section, you are provided with a basic outline of the chapter and key words/points you should know. Use this outline to develop a complete outline of the material. Write the definitions or further explanations for the terms. Use the space provided in this workbook or rewrite that material in your notebook. This will help you study and remember the material in preparation for your tests, assignments, and papers.

the Framers—

Preamble to the United States Constitution—

"best hope" and "last, best hope on earth"—

Government: What It is and Why We Need It

government—

citizen—

politics—

Functions of Government

"to form a more perfect union"—

establishing government—

ensuring domestic tranquility—

providing for the common defense—

promoting the general welfare—

securing the blessings of liberty—

Types of Government

monarchy—

totalitarianism—

oligarchy—

democracy—

Aristotle's Classifications of Government (Table 1.1)—

Roots of American Government: Where Did the Ideas Come From?

The Reformation and the Enlightenment: Questioning the Divine Right of Kings

Enlightenment—

divine right of kings—

Isaac Newton—

the Pilgrims—

social contract—

Hobbes, Locke, and a Social Contract Theory of Government

social contract theory—

Thomas Hobbes—

Leviathan (1651)—

"solitary, poor, nasty, brutish, and short"—

John Locke—

Second Treatise on Civil Government (1698) and *Essay Concerning Human Understanding* (1690)—

natural rights—

life, liberty, and property—

Thomas Jefferson and the original draft of the Declaration of Independence—

Devising a National Government in the American Colonies

Jean-Jacques Rousseau—

Virginia House of Burgesses—

"taxation without representation"—

direct democracy—

indirect democracy (representative democracy)—

republic—

American Political Culture and the Characteristics of American Democracy

political culture—

Personal Liberty

personal liberty—

the change from "freedom from" to "freedom to"—

Equality

political equality—

Popular Consent and Majority Rule

popular consent—

majority rule—

minority rights—

Popular Sovereignty—

popular sovereignty—

natural law—

Civil Society

civil society—

Individualism

individualism—

"certain unalienable rights"—

Religious Faith

religion and religious faith in America—

wall of separation—

Christian evangelicals—

<u>Changing Characteristics of the American People</u>

things Americans have in common—

focus on differences among Americans—

Changing Size and Population

U.S. population today and when Constitution adopted—

U.S. population, 1880-2040 (Figure 1.2)—

population and representation in Congress—

Changing Demographics of the U.S. Population

Changes in Racial and Ethnic Composition

immigration—

Race and Ethnicity in America: 1967 and 2006 (Figure 1.3)—

Huntington Theory of Hispanization—

Changes in Age Cohort Composition

Baby Boomers—

America is Getting Older (Figure 1.4)—

potential effects of aging population—

Changes in Family and Family Size

factors affecting family size and household arrangements—

"ideal" family size in 1949 and 2004—

single-parent families—

Implications of These Changes

illegal immigration: problems and reactions—

anti-immigration sentiments in America—

affirmative action programs—

effects of demographics—

Political Ideology: Its Role in the World and in American Politics

ideologies—

two factors that shaped human history in 20th century (Isaiah Berlin)—

ideologies perform four key functions—

Prevailing American Political Ideologies

Adult Self-Identification as Liberal, Moderate, or Conservative, 1974-2006 (Figure 1.5)—

Conservatism

conservative—

social conservative—

Liberalism

liberal—

liberals favor equality—

Problems with Political Labels

studies show conservatives often take liberal positions on issues and vice-versa—

states are not uniformly "red" or "blue" (Figure 6.1)—

Current Attitudes Toward American Government

American Dream—

major sources of most American's on-the-air news supplemented by growth of news and quasi-news outlets—

growth of Internet and blogs—

effects of news media dynamics (rush to be first with the news, instantaneous nature of communications, focus on personality and scandal)—

High Expectations

Americans' relation to government (federal and state) in the first 150 years of our nation's history—

the rise in public expectations of the federal government—

effect of unmet expectations on citizens—

A Missing Appreciation of the Good

our lack of faith in country's institutions and symbols (Figure 1.7)—

Americans' high standard of living due to governmental programs and protections (Table 1.2)—

everyday pervasive influence of government rulings or regulations in Americans' lives—

the good government can do—

Mistrust of Politicians

Roper poll of Americans' trust in politicians—

examples of scandals and misdeeds—

how most politicians act—

Voter Apathy

reasons presented for not voting—

Redefining Our Expectations

government's role and our expectations—

redefining our ideas and expectations of government: what do we want?—

examples of how various crises led to change—

Research Ideas and Possible Paper Topics

1) Further examine the Enlightenment and some of the political philosophers who developed concepts that the Founders incorporated into our system of government. What were some of the key ideas that formed the predicates for the government we have today?

2) Do you believe government is "good" or government is "bad" intrinsically? Or is government merely a tool, with the good or bad affects it produces a result of the intentions and abilities or those who control it? What are your expectations of government, if any? Does government affect your life in any way? Why or why not?

3) Discuss the nature of the challenges to America posed by the changing racial, ethnic, and age distribution in society. Look at the contemporary controversy regarding illegal immigration from Mexico as well as more philosophical arguments. Has the meaning of the phrase "We the People" from the Preamble to the United States Constitution changed from the meaning vested in that statement by the Founders?

4) What actions by Republicans led in 2006 to Americans turning control of the U.S. House of Representatives and the U.S. Senate from the Republican Party to the Democratic Party? Was public cynicism about government and politics the principal factor? Was public cynicism limited only to the national scene or to states as well? Was public cynicism limited only to Republicans? Do you think public cynicism will continue in such a fashion through the presidential election in 2008, and with what result?

U.S. Census Bureau offers information on the demographic, geographic, and economic make-up of our country. Includes the ability to search for state-level data.

    http://www.census.gov

The University of Michigan Documents Center page titled "Statistical Resources on the Web for Political Science" provides a one-stop academic research site for students, listing numerous links to sites to assist in researching political, racial, ethnic, social, and other demographic information.

    http://www.lib.umich.edu/govdocs/stpolisc.html

The **Gallup Organization** offers up-to-date and historical perspectives on the opinions of the American public.

    www.gallup.com

Brandeis University's Political Philosophy Internet Resources Web page provides links to numerous sites of interest in political philosophy.

    http://people.brandeis.edu/~teuber/polphil.html

To better understand the Enlightenment, go to a marvelous Web site developed by a high school history teacher in Mesquite, Texas titled **TeacherOz.com**. The Enlightenment page lists scores of resources. (The TeacherOz.com Web site received a recommendation by The History Channel.)

    www.teacheroz.com/Enlightenment.htm

PBSKids presents an interactive Web page titled "How Does Government Affect Me?" While prepared for grammar school children, the site nevertheless can engage your thinking as to how government does indeed affect everyday life of students and other Americans. It is also a great site to share with, if you have any, your children or younger siblings.

    http://pbskids.org/democracy/mygovt

PBS P.O.V. developed a Web site for the 2004 election on the question "Why Vote?" Although we have experienced another general election since it's posting, the Web site provides interesting commentary from a wide range of citizens offering their "point of view" about voting or non-voting.

    http://www.pbs.org/pov/pov2004/election

Yahoo.com. Yahoo is a commercial search engine that has a wide variety of information. For our purposes, there is a government subheading of Yahoo that will provide you with links to many topics on government, regime type, ideology, political thought, and more.

    http://dir.yahoo.com/Government

MULTIPLE CHOICE

1) The type of government where the rule of one in the interest of all, a government rejected by the Framers of the Constitution, is called a
   a. monarchy.
   b. totalitarian state.
   c. oligarchy.
   d. democracy.

2) The first political philosopher to argue the necessity of government to control society because of mankind's bestial tendencies, and that without government life would be "solitary, poor, nasty, brutish and short," was
   a. John Locke.
   b. Thomas Hobbes.
   c. Baron de Montesquieu.
   d. Jean Jacques Rousseau.

3) The idea that men form governments largely to preserve life, liberty, and property comes from
   a. John Locke.
   b. Thomas Hobbes.
   c. Baron de Montesquieu.
   d. Jean Jacques Rousseau.

4) In the original draft of the Declaration of Independence, Thomas Jefferson directly quoted which Enlightenment philosopher with regard to rights?
   a. John Locke
   b. Thomas Hobbes
   c. Baron de Montesquieu
   d. Jean Jacques Rousseau

5) The belief that all people are free and equal by natural right and that this requires that a government which rules the people be one of the consent of those governed is called
   a. a monarchy.
   b. political culture.
   c. an oligarchy.
   d. the social contract theory.

6)   A system of government in which representatives of the people are chosen by ballot is called
        a.   hegemonic democracy.
        b.   tutelary democracy.
        c.   indirect democracy.
        d.   direct democracy.

7)   The set of attitudes, beliefs, and values that people have toward how their government should operate is called
        a.   public opinion.
        b.   norms.
        c.   ideology.
        d.   political culture.

8)   The population of the United States around the time of the ratification of the Constitution was
        a.   1 million.
        b.   4 million.
        c.   30 million.
        d.   100 million.

9)   For the first time in our nation's history, the U.S. population is getting
        a.   younger.
        b.   older.
        c.   shorter.
        d.   thinner.

10)   Because people in this country are living longer than ever before, which one of the following issues do you think this burgeoning population of voters might be most interested in?
        a.   public school quality
        b.   college loan programs
        c.   tax cuts for parents of young children
        d.   Social Security

11)   An individual's coherent set of values and beliefs about the purpose and scope of government are called
        a.   individualism.
        b.   attitude.
        c.   political culture.
        d.   political ideology.

12) One who favors a free market and no governmental interference in personal and economic affairs is called a
a. libertarian.
b. conservative.
c. liberal.
d. mercantilist.

13) One who favors governmental regulation of the economy to protect the environment and the rights of workers, who stresses the need for social services to aid the poor, and who seeks to promote the values of equality through governmental action is called a
a. libertarian.
b. conservative.
c. liberal.
d. mercantilist.

14) Many Americans say they don't vote because they
a. have no time.
b. have no real choice.
c. are content.
d. All of the above.

15) Which of the following is an accurate description of Americans' views of government?
a. Americans have high expectations for what government can accomplish.
b. Americans are generally trusting of politicians.
c. Many Americans are apathetic about voting.
d. Many Americans believe that government looks out for "people like me."

TRUE/FALSE

1) The Reformation and the Enlightenment altered the nature of government as people began to believe they could also have a say in their own governance.

2) John Locke argued that man's natural state was war and government was necessary to restrain man's bestial tendencies.

3) A republic is an economic system based on the market.

4) The American system tries to balance the ideals of majority rule and minority rights.

5) A single member of the House of Representatives serves as many as 927,000 constituents in 2006.

6) Since the 1940s, the number of single-parent households in the United States has decreased dramatically.

7) Liberals favor local and state action over federal action and emphasizes less government regulation of the economy.

8) Studies show that people who identify themselves as conservatives never take liberal views on issues.

9) For some, the American dream includes the ability for their children to grow up to be president.

10) American voters get a chance to vote for candidates and issues in far fewer elections than voters in other countries.

COMPARE AND CONTRAST

natural law and social contract theory

the theories of Thomas Hobbes and John Locke

monarchy, oligarchy, aristocracy, and democracy

direct democracy and indirect democracy

conservatism and liberalism

ESSAY AND SHORT ANSWER QUESTIONS

1) The United States, seeking to overthrow the government of Saddam Hussein, invaded Iraq in 2003. Since the invasion and during the subsequent occupation, the U.S. has worked to create a new political, governmental, and economic structure in that country. What success has been achieved toward that goal and what measures has the U.S. used to foster the institution of democracy in Iraq? What type of governmental system existed under Saddam Hussein? What type exists now under Iraqi President Jalal Talabani? Is this an exercise of popular consent?

2) What is popular consent and what are its historical roots?

3) How does the Preamble of the United States Constitution reflect not only the structure of our government but also the character of the nation?

4) What is political culture in general and what is American political culture?

5) Discuss the roots of the American government. Discuss what philosophies guided the Founders of our country as they created a new system of government.

6) What are some of the characteristics of democracy in the United States? Compare democracy in the U.S. to other democracies in the world.

7) In order to understand the nature of the American government, one must know who the American people are. Discuss the demographics of the United States and the effects of these demographics on the political system.

8) Many Americans are displeased with their government and with politicians. Discuss why.

9) Discuss the changing nature of America and what it means to be an American, particularly in the world after September 11, 2001.

10) What expectations do you think most Americans have of their government and its leaders? What expectations do you have toward your government and its leaders? Are those expectations realistic? What is the role of government in meeting the needs of the people of this country and do you think it is meeting those functions?

ANSWERS TO STUDY EXERCISES

MULTIPLE CHOICE ANSWERS

1) a
2) b
3) a
4) a
5) d
6) c
7) d
8) b
9) b
10) d
11) d
12) a
13) c
14) d
15) c

TRUE/FALSE ANSWERS

1) T
2) F
3) F
4) T
5) T
6) F
7) F
8) F
9) T
10) F

CHAPTER 2
THE CONSTITUTION

Chapter Goals and Learning Objectives

To build a house you first must lay a foundation. The foundation buttresses the structure, gives it support and definition. You build your house directly atop the foundation. Anything not built on that foundation will surely fall from lack of definition and support.

The foundation of our system of government is the Constitution. Our nation and its laws are built upon it. The U.S. Constitution is one of the longest-lasting and least-amended constitutions in the world and has endured despite changing demographics, changing technology, and changing ideas. The problems encountered and compromises made by the Framers of the Constitution continue to affect our nation and our political process. Yet, the structure created and supported by our Constitution still stands. It is important to understand why. An understanding of the Constitution and the development of the Constitution is essential to understanding our political system.

This chapter surveys the colonial era and the events that led to the writing of the Declaration of Independence, the main grievances of the colonists against the Crown and Parliament, the first American government under the Articles of Confederation, the writing of the U.S. Constitution, the nature of the U.S. Constitution, and, the ratification debate.

The main topic headings of the chapter are:

- The Origins of a New Nation
- The First Attempt at Government: The Articles of Confederation
- The Miracle at Philadelphia: Writing a Constitution
- The U.S. Constitution
- The Drive for Ratification
- Methods of Amending the Constitution

In each section, there are certain facts and ideas that you should strive to understand. Many are in boldface type and appear in both the narrative and in the glossary at the end of the book. Other ideas, dates, facts, events, people, etc. are more difficult to pull out of the narrative. (Keep in mind that studying for objective tests [multiple choice, T/F] is different than studying for essay tests. See the Study Guide section on test taking for hints on study skills.)

In general, after you finish reading and studying this chapter, you should understand the following:

- the origins of the new nation and the attendant conditions surrounding the Declaration of Independence and the break from Great Britain
- the first attempt at American government created by the Articles of Confederation
- the circumstances surrounding the writing of a constitution in Philadelphia
- the results of the Framer's work in Philadelphia—the U.S. Constitution
- the campaign for ratification of the new government under the new Constitution
- the methods of amending the Constitution

Chapter Outline and Key Points

In this section, you are provided with a basic outline of the chapter and key words/points you should know. Use this outline to develop a complete outline of the material. Write the definitions or further explanations for the terms. Use the space provided in this workbook or rewrite that material in your notebook. This will help you study and remember the material in preparation for your tests, assignments, and papers.

The Origins of a New Nation

the colonists of the New World and their reasons for wanting to govern themselves—

local participation in decision-making allowed the colonists by King James I—

oppressive British traditions absent in the New World—

Trade and Taxation

mercantilism—

French and Indian War—

Treaty of Paris of 1763—I

Stamp Act of 1765—

Quartering Act of 1765—

Samuel Adams and Patrick Henry—

Sons and Daughters of Liberty—

protests and boycotts—

First Steps Toward Independence

Stamp Act Congress of 1765—

Townshend Act of 1767—

Committees of Correspondence—

Tea Act of 1773—

Boston Tea Party—

Coercive Acts of 1774 (Intolerable Acts)—

The First Continental Congress

First Continental Congress (1774)—

Declaration of Rights and Resolves—

The Second Continental Congress

Second Continental Congress (1775)—

Olive Branch Petition—

Thomas Paine and *Common Sense*—

resolution by Richard Henry Lee of Virginia on June 7, 1776—

the three parts of Lee's resolution—

confederation—

The Declaration of Independence

Declaration of Independence—

Thomas Jefferson—

John Locke and the Declaration of Independence—

The First Attempts at Government: The Articles of Confederation

Articles of Confederation—

a confederation derives all its powers from the states—

a "league of friendship" linking the states for limited purposes—

Key provisions of the Articles of Confederation—

1)

2)

3)

4)

5)

Problems Under the Articles of Confederation—

the "critical period" from 1781 to 1789—

effects of the weaknesses of the Articles of Confederation:

1) no power to tax—

2) no resources to back its national currency—

3) no power to regulate commerce among the states or with foreign nations—

4) no chief executive (no president) to execute (implement) the laws—

5) no judicial system—

6) no strong central government---

dissatisfaction of Washington and Hamilton with Articles of Confederation—

Shays's Rebellion

> requirements for voting and holding office—

> factors leading to Shays's Rebellion—

> Daniel Shays—

> Shays's Rebellion—

> national and state response to Shays's Rebellion—

> implications for government of Shays's Rebellion—

The Miracle at Philadelphia: Writing a Constitution

> Constitutional Convention of 1787—

The Characteristics and Motives of the Framers

> secrecy attendant to the convention—

> "Founding Fathers"—

> constitution—

> Charles Beard's *An Economic Interpretation of the Constitution*—

> progeny of Beard's work—

The Virginia and New Jersey Plans

> Virginia Plan—

> New Jersey Plan—

Constitutional Compromises

> problems between small states' desire for equal representation in the new Congress and larger states' demand for proportional representation—

> Great Compromise—

> problems arising from regional differences—

> Three-Fifths Compromise—

Unfinished Business Affecting the Executive Branch

concerns of the Framers over a chief executive—

recommendations of the Committee on Unfinished Portions—

Electoral College—

Hamilton in *Federalist No. 68*—

impeachment and removal—

The U.S. Constitution

early draft of the Preamble—

final draft of the Preamble—

The Basic Principles of the Constitution

Montesquieu—

separation of powers—

checks and balances—

federalism—

federal system—

three key features of separation of powers—

different means of selecting federal officers—

how Senators originally elected under the Constitution—

Seventeenth Amendment (1913)—

Separation of Powers and Checks and Balances Under the U.S. Constitution (Figure 2.1)—

The Articles of the Constitution

Article I: The Legislative Branch

enumerated powers—

necessary and proper clause (elastic clause)—

implied powers—

Article II: The Executive Branch

president—

important powers of the president in section 3—

State of the Union Address—

section 4—

Article III: The Judicial Branch

Supreme Court—

Congress and the lower courts—

appointments for life—

Articles IV Through VII

Article IV and full faith and credit clause—

Article V and amendments—

Article VI and the supremacy clause—

Article VI and no religious test for public office—

Article VII and ratification—

The Drive for Ratification

letter from George Washington with the proposed Constitution sent to the Second Continental Congress—

who favored the proposed Constitution in the Second Continental Congress?—

Federalists Versus Anti-Federalists

Federalists—

Anti-Federalists—

The Federalist Papers

"Publius"—

Alexander Hamilton, James Madison, and John Jay—

The Federalist Papers—

Federalist No. 10—

"Brutus" and "Cato"—

Anti-Federalist arguments—

Madison answers the criticisms raised by the Anti-Federalist in *Federalist Nos. 10* and 51—

Ratifying the Constitution

Article VII—

submission of the Bill of Rights as political compromise to assuage Anti-Federalists fears—

Amending the Constitution: The Bill of Rights

proposed amendments sent to the states for ratification—

Twenty-Seventh [Madison] Amendment—

Bill of Rights sought by the Anti-Federalists—

protections and guarantees of the Bill of Rights—

Methods of Amending the Constitution

reasons for the formal amendment process to be a slow one—

Formal Methods of Amending the Constitution

Article V—

two-stage amendment process—

two methods of proposal—

ratification must occur in one of two ways—

Eighteenth and Twenty-First Amendments—

ERA—

reaction to *Texas* v. *Johnson* (1989)—

Informal Methods of Amending the Constitution

Judicial Interpretation

Marbury v. *Madison* (1803)—

criticisms of judicial review—

Social and Cultural Change

evolution of Constitution to accommodate change—

Great Depression and the New Deal—

Federal Marriage Amendment—

Research Ideas and Possible Paper Topics

1) Examine the Articles of Confederation and pose an argument that they were not inherently flawed and should have been maintained as the American form of government. Examine some of the arguments by conservatives today who endorse a further downsizing of the federal government and the return of many federal powers back to the states. How do these arguments compare to the Articles of Confederation?

2) Those who believe in a literal interpretation of the Constitution look to documents such as the *Federalist Papers* to determine the original intent of the Framers. Research the historical and political importance of the *Federalist Papers* with

regard to the interpretation of the Constitution. Do Hamilton, Madison and Jay in the *Federalist Papers* provide a complete and sound explanation of the Framers' thinking in writing the Constitution or were the *Federalist Papers* a polemic written to sell the new constitution to a skeptical public?

3)   The text gives a few examples of how the Constitution has changed due to interpretations by the judiciary and others. Explore other ways in which the Constitution has changed or will soon change.

4)   One of the major factors in the reelection of George W. Bush as president in 2004 was the issue of same-sex marriages. Social conservatives pushed the president to announce his support of a constitutional amendment banning same-sex marriages. Why do they believe it is necessary to amend the Constitution to achieve the goal of prohibiting same-sex marriages? Put another way, what is one of the constitutional arguments made by proponents of same-sex marriages that contends the Constitution forbids the federal and state governments from banning same-sex marriages?

Web sites

Cornell University site offers the complete text of the Constitution. Many terms are hyperlinked and cross-referenced to other key issues.
  www.law.cornell.edu/constitution/constitution.table.html

The U.S. Constitution OnLine offers many documents, including the Articles of Confederation, Declaration of Independence, the Constitution, and many other links.
  www.usconstitution.net

Search and download the text of the **Federalist Papers** from **The Avalon Project at Yale Law School**.
  http://www.yale.edu/lawweb/avalon/federal/fed.htm

Turn to **GradeSaver's Classic Notes** for background on Alexander Hamilton, James Madison, and John Jay, as well as summaries and analysis of *The Federalist Papers*.
  http://www.gradesaver.com/ClassicNotes/Titles/federalist/

The **Manuscript Division of the Library of Congress** offers a wide variety of documents from the fifteenth to twentieth centuries on American history.
  http://lcweb2.loc.gov/ammem/mcchtml/corhome.html

The **National Archives** offers a thorough explanation of the constitutional amendment process as well as several useful links to **Constitutional Amendment Information** in their Treasures of Congress Exhibit.
  http://www.archives.gov/federal-register/constitution/

National Museum of American History offers timelines, virtual exhibits, music, and other information from American history.

www.americanhistory.si.edu/

The University of Missouri-Kansas City hosts a Web site examining constitutional conflicts including the right to marry.

http://www.law.umkc.edu/faculty/projects/ftrials/conlaw/righttomarry.htm

---

Practice Tests

MULTIPLE CHOICE

1) Colonists came to the New World
   a. to escape religious persecution.
   b. to acquire land.
   c. to be more independent of government.
   d. All of the above.

2) The first official meeting of the colonies and the first step toward a unified nation was the
   a. Stamp Act Congress.
   b. First Continental Congress.
   c. Committees of Correspondence.
   d. Colonial Parliament.

3) The type of government in which the national government derives its powers from subsidiary units, such as states, is called
   a. shared sovereignty.
   b. unitary government.
   c. a confederacy.
   d. federalism.

4) The Articles of Confederation failed due to a number of weaknesses, including that the national government was not allowed to
   a. coin money.
   b. tax its citizens or the states.
   c. pass laws.
   d. All of the above.

5) The concept that the Framers of the Constitution were motivated principally to create a new government to protect their personal economic well-being and the well-being of men of property was first proposed in a book published in 1913 by historian
   a. Edmund Randolph.
   b. Charles Beard.
   c. Edward Everett Horton.
   d. Gordon S. Wood.

6) The proposal that first called for a bicameral legislature at the Constitutional Convention was called the
   a. New Jersey Plan.
   b. Virginia Plan.
   c. New York Plan.
   d. Great Compromise.

7) In general, at the Constitutional Convention, most of the small states felt comfortable with
   a. a stronger central government to deal with the crisis at hand.
   b. concentration of power into a single branch of government.
   c. a unicameral legislature appointed by the president.
   d. the Articles of Confederation.

8) Reflecting the attitude of many of the Framers of the Constitution, including Alexander Hamilton, the election of the president of the United States would be removed from the hands of the "masses" through the creation of
   a. a bicameral legislature.
   b. the Senate, which would be elected by the states' legislatures.
   c. the Committee on Unfinished Portions.
   d. the electoral college.

9) The phrase included by the Framers in the Preamble to the Constitution, "in order to form a more perfect union," reflects the concerns the Framers had with the
   a. Declaration of Independence.
   b. New Jersey Plan.
   c. Federalist Papers.
   d. Articles of Confederation.

10) The powers vested in Congress by the Framers to govern the nation are enumerated in
   a. Article I, section 8.
   b. the Preamble to the Constitution.
   c. Article II.
   d. the Supremacy Clause of Article VI.

11) Over the course of the nation's history under the Constitution, Congress has often coupled the "necessary and proper" clause with a particular enumerated to dramatically expand its authority (e.g., to regulate airlines and railroads, which did not exist when the Constitution was written). Which of the following enumerated powers is often coupled with the elastic clause to expand federal power?
   a. to levy taxes
   b. to regulate commerce
   c. to coin money
   d. to control immigration

12) Article III establishes
   a. the power of judicial review.
   b. the Supreme Court.
   c. the lower federal courts.
   d. judiciary systems of the state courts.

13) Article VI includes the supremacy clause and also requires
   a. that the federal government create no ex post facto laws.
   b. all states to honor the laws and official acts of the other states.
   c. that states may not coin money.
   d. that no religious test for public office be required for holding any public office.

14) In general, the Anti-Federalists
   a. feared the power of a strong central government.
   b. argued that a president would be become far too powerful.
   c. feared the powerful new national government would usurp the individual rights and liberties of the citizens of the states.
   d. All of the above.

15) An example of constitutional modification through social change without amendment occurred during the Great Depression with the adoption by Congress and approval by the Supreme Court of
   a. the New Deal programs.
   b. the doctrine of judicial review.
   c. the Supremacy Clause.
   d. the declaration of war against Japan.

TRUE/FALSE

1) Thomas Paine's *Common Sense* was instrumental in arousing colonists' support for the new Constitution.

2) The Articles of Confederation worked fairly well throughout the Revolutionary War.

3) The phrase "we the people" is found prominently in the Declaration of Independence.

4) The political philosopher Montesquieu heavily influenced the Framers of the Constitution through his writings, which advocated a separation of powers and a system of checks and balances.

5) Article I, section 8, enumerates the powers of the president to direct and manage the government of the United States.

6) The Constitution establishes state court systems in Article III.

7) The Bill of Rights was added to the Constitution in part as a way to garner support from the Anti-Federalists for the ratification of the Constitution.

8) *The Federalist Papers* were designed to explain the new Constitution and encourage people to favor ratification.

9) The Twenty-Seventh Amendment gives young people, aged eighteen to twenty-one, the right to vote.

10) The Constitution can only be changed through a formal amendment process.

COMPARE AND CONTRAST

Stamp Act Congress and Committees of Correspondence

the First Continental Congress and the Second Continental Congress

federation and confederation

Articles of Confederation and the U.S. Constitution

Virginia Plan, New Jersey Plan, and the Great Compromise

the three main compromises at the Constitutional Convention: the nature of the legislature, the executive branch, and representation

Federalists and Anti-Federalists

methods of amending the Constitution

formal and informal techniques for amending the Constitution

ESSAY AND SHORT ANSWER QUESTIONS

1) Discuss three events that led up to the Declaration of Independence.

2) What impact did the publication of *Common Sense* have on the revolutionary process?

3) What type of government did the Articles of Confederation set up, and what powers did each institution of government have?

4) How was slavery treated in the Constitution? Why was it treated in this manner?

5) What powers did the U.S. Constitution allocate to the executive branch and why?

6) Discuss the route that the American colonies took toward independence.

7) Explain the Articles of Confederation, its successes, and the problems that led to its abandonment and the Constitutional Convention.

8) Explain the "Miracle at Philadelphia" and the compromises that had to be made in order to adopt the Constitution.

9) Discuss the controversies over the ratification of the Constitution.

10) Fully explain the basic principles of the Constitution.

ANSWERS TO STUDY EXERCISES

MULTIPLE CHOICE ANSWERS

1) d
2) a
3) c
4) d
5) b
6) b
7) d
8) d
9) d
10) a

11) b
12) b
13) d
14) d
15) a

TRUE/FALSE ANSWERS

1) F
2) T
3) F
4) T
5) F
6) F
7) T
8) T
9) F
10) F

CHAPTER 3
FEDERALISM

Chapter Goals and Learning Objectives

Given the problems the colonists had with arbitrary English rule, early Americans understandably distrusted a strong, central government and its powers. When framing their own government, they reasoned it necessary to divide power as much as possible to prevent tyranny. They accomplished this horizontally with separation of powers and checks and balances, the three branches of government divided and sharing powers under this system. They accomplished this vertically through federalism, a system in which the national government and the states share powers. Because of these two basic divisions of power, according to James Madison in the *Federalist No. 51*, "a double security arises to the rights of the people." The Founders concluded that the national government needed more power than it was allotted under the Articles of Confederation, but the Framers never intended to gut the powers of the states. Instead, they intended to divide powers so that no one branch or level of government got too powerful. The rest of U.S. history and politics has included battles over the way in which the Constitution divvies up these powers, what the vaguely worded passages mean, and the constantly shifting relationship between the national and state governments. From the ratification of the Tenth Amendment to *McCulloch* v. *Maryland*, the Civil War to the New Deal, the Reagan Revolution to the Contract with America, from the expansion of the federal government to deal with terrorism through the Katrina fiasco, the tug of war between the federal government and the states continues unabated into the 21st Century.

This chapter is designed to introduce you to our system of federalism. The main topic headings of the chapter are:

- The Origins of the Federal System: Governmental Powers Under the Constitution
- Federalism and the Marshall Court
- Dual Federalism: The Taney Court, Slavery, and the Civil War
- Cooperative Federalism: The New Deal and the Growth of National Government
- New Federalism: Returning Power to the States?

In each section, there are certain facts and ideas that you should strive to understand. Many are in boldface type and appear in both the narrative and in the glossary at the end of the book. Other ideas, dates, facts, events, people, etc. are more difficult to pull out of the narrative. (Keep in mind that studying for objective tests [multiple choice, T/F] is different than studying for essay tests. See the Study Guide section on test taking for hints on study skills.)

In general, after you finish reading and studying this chapter, you should understand the following:

- the origins of the federal system and governmental powers under the Constitution
- the Marshall Court defining federalism
- the development of dual federalism before and after the Civil War
- cooperative federalism and the growth of national government
- the movement toward returning power to the states under new federalism

Chapter Outline and Key Points

In this section, you are provided with a basic outline of the chapter and key words/points you should know. Use this outline to develop a complete outline of the material. Write the definitions or further explanations for the terms. Use the space provided in this workbook or rewrite that material in your notebook. This will help you study and remember the material in preparation for your tests, assignments, and papers.

The Number of Governments in the U.S. (Figure 3.1)—

The Origins of the Federal System: Governmental Power Under the Constitution

federal system—

confederation—

unitary system—

The Federal, Unitary, and Confederate Systems of Government (Figure 3.2)—

National Powers Under the Constitution

enumerated powers—

necessary and proper clause—

implied powers—

Sixteenth Amendment—

supremacy clause—

Migratory Bird Treaty of 1918—

The Origins of the Federal System (Figure 3.3)—

State Powers Under the Constitution

powers of the states mentioned in the main text of the Constitution—

Tenth Amendment—

reserve or police powers—

Concurrent Powers Under the Constitution

concurrent powers—

Powers Denied Under the Constitution

powers denied Congress under Article I—

bill of attainder—

ex post facto laws—

Relations Among the States

disputes between states settled by Supreme Court—

full faith and credit clause—

1997 Supreme Court case on full faith and credit—

extradition clause—

interstate compacts—

Emergency Management Assistance Compact—

Compacts by the Numbers (Table 3.1)—

Relations Within the States: Local Governments

the Constitution and local governments—

<u>Federalism and the Marshall Court</u>

John Marshall—

McCulloch v. *Maryland* (1819)

McCulloch v. *Maryland*—

Chief Justice Marshall's answers to the two questions raised—

necessary and proper clause today—

Gibbons v. *Ogden* (1824)

Gibbons v. *Ogden*—

commerce clause—

Dual Federalism: The Taney Court, Slavery, and the Civil War

Roger B. Taney—

dual federalism—

Dred Scott and the Question of Slavery

the Taney Court era and the role of the Supreme Court—

Dred Scott v. *Sandford* (1857)—

Missouri Compromise—

The Civil War, Its Aftermath, and the Continuation of Dual Federalism

the Civil War and federalism—

Civil War Amendments—

the Supreme Court's adherence to dual federalism—

Plessy v. *Ferguson* (1896)—

the Supreme Court and the national government's ability to regulate commerce—

Sherman Anti-Trust Act

Setting the Stage for a Stronger National Government

Sixteenth Amendment—

Seventeenth Amendment—

Cooperative Federalism: The New Deal and the Growth of National Government

the end of dual federalism in the 1930s—

economic events in the 1920s as catalyst for end of dual federalism—

Presidents Calvin Coolidge and Herbert Hoover—

The New Deal

rampant unemployment and the Great Depression—

Franklin D. Roosevelt—

New Deal—

"alphabetocracy"—

the New Deal and local governments—

the Supreme Court's *laissez-faire* attitude toward the economy—

FDR's Court-packing plan—

Court reverses itself on anti-New Deal decisions—

NLRB v. *Jones and Laughlin Steel Co.* (1937)

The Changing Nature of Federalism: From Layer Cake to Marble Cake

layer cake metaphor—

marble cake metaphor—

cooperative federalism—

the 1970s energy crisis and the national 55 mph speed limit—

Federal Grants and National Efforts to Influence the States

Congress and Revolutionary War debt payments—

Morrill Land Grant Act of 1862—

FDR and federal dollars to the states—

federal grant-in-aid programs—

categorical grants—

Lyndon B. Johnson—

Great Society—

"War on Poverty"—

control of programs shift toward Washington—

New Federalism: Returning Power to the States?

New Federalism—

The Reagan Revolution

Republican "Reagan Revolution"—

massive cuts in domestic programs—

dramatic alteration of federal-state-local government relationship—

block grants—

four categories of block grants in late 1980s and early 1990s—

The Devolution Revolution

Bill Clinton—

Contract with America—

"devolution revolution"—

unfunded mandates—

Unfunded Mandates Reform Act of 1995

Personal Responsibility and Work Opportunity Reconciliation Act of 1996—

fiscal and economic results of these programs in the short run—

economic conditions, limited federal government and the Bush and Gore presidential campaigns in 2000—

Federalism Under the Bush Administration

George W. Bush—

state budget shortfalls—

federal budget deficit—

sources of the federal deficit—

"No Child Left Behind"—

preemption—

The Supreme Court: A Return to States' Rights?

"a new kind of judicial federalism"—

Webster v. *Reproductive Health Services* (1989), illustrative of trend—

the Court and the authority of states to limit abortion—

Stenber v. *Carhart* (2000) and 2006 Roberts Court unanimous decision—

the Court has decided several major cases on the nature of the federal system since 1989—

The Rehnquist and Roberts Courts and Federalism (Figure 3.4)—

Violence Against Women Act of 1994 and the Supreme Court—

U.S. v. *Lopez* (1995)—

sovereign immunity—

1996 Supreme Court decision on the author of Congress to place requirements on states regarding Indian tribes—

other Supreme Court cases constraining federal power—

cases on Family Medical Leave Act—

Roberts Court's first decision involving federalism—

Research Ideas and Possible Paper Topics

1) Read the *Federalist Papers* on the topic of federalism. Note down the important features of federalism and its intent. Next, do some research on federalism today. How well does what you see today conform to the "intent of the Founding Fathers"? In a paper, discuss your conclusions and why you think federalism today is similar to or different than what was envisioned in 1787.

2) Examine the role of the U.S. Supreme Court regarding federalism prior to the New Deal, during and after the New Deal, and in the current era of New Federalism. What have been some of the factors affecting the Court, internally and externally during these periods? Is the Court returning to the pre-New Deal approach it took toward federalism? Do you, based upon your research, believe this is a good or problematic development?

3) What do you think are the most important federal issues today and why? Some possibilities include "full faith and credit" (particularly regarding same-sex marriages), the use of the "commerce clause," reproductive rights, term limits, child support issues, and others.

4) The response to Hurricane Katrina and its aftermath in the late summer of 2005 dramatically brought to the nation's attention some of the more prominent problems of federalism and how we respond to a disaster, whether it be a natural disaster, as in the case of a hurricane, or a man-made disaster, as in the case of any number of terrorism scenarios. What were some of the problems that became apparent during Katrina and afterward? What structural, political and administrative dynamics led to the failures? What has been done to correct the problems so that future disasters can be more effectively dealt with?

Web sites

National Council of State Legislators site offers analysis and information on intergovernmental relations.
www.ncsl.org/statefed/afipolcy.htm

NGA Federal Relations page, sponsored by the **National Governors' Associations** examines state-focused problems and provides information on state innovations and practices in how states can best work with the federal government to achieve necessary goals for the citizens of the states. The Web site has stories and articles of interest on the states and provides links to similar issues and organizations.

> http://www.nga.org/portal/site/nga/menuitem.67948e4cf7b28b7ae8ebb856a11010 a0/?vgnextoid=455c8aaa2ebbff00VgnVCM1000001a01010aRCRD

Center for the Study of Federalism at Temple University. The Center publishes *Publius: The Journal of Federalism* and *The Federalism Report* and the Web site offers a variety of links as well.

> www.temple.edu/federalism/

Publius: The Journal of Federalism. *Publius,* sponsored by the Section on Federalism and Intergovernmental Relations of the American Political Science Association, offers academic articles on federal issues in the United States and abroad. The journal publishes special issues on the state of federalism in the U.S.

> http://publius.oxfordjournals.org

The General Services Administration gives you the ability to search for information on hundreds of federal grants.

> www.gsa.gov

The Brookings Institution, a moderate-to-liberal think-tank in Washington, provides free access to a recent policy briefing: "Why Federalism Matters"

> http://www.brookings.edu/comm/policybriefs/pb146.htm

American Enterprise Institute, a conservative think-tank, conducts the Federalism Project, which "explores opportunities to restore real federalism—that is, a federalism that limits the national government's power and competes for their citizens' assets, talents, and business."

> http://www.federalismproject.org/

The Urban Institute, a "nonprofit policy research organization established in Washington D.C. in 1968" has prepared a number of articles and reports relating to federalism under the heading "Assessing the New Federalism."

> www.urban.org/content/Research/NewFederalism/AboutANF/AboutANF.htm

"Federalism After Hurricane Katrina" is the title of a report by **The Urban Institute** under its "Assessing the New Federalism" project.

> http://www.urban.org/UploadedPDF/311344_after_katrina.pdf

The Constitution Society provides access to the text of *The Federalist Papers* as well as links to other sites relating to states' rights.

> www.constitution.org/cs_feder.htm

The **Community Rights Counsel** (CRC), a nonprofit, public interest law firm based in Washington, D.C. and formed in provides assistance to state and local government attorneys in defending land use laws and environmental protections. Their Web page, **Redefining Federalism**, offers their position about how the Supreme Court is protecting federalism too little or too much "in striking down federal law where even the states recognize that a federal role is necessary to address a national problem. Too little, in inappropriately limiting state experimentation."

http://www.redefiningfederalism.org/intro.asp

Practice Tests

MULTIPLE CHOICE

1) While most of the delegates to the Constitutional Convention in Philadelphia favored a strong national government, they realized that some compromises regarding the distribution of powers would be necessary, and therefore created
   a. a confederate form of government very similar to one that had existed under the original constitution, the Articles of Confederation.
   b. a highly centralized form of government, similar to Great Britain's.
   c. a direct democracy.
   d. the world's first federal system, in which the states were bound together under one national government.

2) When is the supremacy clause applicable?
   a. when a state and national law concur
   b. when a state law exists where no national law exists
   c. when state and national law conflict
   d. when a law passed by Congress conflicts with god-given rights

3) The Sixteenth Amendment to the Constitution, adopted in 1913, gave what power to the national government that had not existed under the original Constitution?
   a. the power to levy taxes
   b. the power to borrow money
   c. the power to tax personal income
   d. the power to regulate intrastate commerce

4) A power that is not stated explicitly in the Constitution but is considered to reasonably flow from a power stated in Article I, section 8, is called a(n)
   a. derivative power.
   b. implied power.
   c. enumerated power.
   d. concurrent power.

5) The guarantee of states' rights was provided in the Constitution by
   a. Article I, section 8.
   b. the supremacy clause.
   c. the necessary and proper clause.
   d. the Tenth Amendment.

6) Article I denies certain powers to the national and state governments, including
   a. passing bills of attainder.
   b. entering into contracts.
   c. involvement in elections.
   d. the power to tax.

7) Article IV requires that states recognize judicial proceedings, records, and laws of other states. This is known as the _____ clause.
   a. commerce
   b. full faith and credit
   c. contract
   d. necessary and proper

8) The first major decision of the Marshall Court (in 1819) to define the federal relationship between the national government and the states (by upholding the necessary and proper clause and the supremacy clause) was
   a. *Marbury* v. *Madison.*
   b. *Gibbons* v. *Ogden.*
   c. *McCulloch* v. *Maryland.*
   d. *Dred Scott* v. *Sandford.*

9) The Supreme Court ruled in 1824 that Congress had wide authority under the commerce clause to regulate interstate commerce, including commercial activity, in
   a. *Marshall* v. *New York.*
   b. *Gibbons* v. *Ogden.*
   c. *McCulloch* v. *Maryland.*
   d. *Fulton* v. *New Jersey.*

10) In 1937, the Supreme Court reversed its series of decisions against New Deal programs, afterward approving broad extensions of the use by Congress of the commerce clause to regulate and bolster the economy. The Supreme Court reversed its anti-New Deal trend as a result of
   a. the worsening of Great Depression conditions.
   b. the increased participation of city government in federal affairs.
   c. the imminent threat of war with Nazi Germany and Imperial Japan.
   d. the Roosevelt court-packing plan.

11) The type of federalism metaphorically referred to as "marble cake" federalism is known as _____ federalism.
   a. cooperative
   b. dual
   c. competitive
   d. mixed

12) A broad grant of money given to states with few qualifications or restrictions by the federal government for specified activities is called a _____ grant.
   a. creative
   b. categorical
   c. block
   d. federal

13) The practice of the federal government overriding specific areas of state action is called
   a. supremacy.
   b. preemption.
   c. confiscation.
   d. mediation.

14) The 1995 Supreme Court case, *U.S.* v. *Lopez*, is significant because it was the first decision by the Court in many decades in which the Court
   a. restrained Congress's use of the commerce power, thus shifting power from the national government to the states.
   b. expanded Congress's use of the commerce clause in enhancing federal power.
   c. questioned the use of the power of judicial review by the Court.
   d. declared that federal preemption was unconstitutional.

15) The ruling in *Bush* v. *Gore* (2000) was surprising because
   a. more liberal justices sided with George W. Bush.
   b. more conservative justices sided with Al Gore.
   c. the Court had traditionally shown a reluctance to intervene in state issues.
   d. All of the above.

TRUE/FALSE

1) State and local governments are not bound by the provisions of the U.S. Constitution.

2) The Framers chose federalism to imitate the British centralized governmental system.

3)   In some instances, an American citizen needs a passport to go from California to New York.

4)   The Supremacy Clause states that all powers not specifically granted in the Constitution are reserved to the states.

5)   Police powers are among those powers reserved to the states.

6)   Legal controversies between the states can be decided only by the U.S. Supreme Court.

7)   The Supreme Court decision in the *Dred Scott* case contributed to the advent of the Civil War.

8)   The Civil War forever changed the nature of federalism.

9)   The first federal grant program came in the 1930s as a response to the Great Depression.

10)   The current Supreme Court under Chief Justice John Roberts refuses to consider cases brought up on appeal relating to federal excursions into the powers reserved to the states.

COMPARE AND CONTRAST

confederation and unitary system

national powers, concurrent powers, and state powers

enumerated, implied, and denied powers

supremacy clause and reserve (police) powers

dual federalism and cooperative federalism

layer cake and marble cake federalism

categorical and block grants

the expansion and contraction of federal powers under Supreme Court rulings

ESSAY AND SHORT ANSWER QUESTIONS

1) Why did the Framers choose a federated system? (Remember to define federalism.)

2) Discuss the nature and ramifications of the supremacy clause to intergovernmental relations between the states and the national government.

3) Explain the doctrine of implied powers.

4) What is the role of the states in our federal system? How is it dealt with in the Constitution? Is the question of states' rights settled now or is it ongoing?

5) Discuss the significance of the elastic clause and the commerce clause in the growth of federal power.

6) Explain the distribution of power in the federal system.

7) Discuss how *McCulloch* v. *Maryland* and *Gibbons* v. *Ogden* contributed to the development of federalism. Be sure to include the facts and ruling in each case.

8) Discuss the various stages of federalism this country has gone through, from dual federalism to today. What does the evolution of federalism tell us about our system?

9) Explain the uses of preemption and unfunded mandates. How have these methods been used to alter the nature of federalism, and what is their current status?

10) Discuss the impact of decisions by the Rehnquist and Roberts Courts since the late1980s in defining federalism.

ANSWERS TO STUDY EXERCISES

MULTIPLE CHOICE ANSWERS

1) d
2) c
3) c
4) b
5) d
6) a
7) b
8) c

9) b
10) d
11) a
12) c
13) b
14) a
15) d

TRUE/FALSE ANSWERS

1) F
2) F
3) F
4) F
5) T
6) T
7) T
8) T
9) F
10) F

CHAPTER 4
STATE AND LOCAL GOVERNMENT

Chapter Goals and Learning Objectives

In reporting on politics and government in our country, the news media devotes most of its attention (and, as a result, directs most of the public's attention to) the national government, particularly the actions of the president. While the deeds and decisions of the president and the national government are certainly important in your life, most of your day-to-day experiences with government are with local and state governments. You bathed in water today delivered to your home by your municipal government. You drove to school on state highways and city streets. You are probably taking this government course at a university funded by the state or a community college funded locally and with assistance from the state. You were stopped on the way home by a county sheriff or state trooper for speeding. These are all state and local government functions. Decisions were made, taxes were raised, programs funded by your state and local government. And at the same time, the federal government may have provided some funds to assist in these activities or have coinciding laws or regulations affecting your local and state governmental services.

The relationships between the various governments in our country are dynamic. The multiple levels allow citizens a variety of access points where they can get their voices heard; however, it also makes finding the appropriate place to make an argument a complex process that sometimes reduces a citizen's ability to effectively lobby government. Recent events have strengthened the hand of state governments in many aspects of the federal bargain and the Supreme Court seems to be on a trend toward limiting the powers of the national government and enhancing those of the states (although some recent cases may counter that trend in some areas). Therefore, it is becoming even more important to understand the nature of state and local governments.

This chapter is designed to introduce you to the nature and institutions of state and local governments. The main topic headings of the chapter are:

- The Evolution of State and Local Governments
- State Governments
- Local Governments
- Grassroots Power and Politics
- Relations with Indian Nations
- State and Local Finances

In each section, there are certain facts and ideas that you should strive to understand. Many are in boldface type and appear in both the narrative and in the glossary at the end of the book. Other ideas, dates, facts, events, people, etc. are more difficult to pull out of the narrative. (Keep in mind that studying for objective tests [multiple choice, T/F] is different than studying for essay tests. See the Study Guide section on test taking for hints on study skills.)

In general, after you finish reading and studying this chapter, you should understand the following:

- the evolution of state and local governments
- the major institutions of state governments, including state election trends
- different types of local governments, the foundation of their authority, and special characteristics of the institutions
- the nature of grassroots power and politics
- national and state government relations with Indian nations
- the budgeting process for state and local finances

Chapter Outline and Key Points

In this section, you are provided with a basic outline of the chapter and key words/points you should know. Use this outline to develop a complete outline of the material. Write the definitions or further explanations for the terms. Use the space provided in this workbook or rewrite that material in your notebook. This will help you study and remember the material in preparation for your tests, assignments, and papers.

The Evolution of State and Local Governments

in our history, state governments came first—

local government created by—

governmental institutions in the U.S. are not built from the bottom—

district boundaries for state legislators did not change in response to population shifts in the post-Civil War era—

Baker v. *Carr* (1962)—

one-person, one-vote—

federal government added to state and local government responsibilities in the 1960s and 1970s—

recent trends in federalism affecting state and local governments from the 1970s up through 2002—

State Governments

primary responsibilities of state government—

State Constitutions

state constitution—

early state constitutions in the U.S.—

The Northwest Ordinance of 1787—

effect of Civil War on constitutions of southern states—

political machine—

Progressive Movement—

trend since the 1960s of state constitutional amendments—

relative ease of amending state constitutions—

implications of simple amendment process for state constitutions—

Governors

governor—

most important role governors play—

governors and the budget process—

package or general veto—

line-item veto—

executive responsibilities of governors—

methods of limiting gubernatorial power—

pardon—

commute—

parole—

extradite—

gubernatorial participation in the judicial process—

general trend in power and authority of governors since the 1960s—

State Legislatures

role of the legislature—

citizen legislators—

one-person, one-vote rule—

Baker v. *Carr* (1962)—

annual legislative sessions in the country in 1960 and in 2006—

Nebraska state house—

legislative houses in the states—

legislative terms in the states—

term limits—

States with Term Limits for State Legislators (Table 4.1)—

State Courts

primary function of courts—

two separate court systems: state and federal—

the only time state and federal courts converge—

when there is a conflict between state and federal law—

inclusion—

state courts encouraged to consider federal government as setting minimum standards for individual rights—

state court structure—

State Court Structure (Figure 4.2)—

jurisdiction of various trial courts—

characteristics of appellate courts—

how state judges selected for the bench—

Missouri Plan—

Judicial Selection Patterns (Table 4.2)—

Elections and Political Parties

elections—

partisan and non-partisan elections—

recent trends in state legislative seats won by Republicans & Democrats—

one reason for Republican success in the south—

party identification downplayed—

patterns of party competition in state legislatures—

ethnic, racial and gender factors in elections—

Direct Democracy

direct initiative—

indirect initiative—

direct (popular) referendum—

advisory referendum—

recall election—

<u>Local Governments</u>

personal nature of local governance—

responsibilities of local government—

Charters

Dillon's Rule—

counties and school districts: examples of state government creation—

how are cities, towns and villages established—

charter—

special charters—

general charters—

classified charters—

optional charters—

home rule charters—

Types of Local Government

counties—

towns—

municipalities—

special districts—

formal and informal arrangements among local governments—

Executives and Legislatures

town meetings—

decision-making offices of local governments—

local government and separation of powers—

executive and legislative patterns in local government—

political machines—

mayor—

city council—

professional managers—

district-based elections—

at-large elections—

commission form of government—

Galveston, the 1900 hurricane and the city commission—

Major Forms of Municipal Government (Table 4.3) and trends—

public corporation (authority)—

The "Big Seven" Intergovernmental Associations (Table 4.4)—

Grassroots Power and Politics

nonpartisan elections—

role of local news media—

importance of ties and influence—

frequent patters of decision-making—

ad hoc, issue-specific organizations—

Relations with Indian Nations

domestic dependent nation—

trust relationship—

Federal Policies Toward Indian Nations (Table 4.5)—

compacts—

reservation land—

trust land—

Indian Self-Determination and Education Assistance Act of 1975—

State and Local Finances

difference between federal government and state and local governments regarding budgets—

differences between private business and state and local governments—

importance of the level of funding that governments give to one another—

federal funding for state governments declining—

requirements by the federal government on what state and local government must spend on national programs and concerns—

state governments rely primarily on what taxes?—

local government rely primarily on what taxes?—

user fees—

State and Local Government Revenues (Figure 4.3)—

segregated funds—

progressive taxes—

nature of sales taxes—

regressive taxes—

regressive nature of property taxes—

Research Ideas and Possible Paper Topics

1) Find a copy of your state's constitution and another state constitution from outside of your geographic region (i.e., Midwesterners look for a Western state, Southerners look for a New England state, etc.) and compare them. Are they similar or different? Why and how?

2) Go to the Internet and find the homepages of several different cities around the country. Compare the information you find on their methods of government, priorities, and revenues.

3)   Does your community have direct democracy (initiative, referendum, and recall)? If so, research its use in your community and the rules regarding its use. If not, find a community that has these powers and do the same.

4)   Using the library or the Internet, find out information on at least three Indian tribes. At least one tribe must not run casinos. Make sure they are from several different regions of the country as well. Discuss the quality of life of these three tribes. What kinds of decisions can tribes make? What is tribal life like? How are they governed? Compare the similarities and differences you find.

5)   Find out how your community deals with finances. From where does their money come and where does it go? Is their budget balanced? What kind of surpluses, if any, do they maintain? What constraints does the local government operate under? How easy or difficult is it to get this information?

Web sites

The Web site for **Governing Magazine**, a magazine on state and local government, contains a good index of state and local government links.
    http://governing.com

This site titled "State and Local Government on the Web" was created by the **Piper Group**, a private consulting firm, and lists links to all 50 state governments, along with federal sources, multi-state sources, national organizations, and other entities involved in state and local government.
    www.statelocalgov.net/index.cfm

The **Internet Law Library** has links to all 50 state constitutions; it also includes Indian treaties, compacts as well as territorial laws.
    www.lawguru.com/ilawlib/17.htm

The Web site for the **Council of State Governments** has news stories pertaining to the states. The Web site is updated every weekday.
    www.csg.org

National Council of State Legislatures Web site offers analysis and information on intergovernmental relations.
    www.ncsl.org/statefed/afipolcy.htm

NGA On-Line. The **National Governors' Council** is a nonpartisan organization that looks at solving state-focused problems and provides information on state innovations and practices. The Web site has stories and articles of interest to the states and provides links to similar issues and organizations.
    http://www.nga.org/portal/site/nga

Stateline.org been published online since 1999 and was originally intended as a resource for the news media on state government. However, readership expanded far beyond their original target audience and now includes state officials, students of state government and ordinary citizens from throughout the country who seek to keep track of activities in their state capitol and in other states. Funded by the **Pew Center on the States**, Stateline.org offers a wide variety of information on the states written by professional journalists.

www.stateline.org/

The **National Organization of Counties** collects information on county governments such as county officials, courthouse addresses, county seats, cities in a county, and maintains a collection of demographic data on counties.

www.naco.org/counties/counties/index.cfm

The **National City Government Resource Center** serves as a collection of municipal-related URL's from throughout the U.S. in the following categories: General City Links, Functional City Links, Regional City Links and Other City-Related Links. You can access sites on most cities in the U.S. on this page by using City Guide or CityNet. This is a personal Web site maintained by a university professor who is also a professional city manager.

http://www.geocities.com/CapitolHill/1389/

The U.S. **Department of Homeland Security's Office of Domestic Preparedness** hosts a Web page giving state and local governments information on programs, grants and assistance in counter-terrorism activities.

http://www.ojp.usdoj.gov/odp/

Practice Tests

MULTIPLE CHOICE

1) The requirement that state legislative districts have approximately the same number of people so that legislative representation would be equitable was established in *Baker* v. *Carr* (1962). This decision led to decreased control in state legislatures by
   a. rural areas.
   b. big city political machines.
   c. the federal government.
   d. the Democratic Party.

2) Which of the following enhanced the importance of state and local governments?
   a. A 2002 law that allows the federal government to turn over failing public schools to private businesses to manage.
   b. Increased federal government authority in domestic security.
   c. Reduced federal mandates during the Reagan administration.
   d. The prohibition on the ability of states to establish direct ties with other countries to spur economic growth.

3) The federal government has expanded its role in domestic security despite the fact that it has traditionally been the responsibility of
   a. the United States Army.
   b. state and local police and health agencies.
   c. the United Nations.
   d. the Federal Bureau of Investigation.

4) State governments have primary responsibility for
   a. education.
   b. economic development.
   c. public health.
   d. All of the above.

5) The first state constitutions provided for
   a. limits on the authority of state governors, legislatures, and courts.
   b. checks and balances.
   c. strong executives.
   d. All of the above.

6) Direct voter participation was advocated in the states by the
   a. Populists.
   b. Progressives.
   c. Republican Party.
   d. Whigs.

7) In 43 states, governors have the power to
   a. propose budgets.
   b. veto an entire bill.
   c. line-item veto.
   d. package veto.

8) The authors highlight the extensive and creative use of the line-item veto by Governor
   a. George W. Bush (TX).
   b. Gray Davis (CA).
   c. Tommy Thompson (WI).
   d. John Engler (MI).

9) In 1962, the Supreme Court decided the case *Baker* v. *Carr*, the result of which was (were) that
   a. legislatures more accurately represented their states.
   b. agendas became more relevant and policies more appropriate.
   c. state legislatures became more professional.
   d. All of the above.

10) State and federal courts are
   a. separate.
   b. all part of a single system.
   c. share rules, procedures, and routes for appeal.
   d. overlap in virtually every circumstance.

11) The principle that municipalities owe their origins and derive their powers from the states is called
   a. federalism.
   b. Dillon's Rule.
   c. charter power.
   d. the township rule.

12) One of the most important features of home rule is that a local government is authorized to
   a. legislate on any issue.
   b. legislate on any issue that does not conflict with existing state law.
   c. legislate on any issue that does not conflict with existing federal law.
   d. legislate on any issue that does not conflict with existing state or federal law.

13) Half of all cities in the United States have what type of municipal government?
   a. mayor and council
   b. council and professional manager
   c. commission
   d. town meeting

14) Under U.S. law and the Constitution, Indian tribes are
   a. given the same rights and responsibilities as states.
   b. ignored completely.
   c. treated as totally foreign nations.
   d. considered domestic dependent nations.

15) Local and state government budgets rely on _____ as sources of revenue.
   a. sales taxes
   b. property taxes
   c. income taxes and fees
   d. All of the above.

TRUE/FALSE

1) States recognize and authorize the creation of local governments.

2) The state government is the unit of government that licenses and regulates professions such as doctors, lawyers, barbers and dentists.

3) The intent of the authors of the original state constitutions was to empower state governments.

4) State constitutions are relatively easy to amend and amendments occur frequently to many state constitutions.

5) All governors have line-item and package veto powers.

6) Originally, most states had part-time, citizen legislatures.

7) All judges in state courts are selected by nonpartisan elections.

8) Every state is divided into subunits that are called "counties."

9) The commission form of city government is the most widely used form in the United States today.

10) Local governments rely primarily on sales taxes for their revenues.

COMPARE AND CONTRAST

nonpartisan and partisan elections

the goals of the writers of the state constitutions vs. those of the national constitution

compacts, reservation land, and trust land

the powers of state governors and those of state legislatures

state and federal courts and laws

methods of judicial selection: elections (partisan and nonpartisan), choice by legislature or governor, merit plans

initiative, referendum, and recall

county, municipality, and special district governments

municipal governments: mayor-council, mayor-manager, commission, town meeting

types of gubernatorial vetoes

ESSAY AND SHORT ANSWER QUESTIONS

1) Discuss the nature of state constitutions.

2) What was the Northwest Ordinance of 1787, and why was it important?

3) How are state courts structured?

4) Discuss charters. What kinds are there and what impact do they have on local governments?

5) Compare and contrast the various forms of municipal government and their effectiveness.

6) Which people and what groups tend to exercise power at the state, local, and community levels, and what kinds of power do they wield?

7) For what policy areas do states have primary responsibility, and how do these responsibilities relate to the constitutions they have adopted?

8) Discuss the legal status, treaty obligations, and relationships between the national government and Indian nations.

9) What are the roles, powers, and prerogatives of state governors?

10) The Constitution grants states the power to regulate elections. Discuss the various types of elections held including state level, judicial, local, and federal elections. What impact do states have on these processes? Have patterns of party competition changed over the years and, if so, how?

ANSWERS TO STUDY EXERCISES

MULTIPLE CHOICE ANSWERS

1) a
2) c
3) b
4) d
5) a
6) b

7) c
8) c
9) d
10) a
11) b
12) d
13) a
14) d
15) d

TRUE/FALSE ANSWERS

1) T
2) T
3) F
4) T
5) F
6) T
7) F
8) F
9) F
10) F

CHAPTER 5
CIVIL LIBERTIES

Chapter Goals and Learning Objectives

Should the federal government be able to listen to your private phone calls whenever it wants? Can the government seize and hold you indefinitely, without charges and without the ability to consult with an attorney? Should the government be able to examine your reading habits by scrutinizing library records? What if government's reason for all these actions is national security?

These are not simply hypothetical questions to examine in an academic setting. The government has been engaged in these activities over the past few years. And the reasons given by officials all center on national security following September 11, 2001. These governmental actions are controversial and many lawyers, scholars, judges and citizens argue that the actions violate Americans' civil liberties.

Civil liberties are the individual rights and freedoms listed in the Bill of Rights that the federal government cannot abridge. Civil liberties protect citizens from excesses of the government and from the tyranny of the majority. They place limits on the power of government to restrain or dictate how people may act. The civil liberties we possess, however, are not absolute nor are these liberties simple to explain and understand. They are interpreted and reinterpreted by the Supreme Court and common practice over time. The liberty interests guaranteed by the Bill of Rights originally were designed to protect citizens only from the national government. Subsequently, following the adoption of the Fourteenth Amendment and through the use of the doctrine of selective incorporation, the Supreme Court passed most of the Bill of Rights protections onto the states, thus protecting citizens from their state governments as well as the federal government. The Supreme Court tries to balance rights between competing interests. For example, the Court has generally ruled that your right to free speech ends when you incite a riot that would cause immediate physical harm to others. Here the Court balances an individual's right with the rights of the public at large. Each liberty interest faces a similar balancing act in its interpretation. In the age of terrorism, when many in government argue that civil liberties are secondary in importance behind national security, the balancing act becomes even more difficult. In this chapter, we explore what the government may and may not do and which interests are being balanced at a given time.

This chapter is designed to inform you about the individual rights and freedoms granted to you by the Bill of Rights. The main topic headings of the chapter are:

- The First Constitutional Amendments: The Bill of Rights
- First Amendment Guarantees: Freedom of Religion
- First Amendment Guarantees: Freedom of Speech, Press, and Assembly
- The Second Amendment: The Right to Keep and Bear Arms

- The Rights of Criminal Defendants
- The Right to Privacy

In each section, there are certain facts and ideas that you should strive to understand. Many are in boldface type and appear in both the narrative and in the glossary at the end of the book. Other ideas, dates, facts, events, people, etc. are more difficult to pull out of the narrative. (Keep in mind that studying for objective tests [multiple choice, T/F] is different than studying for essay tests. See the Study Guide section on test taking for hints on study skills.)

In general, after you finish reading and studying this chapter, you should understand the following:

- the Bill of Rights and the reasons for its addition to the Constitution and the eventual application of most of the provisions of the Bill of Rights to the states via the incorporation doctrine
- the meaning of the First Amendment's guarantee of freedom of religion in the establishment clause and free exercise clause
- the meaning of the First Amendment's guarantees of freedom of speech, press, and assembly
- the interpretation and controversy over the Second Amendment and the right to bear arms
- rights of the accused or criminal defendant's rights in the Fourth, Fifth, Sixth, and eighth Amendments and how the U.S. Supreme Court has expanded and contracted those rights
- the meaning of the right to privacy and how it has been interpreted by the Court

Chapter Outline and Key Points

In this section, you are provided with a basic outline of the chapter and key words/points you should know. Use this outline to develop a complete outline of the material. Write the definitions or further explanations for the terms. Use the space provided in this workbook or rewrite that material in your notebook. This will help you study and remember the material in preparation for your tests, assignments, and papers.

civil liberties—

civil rights—

The First Constitutional Amendments: The Bill of Rights

state constitutions and personal liberties in 1787—

the concerns of the Anti-Federalists—

George Mason—

James Madison—

Thomas Jefferson—

Bill of Rights—

Ninth Amendment—

Tenth Amendment—

The Incorporation Doctrine: The Bill of Rights Made Applicable to the States

Barron v. *Baltimore* (1833)—

14th Amendment (1868)—

due process clause—

substantive due process—

Gitlow v. *New York* (1925)—

incorporation doctrine—

Near v. *Minnesota* (1931)—

Selective Incorporation and Fundamental Freedoms

selective incorporation—

fundamental freedoms—

Palko v. *Connecticut* (1937)—

The Selective Incorporation of the Bill of Rights (Table 5.1)—

<u>First Amendment Guarantees: Freedom of Religion</u>

First Continental Congress letter of protest against establishment by the British Parliament of Anglicanism and Roman Catholicism as the official religions of the colonies—

Article VI of U.S. Constitution, "no religious test"—

First Amendment—

establishment clause—

wall of separation—

free exercise clause—

1979 Supreme Court case barring polygamy—

The Establishment Clause

Engel v. *Vitale* (1962)—

Lemon v. *Kurtzman* (1971)—

three-part *Lemon* test for establishment issues:

    1)—

    2)—

    3)—

Equal Access Act of 1984—

1990 Supreme Court case involving Bible club meeting during public high school "activity period"

1993 Supreme Court case involving religious groups using public school facilities after hours—

Agostini v. *Felton* (1997)—

Zelman v. *Simmons-Harris* (2002)—

2005 Supreme Court establishment clause case upholding *Lemon* test with regard to a display of the Ten Commandments in a courthouse—

federal court case involving Charles Colson Prison Fellowship Ministry and a government-funded prison program—

Americans United for Separation of Church and State—

The Free Exercise Clause

free exercise clause—

Church of Lukumi Babalu Aye v. *City of Hialeah* (1993) and the right to sacrifice animals during religious services—

Employment Division, Dept. of Human Resources of Oregon v. *Smith* (1990) and use of peyote in Native American religious services—

Religious Freedom Restoration Act—

Gonzales v. *O Centro Espirita Beneficente Uniao Do Vegetal* (2006) and use of hallucinogenic hosaca tea in religious services—

1965 Supreme Court case involving conscientious objector deferments during Vietnam War—

Supreme Court rulings on prisoners' rights to conduct religious services (Catholic, Protestant, Jewish, Buddhist, and Islamic)—

First Amendment Guarantees: Freedom of Speech, Press, and Assembly

Congressional criticism of media content—

Freedom of Speech and Press

free exchange of ideas—

Supreme Court's protection of thoughts, actions, and words—

The Alien and Sedition Acts

prior restraint—

Alien and Section Acts—

Slavery, the Civil War, and Rights Curtailment

writ of habeas corpus—

Ex parte McCardle (1869)—

sedition prosecutions after the Civil War—

hostility toward Socialists and Communists—

state laws punishing seditions speech by end of World War I—

Gitlow v. *New York* (1925)—

World War I and Anti-Governmental Speech

Espionage Act of 1917—

Schenck v. *U.S.* (1919)—

clear and present danger test—

Brandenburg v. *Ohio* (1969)—

direct incitement test—

Military Commissions Act of 2006—

Protected Speech and Publications

Prior Restraint

New York Times v. *United States* (1971)—

Nebraska Press Association v. *Stuart* (1976)—

2005 Supreme Court prior restraint case involving a deceased public figure (Johnnie Cochran)—

Symbolic Speech

symbolic speech—

Stomberg v. *California* (1931)—

Tinker v. *Des Moines Independent Community School District* (1969)—

Texas v. *Johnson* (1989)—

Federal Flag Protection Act of 1989 and 1990 Supreme Court case ruling it unconstitutional—

Hate Speech, Unpopular Speech, and Speech Zones

R.A.V. v. *City of St. Paul* (1992)—

2003 Supreme Court case on cross burning—

free speech zones—

Regents v. *Southworth* (2000)—

Unprotected Speech and Publications

Libel and Slander

libel—

slander—

New York Times v. *Sullivan* (1971)—

actual malice—

public figures—

Fighting Words

Chaplinsky v. *New Hampshire* (1942)—

fighting words—

"Fuck the draft. Stop the War" and *Cohen* v. *California* (1968)—

Obscenity

Roth v. *U.S.* (1957)—

defining "prurient"—

Miller v. *California* (1973)—

1991 Supreme Court case on nude erotic dancing—

Congress and Obscenity

NEA, Congress and the 1998 Supreme Court case upholding statute limiting NEA—

Communications Decency Act of 1996—

Reno v. *ACLU* (1997)—

Child Online Protection Act of 1998—

Ashcroft v. *Free Speech Coalition* (2002)—

2003 anti-crime bill limiting cyber porn—

2004 Supreme Court case striking down further efforts by Congress to limit cyberporn—

Freedoms of Assembly and Petition

DeJonge v. *Oregon* (1937)—

The Second Amendment: The Right to Keep and Bear Arms

Second Amendment—

U.S. v. *Miller* (1939)—

Quilici v. *Village of Morton* (1983)—

Brady Bill—

1997 Supreme Court case on the Brady Bill—

1994 ban on assault weapons—

National Rifle Association—

The Rights of Criminal Defendants

the Fourth, Fifth, Sixth, and Eighth Amendments—

due process rights (also known as procedural guarantees, rights of defendants)—

criticism of Warren Court decisions—

The Fourth Amendment and Searches and Seizures

Fourth Amendment—

English Parliament and general writs of assistance—

Supreme Court has interpreted the Fourth Amendment, over the years, to allow the police to search:

    1)

    2)

    3)

knock and announce—

2006 Supreme Court ruling on case where improperly seized evidence could be used even if police refused to knock—

reasonable suspicion—

warrant—

warrantless searches—

2001 Supreme Court case on California policy regarding probationers and warrantless searches—

the Supreme Court and rulings on consent—

search situations where no arrest occurs—

homes and warrants—

"open fields doctrine"—

thermal imager case—

automobile searches—

cars and searches—

2002 border patrol officer case—

USA Patriot Act—

Drug Testing

1986 executive order by Reagan for executive branch employee drug testing—

1997 law requiring random drug testing of congressional employees—

1989 Supreme Court ruling regarding drug and alcohol testing of employees involved in accidents—

1995 Court ruling on random drug testing of public high school athletes—

2002 Court ruling on mandatory drug testing of high school students participating in any extracurricular activities—

Chandler v. *Miller* (1997)—

greater protection for public employees than private sector employees from drug screening—

2001 Court ruling on compulsory drug testing for pregnant women undergoing medical care—

The Fifth Amendment and Self-Incrimination

Fifth Amendment—

self-incrimination—

use of voluntary confessions—

the third degree—

Miranda v. *Arizona* (1966)—

Miranda rights—

Rehnquist Court and *Miranda* rights—

1991 Rehnquist Court ruling on coerced confessions and "harmless error"—

2000 Rehnquist Court ruling reaffirming central holding of *Miranda*—

2003 Rehnquist Court ruling in case where defendant interrupted officers before they read him his rights—

double jeopardy clause—

Smith v. *Massachusetts* (2005)—

The Fourth and Fifth Amendments and the Exclusionary Rule

Weeks v. *U.S.* (1914)—

exclusionary rule—

"fruits of a poisonous tree"—

Mapp v. *Ohio* (1961)—

1976 Supreme Court case creating the good faith exception—

inevitable discovery—

2006 Supreme Court decision regarding evidence collected under an anticipatory warrant—

The Sixth Amendment and Right to Counsel

Sixth Amendment—

history of providing counsel to defendants too poor to hire a lawyer—

Gideon v. *Wainwright* (1963)—

Abe Fortas—

1972 Burger Court expansion of *Gideon*—

2002 Rehnquist Court expansion of *Gideon*—

actual imprisonment standard—

quality of counsel issue—

2005 Supreme Court ruling on competence of counsel—

The Sixth Amendment and Jury Trials

speedy and public trial by impartial jury—

impartial jury—

1880 and 1975 Supreme Court rulings on systematic exclusion of groups—

Batson v. *Kentucky* (1986)—

1994 Court ruling on exclusion of women from juries—

Maryland v. *Craig* (1990)—

The Eighth Amendment and Cruel and Unusual Punishment

Eighth Amendment—

English Bill of Rights in 1687—

death penalty in America—

Furman v. *Georgia* (1972)—

Gregg v. *Georgia* (1976)—

McKleskey v. *Kemp* (1987)—

McKleskey v. *Zant* (1991)—

2002 mentally retarded convicts case (*Atkins* v. *Virginia*)—

2005 Supreme Court decision on executing those who committed murders as minors—

2000 Illinois moratorium on executions by Gov. George Ryan—

2003 commutation of death sentences by Gov. Ryan—

DNA testing and executions—

House v. *Bell* (2006)—

2006 Court ruling on death-row inmate challenges of drugs and procedures involved in lethal injections—

U.S. Executions by Year, 1976-2006—

The Right to Privacy

right to privacy—

Justice Brandeis and "the right to be left alone"—

Birth Control

Griswold v. *Connecticut* (1965)—

"penumbras" of the Constitution—

zones of privacy—

Abortion

Roe v. *Wade* (1973)—

Hyde Amendment and Supreme Court rulings on its constitutionality—

Webster v. *Reproductive Health Services* (1989)—

Planned Parenthood of Southeastern Pennsylvania v. *Casey* (1992)—

"an undue burden"—

gag rule—

Partial Birth Abortion bills vetoed by President Clinton both in 1996 and 1998—

Stenberg v. *Carhart* (2000)—

Partial Birth Abortion Ban Act of 2003, signed by President George W. Bush—

2007 Supreme Court decisions in *Gonzales* v. *Carhart*, and *Gonzales* v. *Planned Parenthood*—

Homosexuality

Lawrence v. *Texas* (2003)—

The Right to Die

1990 Supreme Court ruling on parents wanting to withdraw a feeding tube from their comatose daughter—

1997 Supreme Court ruling on physician-assisted suicide (*Vacco* v. *Quill*)—

U.S. Attorney General John Ashcroft and Oregon assisted suicide law—

Gonzalez v. *Oregon* (2005)—

Alberto Gonzalez—

Research Ideas and Possible Paper Topics

1) Find out if your campus has a "speech code." (If it doesn't, find a nearby college or university with one.) Would this code stand up to a constitutional test? Why or why not? According to your understanding of the First Amendment, are speech codes constitutional? Do some research at the campus newspaper and see if there was any controversy surrounding the adoption of the speech code and discuss it in class.

2) Explore the current docket of the Supreme Court. What civil liberties issues are going to be or are being heard this term? How do you think they will be decided and why? Follow the process until the rulings are made and see if you are right.

3) Under Chief Justice Rehnquist, the Court has reduced many of the due process rights granted under the Warren and Burger Courts. Find examples of how these rights have changed and why. Has the new Roberts Court heard cases on due process issues and to what end? What has the role of public and political opinion been in these changes?

4) Call your local branch of the American Civil Liberties Union. Visit or ask for written information about their activities and issues. Find out what they do and why. Also check their Web site (see below) for information.

5) The 2003 Supreme Court decision in *Lawrence* v. *Texas* has far-reaching implications for gay rights in the United States. The *Lawrence* decision precipitated activity, for example, in the states and in national politics regarding

same-sex marriages.   What effects did the *Lawrence* decision have on that and other issues relating to gay rights and American politics?

Web sites

The **Legal Information Institute** of Cornell University has an excellent site that offers extensive information about civil liberties. There is a section focused on the First Amendment with definitions, historical background, Supreme Court decisions, and links to numerous First Amendment-related sites. There are also sites at LII for prisoners' rights, employment rights, and constitutional rights generally.
www.law.cornell.edu/topics/first_amendment.html

American Civil Liberties Union (ACLU) offers information on the entire Bill of Rights including racial profiling, women's rights, privacy issues, prisons, drugs, etc. Includes links to other sites dealing with the same issues.
www.aclu.org

The U.S. Information Agency of the Department of State offers an annotated version of the full text of the Bill of Rights and other constitutional documents.
http://usinfo.state.gov/products/pubs/constitution/amendment.htm

The **Cato Institute,** a Libertarian think-tank, hosts a Constitution Studies page on its Web site, examining Amendments 1, 2, 4, 5, 9 and 10 as well as other constitutional issues.
www.cato.org/ccs/issues.html

PBS offers a Web page that presents the background and issues relating to *Texas* v. *Johnson* and *U.S.* v. *Eichman*, the flag-burning cases, freedom of expression cases.
www.pbs.org/jefferson/enlight/flag.htm

The Freedom Forum, based in Arlington, Virginia., is a nonpartisan foundation dedicated to the study of free press and free speech issues, with a particular focus on freedom of the press.
http://www.freedomforum.org

The First Amendment Center is an organization that studies and reports on First Amendment issues. Vanderbilt University hosts and operates the First Amendment Center and its Web site.
http://www.firstamendmentcenter.org

Americans United for Separation of Church and State monitors church-state separation issues and promotes protection of the First Amendment establishment clause in Congress and state legislatures.
www.au.org

Professor Eugene Volkh of the **UCLA Law School** maintains a list of links to sources on the Second Amendment. You can also click on a link to his homepage to find a list of scholarly articles he has written on the Second Amendment and other Bill of Rights issues.

http://www1.law.ucla.edu/~volokh/2amteach/sources.htm

The James Madison Research Library and Information Center Web site is hosted by **The National Rifle Association** to detail their understanding of the Second Amendment.

www.madisonbrigade.com

Fighting Terrorism/Protecting Liberty is a site by the **National Association of Criminal Defense Lawyers.** This site monitors the many bills in Congress and proposals by the Department of Justice to increase the powers of law enforcement in the face of terrorism. The NACDL and other organizations concerned with civil liberties track these measures to ensure the least possible intrusion on liberties consistent with protection from terrorist attacks.

www.criminaljustice.org/public.nsf/freeform/terrorism1?OpenDocument

Also from the **National Association of Criminal Defense Lawyers** is a Web page devoted to the fortieth anniversary in 2003 of the Supreme Court decision in *Gideon* v. *Wainwright.*

http://www.nacdl.org/gideon

NoloPress is a commercial publisher of self-help legal information and it provides a Web page that offers a tour of the ways in which the Bill of Rights attempts to ensure fair treatment for those accused of crimes by the government.

http://www.nolo.com/lawcenter/ency/article.cfm/objectID/6410CC94-3E8F-4A37-A5F85E3348E6431F/catID/D4C65461-8D33-482C-92FCEA7F2ADED29A

The Center for Reproductive Rights Web site has an extensive guide to national and international legal issues dealing with abortion.

http://www.crlp.org

The American Life League Web site has a list of Supreme Court cases and links to information regarding the abortion issue from a pro-life position.

http://www.all.org/issues.php?PHPSESSID=8dba6a130a018d4d1cd6a31d63dab2df

The University of Missouri-Kansas City School of Law hosts a Web page with background of Supreme Court cases dealing with gay rights in the United States.

http://www.law.umkc.edu/faculty/projects/ftrials/conlaw/gayrights.htm

A Web site published by the **University of Washington Libraries** titled *Taking Back America* provides numerous links about the USA Patriot Act and threats to the liberty interests of American citizens raised by the Act.

http://www.lib.washington.edu/Suzref/patriot-act/

Findlaw is a searchable database of S.C. decisions plus legal subjects, state courts, law schools, bar associations, and international law.

www.findlaw.com

Practice Tests

MULTIPLE CHOICE

1) The Bill of Rights, as added to the Constitution originally,
   a. was a compromise between the Federalists and the Anti-Federalists.
   b. listed a number of individual and states' rights to be protected.
   c. was designed to serve as protection against infringement of rights by the new national government.
   d. All of the above.

2) The Constitution was ratified in 1789; Amendments 1 through 10 were ratified
   a. over the course of 20 years, following the adoption of the Constitution.
   b. in 1789 (Amendments 1-5) and 1792 (Amendment 6-10).
   c. in 1791.
   d. in 1789.

3) The Supreme Court ruled that the Bill of Rights limited only the federal government and not the states in
   a. *Barron* v. *Baltimore.*
   b. *McCulloch* v. *Maryland.*
   c. *Cantwell* v. *Connecticut.*
   d. *Reynolds* v. *U.S.*

4) The due process clause is located in the _____ Amendment(s).
   a. Fifth
   b. Sixth
   c. Fourteenth
   d. Fifth and Fourteenth

5) The rationale for the process of selective incorporation protecting against the abridgment only of fundamental freedoms was set out in the 1937 Supreme Court case of
   a. *Cantwell* v. *Connecticut.*
   b. *Reynolds* v. *Sims.*
   c. *Near* v. *Minnesota.*
   d. *Palko* v. *Connecticut.*

6) The clause in the Bill of Rights that prohibits the national government from establishing an official religion is called the
   a. establishment clause.
   b. free exercise clause.
   c. religious freedom clause.
   d. freedom to choose clause.

7) The Supreme Court has ruled that in establishment clause questions, a law is constitutional if it had a secular purpose, neither advanced nor inhibited religion and did not foster excessive government entanglement with religion. The three-part test comes from the case
   a. *Mapp* v. *Ohio.*
   b. *Lemon* v. *Kurtzman.*
   c. *Stenburg* v. *Carhart.*
   d. *Chaplinsky* v. *New Hampshire.*

8) The guarantee of free speech in the First Amendment is not absolute. Among the limitations on speech are
   a. sedition and treason.
   b. slander and libel.
   c. obscenity.
   d. All of the above.

9) The Supreme Court first acknowledged symbolic speech in the case
   a. *Chaplinsky* v. *New Hampshire.*
   b. *Roth* v. *U.S.*
   c. *Stromberg* v. *California.*
   d. *Miller* v. *California.*

10) The amendment that requires the police to get a search warrant to conduct searches of your home in most cases is the _____ Amendment.
   a. Fourth
   b. Fifth
   c. Sixth
   d. Eighth

11)   In 1966, the Court ruled that suspects must be apprised of their rights once
       arrested in the case of
       a.   *Gideon* v. *Wainwright.*
       b.   *Michigan* v. *Tyler.*
       c.   *Mapp* v. *Ohio.*
       d.   *Miranda* v. *Arizona.*

12)   In *Weeks* v. *U.S.* (1914), the Supreme Court barred the use of illegally seized
       evidence at trial. This is called the
       a.   warrant rule.
       b.   exclusionary rule.
       c.   Weeks test.
       d.   search and seizure doctrine.

13)   Death penalty cases are usually dealt with under the _____ Amendment.
       a.   Fourth
       b.   Fifth
       c.   Sixth
       d.   Eighth

14)   The right to privacy was first cited in
       a.   *Furman* v. *Georgia.*
       b.   *McCleskey* v. *Zant.*
       c.   *Griswold* v. *Connecticut.*
       d.   *Roe* v. *Wade.*

15)   Where is the right to privacy found in the U.S. Constitution?
       a.   in the Fourth Amendment
       b.   in the Sixth Amendment
       c.   in the "Right to Privacy Amendment"
       d.   in the "penumbras" of the Constitution

TRUE/FALSE

1)   The Federalists put forward the idea of a Bill of Rights in order to protect the
       liberty of individual citizens from the state governments.

2)   The Court first ruled that prayer in public school was unconstitutional in *Engel* v.
       Vitale.

3)   *New York Times* v. *Sullivan* made it much easier to prove libel which is not
       constitutionally protected speech.

4)   Burning the American flag is considered constitutionally protected symbolic
       speech.

5)   In *New York Times* v. *United States*, the Supreme Court ruled that the U.S. government could prevent the publication of papers harmful to national security.

6)   The Fourth Amendment's purpose was to deny the national government the authority to conduct general searches.

7)   Police officers do not need a warrant if they have consent to search.

8)   The Sixth Amendment guarantees citizens an attorney under all circumstances, civil and criminal.

9)   The Supreme Court has interpreted the Sixth Amendment to mean that jury trials must be available if a prison sentence of six months or more is possible.

10)   The death penalty has more public support today than ever before.

COMPARE AND CONTRAST

civil liberties and civil rights

the Bill of Rights and the Incorporation Doctrine

free exercise and establishment clause

clear and present danger and direct incitement tests

symbolic speech, prior restraint, and hate speech

due process rights: Fourth, Fifth, Sixth and Eighth Amendments

Furman v. *Georgia, Gregg* v. *Georgia,* and *McCleskey* v. *Kemp*

privacy rights: birth control, abortion, homosexual rights, the right to die, medical records, etc.

ESSAY AND SHORT ANSWER QUESTIONS

1)   What is the Bill of Rights, and why was it added to the Constitution?

2)   Explain the establishment clause and its current application.

3)   What is the incorporation doctrine, and how has it been used?

4)   What is the exclusionary rule, and why is it important?

5)   What has the Supreme Court ruled in "right to die" cases?

6)   Explain the First Amendment. What rights and liberties are covered by this amendment, how has the Supreme Court interpreted its meanings, and what rights/liberties is the Court trying to balance in making its rulings on these issues? Be sure to cite cases.

7)   Explain our rights to free speech, freedom of the press, and freedom to petition and assemble. What limits exist on these rights? Be sure to cite cases.

8)   Discuss the application of the Fourth Amendment since 9/11. What has the federal government done that circumvents Fourth Amendment protections? Are these circumventions justified? What are the arguments for and against the federal government's expansive campaign for national security at the cost of many Fourth Amendment protections? Cite cases.

9)   Discuss due process rights stemming from the Fifth, Sixth, and Eighth Amendments. How have these protections changed over time? Be sure to cite cases.

10)   What is the right to privacy? What are the constitutional bases of this right? How has this right been applied and to what might it be applied in the future?

ANSWERS TO STUDY EXERCISES

MULTIPLE CHOICE ANSWERS

1) d
2) c
3) a
4) d
5) d
6) a
7) b
8) d
9) c
10) a
11) d
12) b
13) d
14) c
15) d

TRUE/FALSE ANSWERS

1) F
2) T
3) F
4) T
5) F
6) T
7) T
8) F
9) T
10) F

CHAPTER 6
CIVIL RIGHTS

Chapter Goals and Learning Objectives

Civil rights concern the positive acts that governments take to protect certain classifications of individuals against arbitrary or discriminatory treatment by government or individuals. The Framers were most concerned with creating a new, workable, and enduring form of government than with civil rights. The Fourteenth Amendment introduced the idea of equal protection of the laws and has generated more litigation to determine and specify its meaning than any other constitutional provision. This chapter explores how African Americans, women, and other disadvantaged political groups, groups which had been historically and systematically denied their liberty interests, have drawn ideas, support, and success from one another in the quest for equality under the law. This chapter presents information that may be much more than intellectually interesting to you.   You may have been or will be the victim of arbitrary or discriminatory treatment because of your race, gender, national origin, religion, age, sexual orientation, or disability. How do you obtain protection of the civil rights laws of the nation or your state? What, indeed, are your rights under the law and to where do you turn for protection?

This chapter is designed to inform you about the struggle of women and minorities for civil rights and the privileges of citizenship, including equal protection of the laws and voting rights, and is designed to inform you of how one can seek protection of one's civil rights under the law. The main topic headings of the chapter are:

- Slavery, Abolition, and Winning the Right to Vote, 1800-1890
- The Push for Equality, 1890-1954
- The Civil Rights Movement
- The Women's Rights Movement
- Other Groups Mobilize for Rights
- Continuing Controversies in Civil Rights

In each section, there are certain facts and ideas that you should strive to understand. Many are in boldface type and appear in both the narrative and in the glossary at the end of the book. Other ideas, dates, facts, events, people, etc. are more difficult to pull out of the narrative. (Keep in mind that studying for objective tests [multiple choice, T/F] is different than studying for essay tests. See the Study Guide section on test taking for hints on study skills.)

In general, after you finish reading and studying this chapter, you should understand the following:

- slavery, abolition, and winning the right to vote from 1800 to 1890

- the push for equality by African Americans and women from 1885 to 1954, using the Supreme Court's decisions in *Plessy* v. *Ferguson* to *Brown* v. *Board of Education of Topeka, Kansas* to define the study
- the civil rights movement and its techniques, strategies, and leaders as well as the Civil Rights Act of 1964 and its facilitation and effects
- the development of a new women's rights movement and its push for an equal rights amendment to the U.S. Constitution
- efforts of other groups to expand the definition of civil rights further such as Native Americans, Hispanic Americans, gays and lesbians, and disabled Americans, often using methods borrowed from the struggles of African Americans and women
- continuing controversies in civil rights and workplace discrimination

---

Chapter Outline and Key Points

In this section, you are provided with a basic outline of the chapter and key words/points you should know. Use this outline to develop a complete outline of the material. Write the definitions or further explanations for the terms. Use the space provided in this workbook or rewrite that material in your notebook. This will help you study and remember the material in preparation for your tests, assignments, and papers.

civil rights—

Fourteenth Amendment—

Slavery, Abolition, and Winning the Right to Vote, 1800-90

Slavery and Congress

Congress bans the slave trade—

black population in first half of nineteenth century—

Missouri Compromise of 1820—

The First Civil Rights Movements: Abolition and Women's Rights

abolitionist movement—

NAACP—

Frederick Douglass—

Seneca Falls Convention (1848)—

The 1850s: The Calm Before the Storm

Uncle Tom's Cabin (1852)—

Dred Scott v. *Sandford* (1857)—

The Civil War and its Aftermath: Civil Rights Laws and Constitutional Amendments

Emancipation Proclamation—

Thirteenth Amendment—

Black Codes—

Civil Rights Act of 1866—

Fourteenth Amendment—

due process clause of Fourteenth Amendment—

privileges and immunities clause of Fourteenth Amendment—

Fifteenth Amendment—

National Woman Suffrage Association—

Civil Rights, Congress, and the Supreme Court

"freedmen"—

Jim Crow Laws—

Civil Rights Cases (1883)—

three ways Southern states excluded African Americans from the vote after the Civil War Amendments:

1) poll taxes—

2) property-owning qualifications—

3) literacy tests—

grandfather clause—

The Push for Equality, 1890-1954

The Progressive Era—

Plessy v. *Ferguson* (1896)—

separate but equal—

Jim Crow system expanded—

The Founding of the National Association for the Advancement of Colored People

NAACP—

W. E. B. DuBois—

Niagara Movement—

Key Women's Groups

NAWSA—

Susan B. Anthony—

NCL—

Muller v. *Oregon* (1908)—

suffrage movement—

Nineteenth Amendment—

Litigating for Equality

reasons for turning to the federal courts—

Test Cases

Lloyd Gaines case of 1938—

Thurgood Marshall—

NAACP-LDF—

the *Sweatt* and *McLaurin* cases of 1950—

amicus curiae briefs—

Brown v. *Board of Education*

Brown v. *Board of Education of Topeka, Kansas* (1954)—

Kenneth Clark's doll study—

equal protection clause—

Black Monday—

The Civil Rights Movement

School Desegregation After Brown

Brown v. *Board of Education II* (1955)—

Governor Orval Faubus—

Little Rock Central High School—

Cooper v. *Aaron* (1958)—

A New Move for African American Rights

Rosa Parks—

Montgomery Bus Boycott—

Dr. Martin Luther King, Jr.—

Formation of New Groups

Southern Christian Leadership Council (SCLC)—

Student Nonviolent Coordinating Committee (SNCC)—

sit-in protest—

freedom rides—

March on Birmingham—

The Civil Rights Act of 1964

first significant civil rights legislation passed since the post-Civil War era—

March on Washington, August 1963—

"I Have A Dream" speech—

President Lyndon B. Johnson—

Senator Strom Thurmond—

Elements of Civil Rights Act of 1964:

    1)

    2)

    3)

    4)

    5)

    6)

Malcolm X—

The Impact of the Civil Rights Act of 1964

Education

    Swann v. *Charlotte-Mecklenburg School District* (1971)—

    de jure discrimination—

    de facto discrimination—

    forced busing—

    1995 Supreme Court case on school desegregation—

    trend today regarding school desegregation plans—

Employment

> Title VII of Civil Rights Act of 1964—
>
> 1978 amendment regarding pregnancy—
>
> *Duke Power Company* case (1971)—
>
> "business necessity"—
>
> some examples of job requirements found illegal—

The Women's Rights Movement

several reasons for a separate women's rights movement—

Litigation for Equal Rights

> *Hoyt* v. *Florida* (1961)—
>
> 1961 President's Commission on the Status of Women—
>
> *The Feminine Mystique*—
>
> sex discrimination prohibition added by Southern congressmen to Title VII for what reason?—
>
> Equal Opportunity Employment Commission (EEOC)—
>
> National Organization of Women (NOW)—
>
> Equal Rights Amendment (ERA)—
>
> *Roe* v. *Wade* (1973) and impact on ERA—
>
> ratification record on ERA—

The Equal Protection Clause and Constitutional Standards of Review

> Fourteenth Amendment and equal protection—
>
> suspect classification—
>
> strict scrutiny—
>
> fundamental freedoms—

The Equal Protection Clause and Standards of Review (Table 6.1)—

Supreme Court cases on equal protection in the 1940s and 1950s—

Korematsu v. *U.S.* (1944)—

Supreme Court cases on equal protection in the 1960s and 1970s—

intermediate standard of review—

practices which have been found to violate the Fourteenth Amendment:

    1)

    2)

    3)

    4)

    5)

    6)

governmental practices and laws upheld by the Court:

    1)

    2)

Statutory Remedies for Sex Discrimination

Equal Pay Act of 1963—

key victories under Title VII of the Civil Rights Act:

    1)

    2)

    3)

    4)

Title IX of the Civil Rights Act—

Bush administration position on Title IX provisions—

The Wage Gap, 1990-2006 (Figure 6.1)—

Other Groups Mobilize for Rights

Hispanic Americans

LULAC—

patterns of immigration—

National Council of La Raza—

Cesar Chavez—

United Farm Workers Union—

MALDEF—

Voting Rights Act—

public school discrimination cases—

other areas of MALDEF litigation and lobbying—

legislation proposing crack-down on illegal immigration—

Native Americans

"Indian tribes" under the U.S. Constitution—

Northwest Ordinance of 1787 and Native Americans—

genocide-at-law—

Dawes Act of 1887—

NARF—

land rights and casinos—

large Native American land claim in 1972—

Native Americans and religious freedom—

Bury My Heart at Wounded Knee—

Department of Interior and Indian trust funds—

Indigenous Democratic Network (INDN)—

Gays and Lesbians

Lamda Legal Defense and Education Fund—

"Don't Ask, Don't Tell" policy—

Romer v. *Evans* (1996)—

Lawrence v. *Texas* (2003)—

Wal-Mart and discrimination based on sexual orientation—

2003 Massachusetts Supreme Court ruling on gay marriage—

2004 election and same-sex marriage issue—

George W. Bush and banning same-sex marriages—

Disabled Americans

Americans with Disabilities Act (ADA) of 1990—

the cumulative effect of four 1999 Supreme Court cases in 1999 on the ADA—

Tennessee v. *Lane* (2004)—

American Association of People with Disabilities (AAPD)

<u>Continuing Controversies in Civil Rights</u>

areas of continued discrimination—

2006 poll on a woman as president—

July, 2005 poll on same-sex marriage—

Affirmative Action

affirmative action—

Regents of the University of California v. *Bakke* (1978)—

Ronald Reagan's position on affirmative action—

Public Opinion on Affirmative Action (Figure 6.2)—

five 1989 Supreme Court cases on affirmative action—

Civil Rights Act of 1991 and affirmative action—

Hopwood v. *Texas* (5th Circuit, 1996)—

Grutter v. *Bollinger* (2003)—

Pay Equity and Other Issues of Workplace Discrimination

Wal-Mart discrimination against women—

Wal-Mart discrimination against Hispanic immigrants—

Research Ideas and Possible Paper Topics

1) Look at the current Supreme Court docket. What civil rights cases do you see? What are their constitutional arguments, and how do they differ from the cases the book discusses in the 1950s, 60s and 70s?

2) The use of *amicus curiae* briefs has increased dramatically in the last several decades and many people now argue that public opinion plays a role in Supreme Court decisions. Analyze and discuss these two issues. How would you characterize the role of such influence in civil rights cases?

3) Examine the controversial issue of same-sex marriages and research it in-depth. What constitutional issues are used, what arguments, etc.? How did the issue effect the 2004 presidential election and the recent mid-term elections? How do you feel the Roberts Court would rule on this issue and why? Explore the possibility of a constitution amendment proposed by the Republican Party to prohibit same-sex marriages.

4) Look at the current Supreme Court. Do some biographical and case research on each of the nine justices in the area of civil rights. Build a typography

(classify the judges into groups of like-minded individuals) on how the current justices rule on civil rights. (Example: The simplest typography would be liberal—moderate—conservative. But be sure to define each of those categories. A more complex system would provide better analysis of the Court.) What has been the impact of the new Court members appointed by President George W. Bush in his second term?

5) Congress also plays a role in civil rights. Do some research to determine what types of civil rights issues Congress has been dealing with in the last four years. What are the separate roles of Congress and the courts in civil rights?

Web sites

Civil Rights Division, U.S. Department of Justice Web site offers an overview of the activities and programs of the DOJ on civil rights as well as links to documents, legislation, cases, and the Civil Rights Forum Newsletter.
www.usdoj.gov/crt/crt-home.html

U.S. Commission on Civil Rights is a bi-partisan, fact-finding agency established within the executive branch. The Web site offers news releases, publications, a calendar of events, and multimedia coverage of civil rights events.
www.usccr.gov

The **Legal Information Institute** of Cornell University has an excellent site that offers extensive information about the legalities and definitions of civil rights. It begins with a prose definition of a civil right and includes links to U.S. Government laws, state laws, Supreme Court rulings, international laws on civil rights, and more.
www.law.cornell.edu/topics/civil_rights.html

The **National Association for the Advancement of Colored People** (NAACP) Web site offers information about the organization, membership, and issues of interest to proponents of civil rights.
www.naacp.org

The **Southern Poverty Law Center (SPLC)** is a nonprofit group dedicated to fighting hate and intolerance. Their Web site includes information on the center and their activities including a program titled "Teaching Tolerance," the Klanwatch, and Militia Task Force. They also have a state-by-state listing of "hate incidents."
www.splcenter.org

National Organization of Women (NOW) Web site offers information on the organization and its issues/activities, including women in the military, economic equity and reproductive rights. They offer an e-mail action list and the opportunity to join NOW online. Also has links to related sites.

www.now.org

Mexican-American Legal Defense and Education Fund (MALDEF) Web site offers information on scholarships, job opportunities, legal programs, regional offices information, and more.

www.maldef.org

Native American Rights Fund (NARF) Web site offers profiles of issues, an archive, resources, a tribal directory, and treaty information as well as a lot of other information.

www.narf.org

80-20 Initiative is a nonprofit group working to further civil rights for Asian-Americans. Its Web page presents information related to legal and political issues central to the organization's activities.

http://80-20initiative.blogspot.com/2004_08_01_80-20initiative_archive.html

America with Disabilities Act (ADA) offers information on this legislation and rights of the disabled.

www.usdoj.gov/crt/ada/adahom1.htm

EthnicMajority.com is a Web site promoting equal rights and opportunities for African, Latino and Asian Americans. Its page on affirmative action gives an extensive background on the issue and numerous links to organizations promoting and protecting affirmative action.

www.ethnicmajority.com/affirmative_action.htm

The Council on American-Islamic Relations offers a Web page detailing discrimination problems facing Islamic Arab American citizens following 9/11.

http://www.cair-net.org/default.asp?Page=knowYourRightsPocketGuide

Anti-Defamation League's Web page on civil rights focuses on several issues, including anti-Semitism.

http://www.adl.org/civil_rights

The **Legal Information Institute** of Cornell University has an excellent site that offers extensive information about the legalities and definitions of employment discrimination law. It begins with a prose definition of employment law and includes links to U.S. government laws, state laws, Supreme Court rulings, and more.

http://www.law.cornell.edu/topics/employment_discrimination.html

Findlaw is a searchable database of SC decisions plus legal subjects, state courts, law schools, bar associations, and international law.
www.findlaw.com

Practice Tests

MULTIPLE CHOICE QUESTIONS

1)   Congress banned the slave trade in
       a.   1787.
       b.   1791.
       c.   1808.
       d.   1860.

2)   Slavery and involuntary servitude were banned by the _____ Amendment.
       a.   Tenth
       b.   Thirteenth
       c.   Fifteenth
       d.   Seventeenth

3)   Why was the Civil Rights Act of 1866 passed?
       a.   to invalidate Black Codes
       b.   to encourage Southern resistance
       c.   to discourage integration
       d.   to overturn *Brown* v. *Board of Education of Topeka, Kansas*

4)   The doctrine of "separate but equal" was first enunciated in the case
       a.   *Dred Scott* v. *Sandford.*
       b.   *Bradwell* v. *Illinois.*
       c.   *Minor* v. *Happersett.*
       d.   *Plessy* v. *Ferguson.*

5)   Women were granted the right to vote in 1920 through the _____ Amendment.
       a.   Fifteenth
       b.   Seventeenth
       c.   Nineteenth
       d.   Twenty-First

6)   During the 1930s, the NAACP decided it was time to launch a challenge to the precedent set by *Plessy*. To do so, they used a strategy of
       a.   litigation.
       b.   strikes and protests.
       c.   boycotts.
       d.   All of the above.

7) The following state laws (no longer in effect) are examples of what kind of laws?

Lunch Counters: No persons, firms, or corporations, who or which furnish meals to passengers at station restaurants or station eating houses, in times limited by common carriers of said passengers, shall furnish said meals to white and colored passengers in the same room, or at the same table, or at the same counter. *South Carolina*

Libraries: Any white person of such county may use the county free library under the rules and regulations prescribed by the commissioners court and may be entitled to all the privileges thereof. Said court shall make proper provision for the negroes of said county to be served through a separate branch or branches of the county free library, which shall be administered by [a] custodian of the negro race under the supervision of the county librarian. *Texas*

Education: [The County Board of Education] shall provide schools of two kinds; those for white children and those for colored children. *Texas*

- a. civil rights laws
- b. affirmative action laws
- c. constitutional laws
- d. Jim Crow laws

8) In *Brown* v. *Board of Education II*, the Supreme Court ordered that racially segregated public school must be integrated
- a. with all deliberate speed.
- b. immediately.
- c. in the South but not the North.
- d. only if civil and political unrest can be avoided in the process.

9) In *Craig* v. *Boren*, the issue at stake was
- a. single-sex public schools.
- b. different drinking ages for men and women.
- c. that only women were allowed to receive alimony.
- d. that women could be barred from jury service.

10) The civil rights organization founded in the late 1970s at the same time litigation was being filed by activities trained at the American Indian Law Center at the University of New Mexico was the
- a. Lambda Legal Defense Fund.
- b. Legal Defense Fund for Women.
- c. Native American Rights Fund.
- d. Equal Opportunity Employment Commission.

11) U.S. policy toward Native Americans in the Dawes Act of 1887 favored
- a. dependent status.
- b. foreign status.
- c. separation.
- d. assimilation.

12) MALDEF is a civil rights group that tends to litigation in a wide range of areas of concern to
   a. blacks.
   b. Anglos.
   c. Native Americans.
   d. Hispanics.

13) In 2003, the Supreme Court ruled for the rights of homosexuals in the case of
   a. *Gregg* v. *Georgia.*
   b. *Romer* v. *Evans.*
   c. *Furman* v. *Georgia.*
   d. *Missouri* v. *Jenkins.*

14) What group won greater protection against discrimination through this legislation fueled largely by a group of veterans?
   a. Americans with Disabilities Act
   b. Civil Rights Act
   c. Voting Rights Act
   d. Fair Housing Act

15) In 1978, the Supreme Court first addressed the issue of affirmative action in *Regents of the University of California* v. *Bakke.* They ruled that
   a. all affirmative action is unconstitutional.
   b. race could not be taken into account in admissions decisions.
   c. race could be taken into account, but strict quotas were unconstitutional.
   d. if affirmative action policies discriminated against a member of the majority who was more qualified, they were unconstitutional.

TRUE/FALSE

1) Black Codes were laws of the Reconstruction South that allowed blacks to vote and exercise their constitutional rights.

2) Some women opposed the Fourteenth Amendment because it introduced gender to the Constitution for the first time.

3) The Nineteenth Amendment guaranteed women the right to vote in the United States.

4) President Harry Truman, through an executive order, desegregated the United States military services.

5) The Supreme Court's decision in *Brown* v. *Board of Education* overturned its earlier separate-but-equal ruling in *Plessy* v. *Ferguson.*

6) The Montgomery Bus boycotts were started by Dr. Martin Luther King, Jr. when he refused to give up his seat on a public bus to a white woman in Montgomery, Alabama, on December 1, 1955.

7) The Civil Rights Act of 1964 prohibits employment discrimination based on race, sex, age and national origin in Title VII of the Act.

8) Among the Southern Senators who opposed the passage of the Civil Rights Act of 1964 was Strom Thurmond of South Carolina, who later switched from the Democratic Party to the Republican Party.

9) The ERA was adopted as the Twenty-seventh Amendment to the Constitution in 1982.

10) Affirmative action in higher education was ended completely in the 2003 Supreme Court decision of *Grutter* v. *Bollinger*.

COMPARE AND CONTRAST

slavery and abolition

African American suffrage movement and the women's suffrage movement

Plessy v. *Ferguson* and *Brown* v. *Board of Education, Topeka, Kansas*

Thirteenth, Fourteenth, Fifteenth Amendments

Black Codes, grandfather clauses, and Jim Crow

NAACP and NAWSA

Civil Rights Act of 1964 and Voting Rights Act of 1965

de jure and *de facto* discrimination

intermediate level scrutiny and strict scrutiny

ESSAY AND SHORT ANSWER QUESTIONS

1) Define civil rights and discuss their constitutional bases.

2) What was the abolitionist movement?

3) Discuss the importance of the Thirteenth, Fourteenth, and Fifteenth Amendments, the Civil War Amendments.

4) Discuss the role the *Brown* decision has had on American society. Has racial equality improved because of it? Was public school desegregation successful in promoting racial equality? What U.S. Supreme Court decision in 2006 curtailed some of the requirements set forth by *Brown*?

5) With regard to civil rights, discuss the 1944 Supreme Court case of *Korematsu* v. *U.S.* Is the law established in that case still in effect today?

6) Discuss the development of civil rights through from 1800-1890 in American political history.

7) Discuss the history of the women's suffrage and rights movement up to and including the ERA and its ratification drive.

8) The NAACP chose to use a litigation strategy to achieve desegregation and equal rights. How did they implement this strategy, and what were their other choices?

9) Explain the equal protection clause and the constitutional standards of review. Use examples of Supreme Court cases.

10) Once African Americans and women had some success in the battle for equal rights, other groups mobilized to gain their rights. Discuss these groups, the tactics they used, and how successful they have been.

ANSWERS TO STUDY EXERCISES

MULTIPLE CHOICE ANSWERS

1) c
2) b
3) a
4) d
5) c
6) a
7) d
8) a
9) b
10) c
11) d
12) d
13) b
14) a
15) c

TRUE/FALSE ANSWERS

1) F
2) T
3) T
4) T
5) T
6) F
7) T
8) T
9) F
10) F

CHAPTER 7
CONGRESS

Chapter Goals and Learning Objectives

Since our country's earliest days, a national Congress has existed in one form or another. First, the Continental Congress represented the colonies, and it had little to no authority over them. Then, the states were represented in Congress under the Articles of Confederation, a national legislature that had but a few more powers than the Continental Congress over the colonies. Article I of the Constitution, however, vested the governing powers of the United States squarely in the hands of "the first branch of government," Congress. Indeed, Congress alone was given the power to create legislation, control the purse, declare war, raise an army, control commerce as well as other national governing authority under Article I, section 8. The United States had no president under its early government until the adoption of the new Constitution. And even under the new Constitution, the chief executive came in second place (Article II). Despite a balance of powers among the three branches of government, Congress was first among equals.

Today, the president of the United States is first among equals. Structurally under the Constitution, the powers of Congress have not been diminished. However, few would argue today that the president of the United States stands preeminent over the Congress in many ways. Yet, through much of our history as a nation, the reverse was true: Congress was preeminent over the presidency. Today, the president is, in terms of real and perceived power, the chief policymaker of the country. What changed over the course of our history regarding Congress? Why can virtually all Americans readily name the president but few can identify their own representatives in Congress?

The Congress of the United States consists of the House of Representatives and the Senate. It enacts our federal laws and sets the federal budget. Members of Congress work to represent their states and districts within their states. Individually, each member of Congress shares power with his or her colleagues. As a body, Congress, the institution, makes laws and policy. Individually, its members work to better the conditions of their states and districts. The Congress is organized along political party lines and the party in the majority in the House and in the Senate has enormous power to set and control its operations and agenda. The Republican controlled House during the first six years of George W. Bush's presidency, along with the Senate under Republican control for most of those six years, gave the Republican president numerous political victories. With the election in 2006 of a Democratic majority in the House and the Senate, the direction Congress took changed significantly. It is important to understand the role of Congress and its members, how the Congress goes about its business, and the extent of its constitutional powers. This chapter discusses how Congress is organized, how it makes laws as a body, how the individual members of Congress make decisions, how the relationship between Congress and the executive branch works.

This chapter is designed to inform you about the institution of Congress. The main topic headings of the chapter are:

- The Constitution and the Legislative Branch of Government
- How Congress is Organized
- The Members of Congress
- How Members Make Decisions
- The Law-making Function of Congress
- Congress and the President
- Congress and the Judiciary

In each section, there are certain facts and ideas that you should strive to understand. Many are in boldface type and appear in both the narrative and in the glossary at the end of the book. Other ideas, dates, facts, events, people, etc., are more difficult to pull out of the narrative. (Keep in mind that studying for objective tests [multiple choice, T/F] is different than studying for essay tests. See the Study Guide section on test taking for hints on study skills.)

In general, after you finish reading and studying this chapter, you should understand the following:

- what the Constitution says about the legislative branch of government
- how Congress is organized, comparing the House and the Senate and how the differences between the two chambers affect the legislative process
- how members of Congress are elected and what they do
- how members of Congress make decisions and what factors influence those decisions
- the law-making function of Congress
- how members of Congress make decisions
- the relationship between Congress and the presidency and its many permutations over our history
- the relationship between Congress and the judicial branch

Chapter Outline and Key Points

In this section, you are provided with a basic outline of the chapter and key words/points you should know. Use this outline to develop a complete outline of the material. Write the definitions or further explanations for the terms. Use the space provided in this workbook or rewrite that material in your notebook. This will help you study and remember the material in preparation for your tests, assignments, and papers.

the Framers' original concept of Congress's representational function—

the dual role Congress plays—

The Constitution and the Legislative Branch of Government

Article I of the Constitution—

the Great Compromise—

bicameral legislature—

requirements for membership in the House and Senate—

term of office for Senators and staggered election—

how Senators elected under Article I—

Seventeenth Amendment—

term of office for members of U.S. House of Representatives—

how House members are elected and related expectations of the Framers for the House—

census—

size of House in 1790—

expansion of the House—

House membership set by statute in 1929—

average number of people in a House district in 2006—

apportionment—

redistricting—

The Powers of Congress (Table 7.1)—

powers constitutionally shared by both houses—

bill—

necessary and proper clause—

formal law-making power—

exclusive powers of each house—

impeachment—

role of the two houses in impeachment—

Senate's sole power of "advise and consent"—

Wilson and the Treaty of Versailles—

Key Differences Between the House of Representatives and the Senate (Table 7.2):

        constitutional differences—

        differences in operation—

        changes in the institution—

How Congress is Organized

a new Congress is seated every _____ years—

among first items on agenda of new Congress—

hierarchical leadership structure—

Organizational Structure of the House of Representatives and the Senate in the 110th Congress (Figure 7.1)—

The Role of Parties in Organizing Congress

The 110th Congress (Figure 7.2)—

majority party—

minority party—

role of parties regarding committees—

what happens at start of new Congress in party caucus or conference?—

Committee on Committees—

Steering Committee—

The House of Representatives

the first Congress in 1798—

more tightly organized, more elaborately structured, governed by stricter rules—

loyalty to leader and party line votes—

the leadership: Speaker, majority and minority leaders, Republican and Democratic House whips—

The Speaker of the House—

    how elected—

    elected by majority party—

    duties of Speaker—

    the first powerful House speaker—

    new professionalism of House and Speaker—

    Speaker Joe Cannon—

    House revolt in 1910 and 1911 against strong Speakers—

    Newt Gingrich—

    Dennis Hastert—

    2006 election and Mark Foley scandal—

    Minority-Party Rights in Congress—

    Speaker Nancy Pelosi in 2007—

Other House Leaders—

    party caucus or conference—

    majority leader—

    were the two parties sit in the House chamber—

minority leader—

whips—

Tom DeLay—

The Senate

presiding officer of the Senate, status and duties—

Dick Cheney—

official chair of the Senate—

how president pro tempore elected and his duties—

duty of presiding over Senate rotates—

majority leader of the Senate and duties—

majority leader's power compared to Speaker's power—

whips—

Senate rules give tremendous power to individual senators—

why called a "gentlemen's club"?—

senators in the 1960s and 1970s—

majority leaders' difficulty in controlling today's Senate—

The Committee System

real legislative work of Congress takes place in committees—

bills moving through committee—

institutional committee system created in 1816—

Republican reorganization of committee structure in 1995—

House committees weakened since 1995—

House committee organization under Democratic control in 100th Congress—

Types of Committees:

    standing committees—

    joint committees—

    conference committees—

    select (or special) committees—

Committees of the 109th Congress (Table 7.3)—

House Committee on Rules—

power of standing committees—

discharge petition—

committee assignments in House and Senate—

framing legislation in House and Senate—

more individual input in Senate—

Committee Membership:

    value of committee assignments to members—

    pork—

    earmarks—

    value of public works programs to members—

    value of membership on some committees to campaign contributions—

    Appropriations and Budget Committees—

    party distribution and committee membership—

    share of committee membership for majority Democrats in 110th Congress—

Committee Chairs:

power and prestige—

staff—

seniority—

role of seniority in selecting committee chairs in House and in Senate—

The Members of Congress

congressional careerists—

why some members of Congress do not seek reelection—

how former members of Congress can make a lot of money in private sector—

former members of Congress as lobbyists—

constituencies that members of Congress must attempt to appease—

A Day in the Life of a Member of Congress (Table 7.4)—

Running for Office and Staying in Office

incumbency—

success of incumbents in reelection—

The Advantages of Incumbency (table 7.5)—

2006 election, incumbents, and scandal—

other reasons incumbents lost in 2006—

Congressional Demographics

general demographics of members of Congress—

education—

wealth—

"Millionaires Club"—

age—

women—

minorities in 2007 in the House and Senate—

Barack Obama—

Female and Minority-Group Members of Congress, Selected Years (Figure 7.3)—

occupations—

Iraq veterans—

Theories of Representation

Edmund Burke—

trustee—

delegate—

politico—

minority representation in Congress—

studies regarding women in Congress—

<u>How Members Make Decisions</u>

Party

members look to party leaders—

increase of party votes where majorities of the two parties took opposing sides (from 1970 to mid-1990)—

unanimity of votes in 107th and 108th Congress—

election of George W. Bush and "harder edge" taken by House Republicans—

voter discontent over Republican control of Congress and the 2006 midterm election results—

divided government—

percentage of voters in 2006 general election-day poll who stated a preference for divided government—

Constituents

constituents—

how often do members vote in conformity with people in the districts?—

how members of Congress gauge constituents' positions—

when do legislators act as trustee?—

when do legislators act as representatives, acting on voting cues?—

Colleagues and Caucuses

logrolling—

special-interest caucuses—

Interest Groups, Lobbyists, and Political Action Committees

primary functions of most lobbyists—

grassroots appeals—

do members of Congress tend to vote for interests of lobbyists who have contributed to their campaigns and why?—

Staff and Support Agencies

members reliance on staff—

duties of staff—

committee staff—

influence of staff on voting—

Congressional Support Agencies (Table 7.6):

116

Congressional Research Service (CRS)—

Government Accountability Office (GAO)—

Congressional Budget Office (CBO)—

The Law-making Function of Congress

who can formally submit a bill for congressional consideration—

approximate number of bills introduced in 109th Congress—

approximate number of bills introduced in 109th Congress that were made into law—

How a Bill Becomes a Law: The Textbook Version

How a Bill Becomes a Law (Figure 7.4)—

bill introduced—

sponsors and co-sponsors—

one role of clerk of House and of Senate—

three stages of bill becoming a law: committee, on the floor, when two chambers approve different versions of the same bill—

first action, with the committee—

role of committee and subcommittee—

if bill returned to full committee—

markup—

second stage, on the House or Senate floor—

House Committee on Rules—

House budget bills—

Committee of the Whole—

actions taken on floor—

if bill survives—

hold—

filibusters—

cloture—

third stage, when two chambers of Congress approve different versions of same bill—

conference committee (a bill must pass both houses in the same language to go to the president)—

no changes or amendments—

if bill passes—

veto—

four options of president regarding veto within the 10 days he has to consider the bill—

    1)

    2)

    3)

    4)

pocket veto—

How a Bill Really Becomes a Law: The China Trade Act of 2000

<u>**Congress and the President**</u>

the relationship before and after the 1930s—

The Shifting Balance of Power

post Civil War Congress—

impeachment of Andrew Johnson—

FDR presidency—

Congress cedes a major role in the legislative process—

critics of Congress—

the power void and George W. Bush's claim to unprecedented power—

Bush refusal to honor congressional subpoenas—

search of member of Congress's office by FBI—

Congressional Oversight of the Executive Branch

oversight—

key to Congress's performance of its oversight function—

committee hearings—

Republican Congress lessens oversight role of Congress after election of President George W. Bush—

unprecedented decline in congressional oversight during Bush years—

changes in oversight role of Congress under Democratic Party controlled Congress in 2007—

Congressional Review Act of 1996—

congressional review—

federal agency regulations and the Congressional Review Act—

Foreign Policy and National Security

division of foreign policy powers between the Congress and the president under the Constitution—

War Powers Act of 1973—

limited effectiveness of War Powers Act—

2001 joint resolution authorizing president to use force against terrorists—

concerns raised by Vietnam veterans over the 2001 open-ended joint resolution—

troubling issue of oversight while nation waging war—

Senator Jay Rockefeller and Vice President Dick Cheney—

Confirmation of Presidential Appointments

Senate's special oversight function—

confirmation of key members of executive branch and presidential appointments to the federal courts—

what a wise president does before making controversial nominations—

Impeachment Process

ultimate oversight—

Constitution vague about impeachment—

treason, bribery, or other "high crimes and misdemeanors"

what did Framers intend?—

Hamilton in *Federalist No. 65*—

The Eight Stages of the Impeachment Process (Table 7.7)—

only four resolutions against presidents have resulted in further action:

1)

2)

3)

4)

Congress and the Judiciary

power of judicial review and the acts of Congress—

120

ways in which Congress can exercise control over the federal judiciary—

senatorial courtesy—

setting jurisdiction of federal courts—

Research Ideas and Possible Paper Topics

1) Do some research and compare the 100th Congress to the 110th Congress in terms of party majority, leadership, representation, minorities, women, structure, incumbency advantage, and rules. What were the major changes? What accounts for the similarities and differences?

2) Using the Congressional Web site or government documents, research the transition between the 109th and 110th Congresses. What happened from election day 2006 to office-taking in January 2007? How are new members introduced to the rules, protocols, and traditions of the House and Senate? What happens to staff if their member is defeated? How do new members recruit staff? How are leaders chosen? How are rules made? Are there any "left-over issues" from the 109th? What impact has the 110th Congress had on the country?

3) Pick a piece of legislation from the current session of Congress. Write a legislative history of that bill or law. Outline the steps it took, who supported it, who opposed it, and various other influences on its passage. Were there hearings, witnesses, or controversy? Does this compare with what you learned in the text about the law-making process? How?

4) Most Americans claim to dislike and distrust Congress but like and trust their own member of Congress. What explains this paradox? Do some research on public opinion and voting behavior, analyze the media coverage of Congress, think about what members of Congress do, and why this would be the case. Prepare a presentation explaining this phenomenon for class. See if you can determine how your own U.S. Representative is perceived in your area as well.

5) There have been a number of high-profile scandals in the Congress throughout history. Americans now seem quite concerned about the ethics of the legislature. Do some research on scandals in Congress. What were some of major scandals in history? How severe have they been? How widespread have they been? Is it a few bad apples or the whole barrel? Be sure to look at how the media have covered these scandals and the lack thereof in your discussion of the ethical nature of Congress. Be sure to discuss the scandals of the 109th Congress that led to the Republicans' loss of control of both houses in the 2006 general election.

Web sites

Thomas is the official government Web site about the United States Congress from the **Library of Congress** with information on legislation, the *Congressional Record*, as well as numerous links to Congress-related sites.

http://thomas.loc.gov

Official site of the **U.S. House of Representatives**.

http://www.house.gov

Official site of the **U.S. Senate**.

www.Senate.gov

C-SPAN provides the most extensive coverage of Congress available on television over its three cable channels. Its Web site allows you to follow congressional action as it is broadcast on C-SPAN with streaming video or audio. C-SPAN's **Capitol Spotlight** Web page is sponsored by C-SPAN and **Congressional Quarterly** and has headings such as Write to Congress, Directory of Congress, Vote Library, Bills to Watch, Live Hearings and many more.

www.c-span.org/capitolspotlight/index.asp

Congressional Quarterly (CQ) is a nonpartisan publication whose mission is to inform the electorate. Access to most of the material on the CQ Web site requires a paid subscription, however some free information is available. Check with your college library to see if your school has a CQ subscription which you can use to obtain information from the site which includes information on Congress such as bios, votes, election information, and so on. They also have a link to their state and local level publication.

www.cq.com

GPO Access by the U.S. Government Printing Office offers the full text of many federal government publications on the Web, including the Congressional Record. Among the growing list of titles available are the Federal Register, Congressional Bills, United States Code, Economic Indicators and GAO Reports.

http://www.gpoaccess.gov/legislative.html

The Hill: The Capital Newspaper. From their Web site: " The Hill reports and analyzes the actions of Congress as it struggles to reconcile the needs of those it represents with the legitimate needs of the administration, lobbyists, and the news media. We explain the pressures confronting policymakers, and the many ways—often unpredictable—that decisions are made. But Capitol Hill is more than the focal point of the legislative branch of government. It is also a community not unlike a small city, and we report on its culture, social life, crime, employment, traffic, education, discrimination, shopping, dining, travel, and recreation. Our editorial viewpoint is nonpartisan and nonideological."

www.hillnews.com

RollCall On-Line. "Roll Call is widely regarded as the leading source for Congressional news and information both inside the Beltway and beyond." RollCall On-Line publishes many of the same stories, classifieds, etc. that the print edition publishes. Published on Mondays and Thursdays.

www.rollcall.com

Congress.Org is a joint venture of two Washington, D.C. area firms with expertise in communicating with Congress. Capitol Advantage and Knowlegis, LLC, two non-partisan companies that specialize in facilitating civic participation, started Congress.Org in 1996. Some search engines refer to it as a "one stop shop" for legislative information including contact information on members, committee assignments, etc.

www.congress.org

Public Citizens' Congress Watch is a consumer interest group that monitors and lobbies Congress. Its Web page reports on its actions and issues in the current Congress.

http://www.citizen.org/congress

The Washington Post. Check out the "Today in Congress" section, which offers comprehensive coverage of the Congress, including committee hearings and votes. A free subscription is required.

http://www.washingtonpost.com/wp-dyn/content/politics/congress/?nav=left

Project Vote-Smart is a nonpartisan information service funded by members and nonpartisan foundations. It offers "a wealth of facts on your political leaders, including biographies and addresses, issue positions, voting records, campaign finances, evaluations by special interests." It also offers "CongressTrack," a way for citizens to track the status of legislation, members and committees, sponsors, voting records, clear descriptions, full text, and weekly floor schedules, as well as access to information on elections, federal and state governments, the issues, and politics. Includes thousands of links to the most important sites on the Internet.

www.vote-smart.org

Practice Tests

MULTIPLE CHOICE QUESTIONS

1) The first woman in history to win the office of Speaker of the U.S. House is
   a. Shirley Chisolm.
   b. Kay Bailey Hutchinson.
   c. Nancy Pelosi.
   d. Susan B. Anthony.

2) The Senate was originally chosen by state legislators. This was changed to direct election in 1913 with the passage of the _____ Amendment.
   a. Seventeenth
   b. Eighteenth
   c. Nineteenth
   d. Twentieth

3) The clause of the Constitution that has allowed Congress to expand its powers without constitutional amendment is called the
   a. supremacy clause.
   b. necessary and proper clause.
   c. enumerated powers clause.
   d. executive powers clause.

4) Revenue bills are introduced by
   a. only the president.
   b. the House or Senate.
   c. only the Senate.
   d. only the House.

5) The failure of the Senate to ratify the Treaty of Versailles at the end of the first World War prevented U.S. participation in the League of Nations, which President Woodrow Wilson considered crucial to world peace. This action by the Senate was an exercise of the
   a. necessary and proper clause.
   b. advice and consent power.
   c. impeachment power.
   d. foreign policy power of the president.

6) Among the main differences between the House and the Senate is that
   a. House members are highly specialized.
   b. operation of the Senate is less centralized and less formal.
   c. the House has a Rules Committee.
   d. All of the above.

7) The only House officer specifically mentioned in the Constitution is the
   a. president pro tempore.
   b. majority leader of the Senate.
   c. Speaker of the House.
   d. sergeant at arms.

8) The Speaker in the 110th Congress is
   a. Nancy Pelosi.
   b. Tom DeLay.
   c. Dennis Hastert.
   d. Joseph Cannon.

9) The presiding officer of the Senate, according to the Constitution, is the
   a. vice president of the United States.
   b. president pro tempore of the Senate.
   c. majority leader of the Senate.
   d. speaker.

10) The House committee which reviews most bills after they come from committee and before they go to the full House for consideration is called
   a. a joint committee.
   b. the Governmental Affairs Committee.
   c. the Rules Committee.
   d. the Ways and Means Committee.

11) Approximately _____ bills were introduced in the 109th session of Congress.
   a. 4,500
   b. 5,000
   c. 7,500
   d. 10,000

12) A tactic by which a senator asks to be informed before a particular bill is brought to the floor, in effect stopping the bill, is called a
   a. discharge petition.
   b. cloture.
   c. block.
   d. hold.

13) The growth of presidential powers over congressional powers began particularly with the presidency of
   a. Franklin D. Roosevelt.
   b. Lyndon B. Johnson.
   c. Richard Nixon.
   d. Ronald Reagan.

14) Since 1961, there has been a substantial increase in the use of one of Congress's functions in which it questions members of the president's administration on issues pertaining to execution of congressional directives. That is called
   a. law-making.
   b. oversight.
   c. impeachment and removal.
   d. advise and consent.

15) The War Powers Act was passed by Congress over the president's veto in reaction to presidential expansion of military powers during the
   a. Vietnam War.
   b. second World War.
   c. first Gulf War.
   d. second invasion of Iraq.

TRUE/FALSE QUESTIONS

1) In 1929, the size of the House of Representatives was fixed at 435 by statute.

2) The House of Representatives has the authority to approve presidential appointments.

3) The Senate Rules Committee is very powerful and controls the flow of legislation in the Senate.

4) Every two years, a new Congress is seated.

5) Newt Gingrich, elected Speaker in 1995, was the first Republican speaker after four decades of Democratic control of the House.

6) The officer who has actual power over the operation and administration of the Senate is not the vice president but the Senate majority leader.

7) Much of the actual legislative work of Congress is done within the committee system.

8) Increasing partisanship in Congress has played a role in a number of recent retirements from that body.

9) Any federal governmental official may introduce a bill for the consideration of Congress.

10) Congress has the power to establish the size of the U.S. Supreme Court.

COMPARE AND CONTRAST

apportionment, redistricting, and gerrymandering

bill and law

impeachment and removal

differences in operation between the House and Senate

powers of House and Senate

officers of House and Senate

trustees, delegates, and politicos

standing, ad hoc, and conference committees

rules in the House and the Senate on speaking about issues and bills

general veto, line-item veto, and legislative veto

SHORT ANSWER AND ESSAY QUESTIONS

1) Discuss the history of the legislative branch prior to the adoption of the U.S. Constitution.

2) Define apportionment and redistricting and discuss their implications?

3) Discuss the incumbency advantage for members of Congress.

4) How representative is Congress? (Be sure to discuss the definition and theories of representation.)

5) Discuss the types of committees in Congress.

6) What are the constitutional powers of Congress?

7) How do the powers and functions of the House and Senate differ?

8) Discuss the role of political parties in the House and Senate.

9) What is the law-making function of Congress? Compare and contrast the two ways the text discusses about how a bill becomes a law. Be sure to specify all points at which a bill could die.

10) How do members of Congress make decisions?

ANSWERS TO STUDY EXERCISES

MULTIPLE CHOICE ANSWERS

1) c
2) a
3) b
4) d
5) b
6) d
7) c
8) a
9) a
10) c
11) d
12) d
13) a
14) b
15) a

TRUE/FALSE ANSWERS

1) T
2) F
3) F
4) T
5) T
6) T
7) T
8) T
9) F
10) T

CHAPTER 8
THE PRESIDENCY

Chapter Goals and Learning Objectives

Ask a friend, "Who is your Congressman?" and you are likely to get a blank stare in return. Ask her, however, "Who is the president?" and she will respond instantly, "George Bush, of course!" Congress, constitutionally the first branch of government, has taken a back seat in American politics and government to the president, not only in public awareness but in raw power. The constitutional authority, statutory powers, and burdens of the modern presidency make it a powerful position and an awesome responsibility. Most of the men who have been president in the past two decades have done their best in the job; yet, in the heightened expectations of the American electorate, most have come up short. Our awareness of the president in our public life is high, and our expectations of the person in that office are even higher. Not only did the Framers not envision such a powerful role for the president, they could not have foreseen the skepticism with which many presidential actions are now greeted by journalists and the public. These expectations have also led presidents into policy areas never dreamed of by the Framers.

This chapter is designed to give you a basic understanding of the presidency as an institution, as well as some information on the men who have occupied the office. The main topic headings of the chapter are:

- The Origins of and Rules Governing the Office of President of the United States
- The Constitutional Powers of the President
- The Development and Expansion of Presidential Power
- The Presidential Establishment
- The President as Policy Maker
- Presidential Leadership and the Importance of Public Opinion

In each section, you will find certain facts and ideas that you should work to understand. Many are in boldface type and appear in both the narrative and in the glossary at the end of the book. Other ideas, dates, facts, events, people, etc. are more difficult to find in the narrative. (Keep in mind that the process of reading and studying for objective exams [multiple choice, T/F] is different than for essay tests. See the Study Guide section on test taking for help with study skills.)

In general, after you finish reading and studying this chapter, you should understand the following:

- the roots and rules of the office of president of the United States and the Framers' creation of a chief executive officer under the new constitution
- Article II and the constitutional powers of the presidency

- the development and expansion of presidential power and a more "personalized" presidency; how presidential success now depends on his (or her) personality, popularity, leadership style, and position on the range of presidential authority
- the ever burgeoning presidential establishment made up of advisors, assistants, and departments, all helping the president do his job, but making it easier for him to lose touch with the people
- the president as maker of policy
- presidential leadership and the significance of public opinion: how public opinion affects the presidency and how the president affects public opinion

---

Chapter Outline and Key Points

In this section, you are provided with a basic outline of the chapter and key words/points you should know. Use this outline to develop a complete outline of the material. Write the definitions or further explanations for the terms. Use the space provided in this workbook or rewrite that material in your notebook. This will help you study and remember the material in preparation for your tests, assignments, and papers.

power to persuade—

The Roots of and Rules Governing the Office of President of the United States

the Royal Governor—

executive branch and the Articles of Confederation—

president of the Congress—

the Constitutional Convention and the executive branch—

the Framers and the president—

Presidential Qualifications and Terms of Office

qualifications—

fear of "constitutional monarch"—

term limit under Article II of Constitution—

Twenty-Second Amendment—

office of vice-president—

impeachment—

only presidents to have been impeached—

only president to resign—

executive privilege—

U.S. v. *Nixon* (1974)—

Personal Characteristics of the U.S. President (Table 8.1)—

Rules of Succession

first president to die in office—

first president to be assassinated—

Constitutional Line of Succession (Table 8.2)—

Presidential Succession Act of 1947—

Twenty-fifth Amendment—

Lyndon B. Johnson—

Gerald R. Ford—

Spiro T. Agnew—

Nelson A. Rockefeller—

when president unable to fulfill duties—

president can voluntarily relinquish power (example)—

The Constitutional Powers of the President

Article II—

first sentence of Article II—

The Appointment Power

appointment of ambassadors, federal judges, executive positions—

powerful policy making tool—

president's enforcement power—

President Teams (Table 8.3)—

George W. Bush minority appointments—

Cabinet—

The Power to Convene Congress

The State of the Union—

power to convene Congress—

Hamilton in *Federalist No. 77*—

power to convene Congress only symbolic significance now (why?)—

The Power to Make Treaties

advise and consent of the Senate—

historically, Senate ratified what percentage of treaties submitted to it by the president?—

Woodrow Wilson, Treaty of Versailles and League of Nations—

Jimmy Carter and Panama Canal Treaty—

George W. Bush and International Criminal Court (ICC)—

"fast track" authority—

executive agreement—

Treaties and Executive Agreements Concluded by the United States, 1789-2002 (Table 8.4)—

Veto Power

veto power—

Madison's argument in Constitutional Convention for veto—

"qualified negative"—

congressional override—

Presidential Vetoes (Table 8.5)—

line-item veto—

1996 bill giving president line-item veto—

Clinton v. *City of New York* (1998)—

The Power to Preside over the Military as Commander in Chief

Commander in Chief—

Gulf of Tonkin Resolution—

Pentagon Papers—

The War Powers Act of 1973—

opinion of presidents since Nixon on constitutionality of War Power Act—

George W. Bush and request to Congress for use of force in 2001 and 2002—

The Pardoning Power

pardon—

Gerald Ford and Richard Nixon—

general amnesties—

Jimmy Carter's unconditional amnesty to draft evaders—

<u>**The Development and Expansion of Presidential Power**</u>

forty-three presidents, only forty-two men held office—

Harry Truman's predictions for incoming president, Dwight Eisenhower—

limits on presidential powers—

factors influencing a president's use of his powers—

The Best and the Worst Presidents (Table 8.6)—

Establishing Presidents' Authority: The First Presidents

George Washington and the first presidency—

precedents set by presidency of George Washington:

1)

2)

3)

4)

inherent powers—

contributions of John Adams—

contributions of Thomas Jefferson—

Louisiana Purchase of 1803—

Incremental Expansion of Presidential Powers: 1804-1933

balance of power weighed heavily in favor of Congress—

the Framers' fear—

Andrew Jackson—

Jacksonian democracy—

Jackson's use of his image and personal power—

Lincoln's "questionable acts"—

FDR and the Growth of the Modern Presidency

Congress as decision maker before instantaneous communications—

effects to technological changes on public expectations—

The Expansion of Presidential Powers—

four terms of Franklin D. Roosevelt and growth of presidential power—

Great Depression—

New Deal—

FDR personalized the presidency—

FDR's use of radio—

modern presidency—

The Presidential Establishment

The Vice President

John Adams on the vice presidency—

reason president historically chose their vice presidents—

John Nance Garner—

Dick Cheney—

John Edwards—

Walter Mondale—

Lewis "Scooter" Libby—

The Cabinet

role of the Cabinet as a body—

no provision for Cabinet in Constitution—

new areas of presidential concern leads to new Cabinet offices—

The U.S. Cabinet and Responsibilities of Each Executive Department (Table 8.7)—

most recently created Cabinet office—

The First Lady

First Lady—

Abigail Adams—

Edith Bolling Galt Wilson—

Eleanor Roosevelt—

Hillary Rodham Clinton—

Laura Bush—

The Executive Office of the President (EOP)

The Executive Office of the President—

prime policy makers—

National Security Council (NSC)—

acting as mini-agencies—

Office of Faith-Based and Community Initiatives—

The White House Staff

more directly responsible to the president often—

personal assistants to the president—

how the power of the staff is derived—

size and growth of president's White House staff—

Executive Office Building—

importance of proximity to Oval Office—

The President as Policy maker

FDR's new model of law-making and policy making—

"…duty of the President…privilege of the Congress…."—

The President's Role in Proposing and Facilitation Legislation

Contract with America and presumed reassertion of congressional power—

Clinton's forceful presence in budgetary process—

George W. Bush, his forceful budgetary presence, and 2006 concern over his continuing deficit spending requests—

president's most important power (in addition to support of the public)—

presidents' difficulty in getting Congress to enact their programs—

divided government—

bills central to a president's announced agenda more successful (e.g., George W. Bush's Iraq war resolution)—

honeymoon period and its importance—

patronage—

use of personal rewards—

Speaker Tip O'Neill and the Carter White House—

president's use of political party loyalty—

the most effective president as a legislative leader—

The Budgetary Process and Legislative Implementation

importance of budget process for the president—

FDR and the Bureau of the Budget (1939)—

Office of Management and Budget (OMB)—

Policy Making Through Regulation

executive order—

Harry Truman ended segregation in the military—

LBJ and Executive Order 11246—

Ronald Reagan's executive orders on abortion counseling and fetal tissue research—

George W. Bush's executive orders on stem cell research and military tribunals—

President Bush evisceration of the Presidential Records Act—

thwarting the wishes of Congress—

Presidential Leadership and the Importance of Public Opinion

Presidential Leadership

Barber's Presidential Personalities (Table 8.8)—

usefulness of presidents increasing public attention to particular issues—

significance of a president's ability to grasp the importance of leadership style—

power to persuade—

The President and Moral Leadership—

Going Public: Mobilizing Public Opinion

Theodore Roosevelt and the bully pulpit—

development of communications technology—

"going public"—

Bill Clinton's effective use of the media as candidate and president—

George W. Bush and going directly to the people—

The Public's Perception of Presidential Performance

cyclical pattern of presidential popularity—

highest level of approval at what point?—

every action a president takes is divisive—

only four presidents since Lyndon Johnson have left office with approval ratings over 50 percent—

Presidential Approval Ratings Since 1953, by Party—

surge in president's approval ratings in his term—

George W. Bush "rallying" point due to foreign events—

George W. Bush low approval ratings and Democratic takeover of U.S. House and Senate in 2006 election—

resignation of Defense Secretary Donald Rumsfeld—

Research Ideas and Possible Paper Topics

1) Examine the growth and impact of the modern presidency. Compare it to the role of the president through the first century-and-a-half of the history of the United States. What precipitated the development of the modern presidency and what fueled its tremendous development over the past 70 years? Discuss what you think James Madison and Alexander Hamilton might say about the modern status of the limited chief executive they helped create?

2) Do some research on the vice presidency of Dick Cheney. How does his role compare and contrast with other recent vice presidents? What types of activities has he been involved in and why? Is it a function of his personal relationship with Bush or a permanent change in the office of the vice president? What role, if any, did 9/11 and the invasion of Iraq have in Cheney's role? Discuss.

3) We have experienced periods of "divided government" where the Congress is of one party and the presidency of another. The executive and legislative branches have also recently been controlled by one party. Do some research into public opinion on this issue. Which situation do Americans prefer? Why? Also research the impact divided government has had on the policy process versus the impact of single-party control. Do more bills fail in a divided government? Are Congress and the president more confrontational due to partisan differences in a divided government? Which scenario works better for our democracy? Was the Democratic takeover of control of both the U.S. House and Senate in the 2006 midterm elections due, in part, to a desire by Americans for a return to divided government, and, if so, why? Discuss.

4) Choose two presidents from history and write a paper discussing the impact they had on the office. Two interesting variants might be to choose one president who had a positive effect and one who had a negative effect, or to choose two extremely different personalities who seem equally successful and explain why.

5)   Group Project: Do an analysis of the media's coverage of President Bush during his second term. For one month, watch a variety of network and cable news programs, read a variety of newspapers and weekly news magazines, listen to talk radio (be sure to get right- and left-wing programs), and check out Internet news sites. How is the president covered? What gets the attention of the media and why? Is the president "staging" or "spinning" any of the coverage or are the media in control? Also look at how the president is portrayed in entertainment programming. What implications do your findings have on how we perceive the president? What role, if any, do you believe the news media played in the president's popularity in the polls, both positively and negatively?

Web sites

The official **White House** site for information on George W. Bush and the office of the president.
> http://www.whitehouse.gov

The **National Archives and Records Administration** offers links to all presidential libraries.
> http://www.archives.gov/presidential_libraries/addresses/addresses.html

The **National Portrait Gallery's Hall of Presidents** has information on and portraits of American presidents.
> http://www.npg.si.edu/collect/hall.htm

The **University of North Carolina** site offers biographies of the presidents and first ladies, including links to presidential libraries.
> http://www.ibiblio.org/lia/president

POTUS: Presidents of the United States is assembled by the Internet Public Library and provides background information, election results, Cabinet members, notable events, and some points of interest on each of the presidents. Links to biographies, historical documents, audio and video files, and other presidential sites listed.
> http://www.ipl.org/div/potus/

You can search the **Public Papers of the Presidents of the United States** online at this site provided by the Office of the Federal Registrar. Not all presidential papers are available currently online. Presidential photographs can be accessed as well.
> http://www.gpoaccess.gov/pubpapers/search.html

Statistics, facts, and biographies of U.S. vice presidents are available at **Vice-Presidents.Com**.
> http://www.vicepresidents.com/

Current events and video clips about the presidency of George W. Bush are available on the **C-SPAN** Web site page. Use the URL below, then click on the link titled **Bush Administration** under "Featured Topics" on top left of the main page. Also, you can hear recordings made by President Lyndon B. Johnson of his office telephone calls, tapes which have been release by the LBJ Library. Click on **LBJ White House Tapes** under "C-SPAN Radio" on the left side of the main page.

http://www.c-span.org

The **Museum of Broadcast Communications** offers a Web page titled **U.S. Presidency and Television** which discusses some of the most significant developments in the relationship between the presidency and television since the 1950s.

http://www.museum.tv/archives/etv/U/htmlU/uspresiden/uspresiden.htm

The Web site of the **Virginia Quarterly Review** has posted a fascinating article titled **"Why the Media Love Presidents and Presidents Hate the Media"** which offers a history of the expansion of broadcast technology in American and the modern presidency.

http://www.vqronline.org/articles/2000/spring/nelson-why-media

---

Practice Tests

MULTIPLE CHOICE QUESTIONS

1) Which of the following is not a constitutional requirement to hold the office of the presidency?
   a.   must be male
   b.   must be at least 35 years old
   c.   must be a resident of the United States for at least fourteen years
   d.   must be a natural-born citizen

2) Article II of the Constitution says the president
   a.   may serve only two terms.
   b.   is limited to a maximum of ten years in office.
   c.   serves for a four-year term.
   d.   serves a six-year term.

3) The Presidential Succession Act of 1947 states that if the president should die and the vice president cannot succeed him, then the next in line is the
   a. speaker of the house.
   b. president pro tempore of the Senate.
   c. secretary of state.
   d. majority leader of the Senate.

4) The first president to assume that office after appointment, not election, to the office of the vice presidency was
   a. William H. Harrison.
   b. Dwight D. Eisenhower.
   c. Gerald R. Ford.
   d. George Bush.

5) Which of the following offices is the president not constitutionally empowered to appoint?
   a. members of the U.S. Supreme Court
   b. U.S. ambassadors to foreign countries
   c. officers of the United States (such as Cabinet officers)
   d. speakers of the house and president pro tempore of the Senate

6) An example of the Senate using its advise and consent power to reject a treaty signed by the president was when the Senate rejected the Treaty of Versailles, which had been negotiated and signed by

   a. Theodore Roosevelt.
   b. Franklin Roosevelt.
   c. Woodrow Wilson.
   d. Dwight D. Eisenhower.

7) The president can enter into treaty-like relations with foreign countries for his term only without Senate approval on the basis of
   a. executive powers.
   b. executive privilege.
   c. executive orders.
   d. executive agreements.

8) In 1996, Congress voted to give the president line-item veto power. What is the status of that power now?
   a. President Clinton refused to use it, claiming that the Republican Congress was attempting to trick him.
   b. The Congress voted to repeal the line-item veto given to the president saying that the president was trying to trick them.
   c. In 1998, the U.S. Supreme Court struck down the line-item veto as unconstitutional.
   d. The president continues to use the line-item veto and has done so over twenty times during the past year.

9) Thomas Jefferson expanded the powers of the presidency through
   a. the Louisiana Purchase.
   b. the use of veto powers.
   c. the use of political parties to cement ties with Congress.
   d. the doctrine of enumerated powers.

10) The first president who acted as a strong national leader was
    a. Thomas Jefferson.
    b. Andrew Jackson.
    c. James Monroe.
    d. Franklin D. Roosevelt.

11) The growth of the modern presidency began with
    a. Thomas Jefferson.
    b. Abraham Lincoln.
    c. Franklin Roosevelt.
    d. Ronald Reagan.

12) The most recent Cabinet department established was in 2002 and is the Department of
    a. Homeland Security
    b. Energy.
    c. Veteran's Affairs.
    d. Education.

13) The president most scholars consider to be the most effective in working with Congress, getting 60 percent of his programs through Congress, was
    a. Lyndon B. Johnson.
    b. Richard M. Nixon.
    c. Gerald R. Ford.
    d. Bill Clinton.

14) According to Richard Neustadt, the most important presidential power is
    a. his constitutional power.
    b. the mandate power.
    c. the power to persuade.
    d. his commander in chief power.

15) The term "bully pulpit" was used first by what president to describe the power of the president to reach out to the American people to gain support for his programs?
    a. Theodore Roosevelt
    b. Woodrow Wilson
    c. Franklin Roosevelt
    d. John F. Kennedy

TRUE/FALSE QUESTIONS

1) Under the Articles of Confederation, no executive branch, and therefore no president of the United States, existed.

2) The president is limited to two terms in Article II of the Constitution.

3) In 1967, the Twenty-Fifth Amendment was added to the Constitution to allow a president to nominate a replacement to fill a vacancy in the office of vice president.

4) The first use of the Twenty-Fifth Amendment was when Gerald R. Ford appointed Nelson Rockefeller to be his vice president.

5) Article II gives the president power to appoint members of the congressional leadership, with the approval of the Senate.

6) The president's power to make treaties is limited by the requirement of a vote of two-thirds of the Senate to ratify the treaty.

7) The president has the power to reject all or part of any bill passed by Congress.

8) While only the Congress has the power to declare war, the president has the power to make and wage war.

9) Since the 1973 adoption of the War Powers Act by Congress, every president since Richard Nixon has vigorously supported the War Powers Act as a constitutionally permissible limit on his executive power.

10) Direct, personal appeals to the American people by the president, going over the heads of Congress via radio and television (called "going public") effectively empowers the president to influence Congress.

COMPARE AND CONTRAST

executive agreement and executive order

general and line-item veto

presidential and congressional war powers

the Cabinet and the EOP

presidential and congressional roles in the budget-making process

the Article II presidency versus the modern presidency

ESSAY AND SHORT ANSWER QUESTIONS

1) What are the formal requirements for the presidency? Are there also informal requirements? What are they?

2) How is the vice president chosen, and what are the duties of the office? Have they changed over time? Why?

3) How did the first three presidents affect the powers of the presidency?

4) Compare and contrast the nature and functions of the Cabinet, the Executive Office of the President, and other advisors.

5) Discuss the nature of war powers. What are the presidential and congressional powers at issue and has this conflict been solved?

6) Discuss the origins of the office of president and the constitutional convention debate surrounding the office of the presidency, including a full discussion of the result—Article II of the Constitution.

7) How has presidential power developed? What makes for a powerful president?

8) Analyze the nature and functions of the "presidential establishment."

9) What is the role of the president in the legislative process? What makes a president most effective in this role?

10) Discuss why Americans are dissatisfied with the office of the presidency and whomever inhabits it. What proposals have been made to reform the presidency? Do they adequately reflect the problems and conflicts of the office? Can we "fix" the presidency so that the majority of Americans are satisfied? What elements of the presidency do Americans find satisfying? Discuss.

ANSWERS TO STUDY EXERCISES

MULTIPLE CHOICE ANSWERS

1) a
2) c
3) a
4) c
5) d
6) c
7) d
8) c

9) a
10) b
11) c
12) a
13) a
14) c
15) a

TRUE/FALSE ANSWERS

1) T
2) F
3) T
4) F
5) F
6) T
7) F
8) T
9) F
10) T

CHAPTER 9
THE EXECUTIVE BRANCH AND FEDERAL BUREAUCRACY

Chapter Goals and Learning Objectives

Often called the "fourth branch of government" because of the power its agencies and bureaus exercise, the federal bureaucracy draws criticism from many sectors. Political conservatives charge that the bureaucracy is too liberal and that its functions constitute unnecessary government inference in the business sector. In contrast, liberals view the bureaucracy as too slow, too unimaginative to solve America's problems, and too zealous a guardian of the status quo. And, while many Americans complain of high taxes and inefficiency in government, most Americans regard the government services they receive through the bureaucracy important to their lives. Indeed, it is the executive branch organizations that deliver the myriad of services citizens have come to expect from their government. A basic knowledge of these organizations is important to you, a taxpayer and a consumer of these services.

This chapter is designed to give you a better understanding of the executive branch and federal bureaucracy. The main topic headings of this chapter are:

- The Origins and Growth of the Federal Bureaucracy
- The Modern Bureaucracy
- How the Bureaucracy Works
- Holding Agencies Accountable

In each section, there are certain facts and ideas that you should strive to understand. Many are in boldface type and appear in both the narrative and in the glossary at the end of the book. Other ideas, dates, facts, events, people, etc. are more difficult to pull out of the narrative. (Keep in mind that studying for objective tests [multiple choice, T/F] is different than studying for essay tests. See the Study Guide section on test taking for hints on study skills.)

In general, after you finish reading and studying this chapter, you should understand the following:

- the origins and growth of the federal bureaucracy in the executive branch
- the modern bureaucracy, bureaucrats and the formal organization of the bureaucracy
- how the bureaucracy works
- how to make executive branch agencies accountable

In this section, you are provided with a basic outline of the chapter and key words/points you should know. Use this outline to develop a complete outline of the material. Write the definitions or further explanations for the terms. Use the space provided in this workbook or rewrite that material in your notebook. This will help you study and remember the material in preparation for your tests, assignments, and papers.

bureaucracy—

"fourth branch of government"—

polling results regarding the bureaucracy—

The Origins and Growth of the Federal Bureaucracy

the three governmental departments under the Articles of Confederation—

early development of the Cabinet under the first President of the United States, George Washington—

expansions of the federal executive branch and bureaucracy from 1816 to 1861—

the Post Office—

spoils system—

patronage—

The Civil War and the Growth of Government

expansions of the federal government as a result of the Civil War—

Department of Agriculture—

post-Civil War development—

Pension Office—

Justice Department—

From Spoils System to the Merit System

Pendleton Act—

civil service system—

merit system—

Regulating the Economy

Interstate Commerce Commission—

independent regulatory commissions—

Theodore Roosevelt and movement toward governmental regulation—

Woodrow Wilson and regulation—

Sixteenth Amendment—

The Ebb and Flow of Federal Employees in the Executive Branch, 1789-2005—

Growth of the Government in the Twentieth Century

Great Depression—

Franklin D. Roosevelt and economic regulation—

change in beliefs of Americans regarding intervention by government into the economy—

WPA—

effect of World War II on the U.S. economy—

post-war infusion of new monies into the economy and demands of veterans for services—

G. I. Bill—

Lyndon B. Johnson and the expansion of the bureaucracy—

<u>The Modern Bureaucracy</u>

ways in which the national government differs from private business—

how public sector employees view risks and rewards—

Who Are Bureaucrats?

Distribution of Federal Civilian Employment, 2004 (Figure 4.1)—

federal bureaucrats—

number of federal workers in the executive branch—

General Schedule (GS)—

how most civilian federal government employees selected today—

selection process for lower levels of the U.S. Civil Service—

selection process for mid-level to upper ranges of U.S. Civil Service—

types of federal government jobs not covered by the civil service system—

Characteristics and Rank Distribution of Federal Civilian Employees, 2004 (Figure 9.2)—

where federal workers work—

Federal Agency Regions and City Headquarters (Figure 9.3)—

graying of the federal workforce—

outside contractors—

Formal Organization

approximate number of civilian agencies—

four general types of agencies—

Cabinet Departments

departments—

president's formal Cabinet—

The Executive Branch (Figure 9.4)—

responsibilities of secretaries and Cabinet secretaries—

features shared by departments—

basis for divisions within departments—

clientele agencies—

Government Corporations

government corporations—

examples of government corporations—

U.S. Postal Service—

some reasons for creation of government corporations—

Independent Executive Agencies

independent executive agencies—

heads of independent executive agencies—

reasons for existence of independent agencies—

NASA—

EPA—

Independent Regulatory Commissions

independent regulator commissions—

reasons for independent regulatory commissions—

examples of independent regulatory commissions—

selecting members of boards and commissions—

Government Workers and Political Involvement

Political Activities Act of 1939 (Hatch Act)—

Federal Employees Political Activities Act of 1993—

public employees of the District of Columbia and political activities regulation—

examples of permissible and prohibited actions under the Federal Employees Activities Act (Table 9.1)—

How the Bureaucracy Works

Max Weber and characteristics of model bureaucracies—

congressional delegation of Article I, section 8, powers—

implementation—

iron triangles—

issue networks—

interagency councils—

policy coordinating committees—

U.S. Interagency Structure for National Security in the George W. Bush Administration (Figure 9.6)—

Making Policy

policy making—

administrative discretion—

Rule Making

rule-making—

regulations—

1946 Administrative Procedures Act three part rule-making procedures—

formal hearings—

How a Regulation is Made (Figure 9.7)—

Administrative Adjudication

administrative adjudication—

compared to a trial—

administrative law judges—

Making Agencies Accountable

to whom or what are agencies answerable?—

IRS example—

factors that work to control the power of the bureaucracy—

Making Agencies Accountable (Table 9.2)—

Executive Control

presidents' delegation of control of power to bureaucracy—

presidents find difficult to regain control over power delegated to the bureaucracy—

presidential appointments to the bureaucracy—

how the president can reorganize the bureaucracy—

Thomas Jefferson and bureaucratic responsibility—

reform during the Progressive Era—

Calvin Coolidge and bureaucratic responsibility—

executive orders—

Congressional Control

role of Congress in checking the power of the bureaucracy—

investigatory powers—

police patrol oversight—

fire alarm oversight—

most frequently used form of oversight—

most effective communication—

power of the purse—

House Appropriations Committee—

appropriations process in Congress—

GAO—

OMB—

CRS and CBO—

citizens' appeals of adverse bureaucratic decisions—

congressional review (adopted by 104th Congress)—

Judicial Control

judiciary's oversight less apparent—

courts can issue injunctions or orders even before a rule is formally promulgated—

courts have ruled that agencies must give due process rights to those affected by bureaucratic action (example)—

influence of litigation or threat of litigation on bureaucrats—

degree to which agencies appear to respond to Supreme Court decisions—

specialized courts—

Research Ideas and Possible Paper Topics

1) Service Learning (learn by doing): Visit at least three federal offices in your area. Research each agency (or department or commission) on the Internet prior to your visit. Watch what goes on. Ask questions. Investigate the functions and efficiencies of the procedures used. If possible, schedule interviews with managers and staff at these offices. Ask about misconceptions and problems with the bureaucracy. How does what you find compare with what you learned in the text?

2)   The newest bureaucratic departments is the Department of Homeland Security. Research to determine how the department's genesis, organization, and purpose. How large is the Department of Homeland Security? What is its budget? What former federal agencies were subsumed into DHS? How effective has it been in carrying out its goals? In addition, analyze whether the current Secretary of Homeland Security has managed to change the culture of the department. If so, how?

3)   The U.S. Postal Service has changed its relationship with the government and the American people over time. Research the history of the postal service, its past and present ties to the government, its effectiveness, and reputation. Many of us complain incessantly about the mail. Are we justified? How are rate increases determined? If we are truly unhappy, what avenues of complaint are open?

4)   Service Learning (learn by doing): Write to or visit your local congressional office. Ask to speak with one of the caseworkers who deals with bureaucratic snafus and red tape. Find out how they intervene on behalf of constituents, how effective they are, how many constituents avail themselves of this service, and their impressions of the bureaucracy. Write a paper or discuss in class what you have learned.

5)   How does the bureaucracy affect you? Consider the innumerable ways you perceive government helps or hinders your life. Keep a journal for the semester and note in it ways you interact with bureaucracy and government. At the end of class, compare notes with friends and colleagues. Discuss whether, in total, your experiences with government are positive, negative, or neutral.

Web sites

President Bush's Cabinet is a Web site hosted by the White House presenting photographs of Cabinet officers and biographies. You can go to each of the individual departments via links for each on this Web site.
   www.whitehouse.gov/government/cabinet.html

Federal Web Locator provided by the Villanova Center for Information Law and Policy has links to all government Web sites, including all governmental departments, agencies, corporations, and affiliates.
   http://www.lib.auburn.edu/madd/docs/fedloc.html

FedWorld, hosted by the Department of Commerce, is a comprehensive index of federal government agencies, searchable by keyword. Access to thousands of U.S. government Web sites, more than a 1/2 million U.S. government documents, databases, and other information products with links to the FedWorld File Libraries and other sources.
   www.fedworld.gov

GovExec.com is online version of a magazine for federal employees called **Government Executive.** The Web site offers breaking news stories, analysis, and information about the federal community

www.govexec.com

The Washington Post reports on the activities of the federal bureaucracy for an audience keenly interested in news about it—Washington-based employees of the federal government—in a section entitled **Federal Page**. (Free registration is required for access to the Washington Post.)

http://www.washingtonpost.com/wp-dyn/politics/fedpage

Practice Tests

MULTIPLE CHOICE QUESTIONS

1) The first independent regulatory commission, established to regulate railroad rates after the Civil War, was called the
   a. Independent Transportation Commission.
   b. Federal Trade Commission.
   c. National Railroad Relations Board.
   d. Interstate Commerce Commission.

2) The reform measure that created the merit-based civil service is commonly referred to as the
   a. Anti-Patronage Act.
   b. Hatch Act.
   c. Pendleton Act.
   d. Garfield Act.

3) In 2004, the executive branch had approximately __ million federal workers.
   a. 1.8
   b. 2.7
   c. 3.9
   d. 6.9

4) An agency created by Congress that is concerned with a specific economic activity or interest is called a(n)
   a. Cabinet department.
   b. clientele agency.
   c. independent regulatory commission.
   d. government corporation.

5)   Hundreds of new federal agencies were created to regulate business practices and various aspects of the economy in an attempt to mitigate the effects of the Great Depression during the administration of President
     a.   Theodore Roosevelt.
     b.   Franklin Roosevelt.
     c.   James Garfield.
     d.   Lyndon Johnson.

6)   Which of the following is *not* a type of federal executive agency?
     a.   Government Accounting Office
     b.   government corporation
     c.   independent agency
     d.   regulatory commission

7)   There are currently _____ Cabinet departments.
     a.   10
     b.   12
     c.   13
     d.   15

8)   Executive departments directed by law to foster and promote the interests of a specific segment or group in the U.S. population (and, thus, are particularly subject to lobbying from outside organized interests) is called a(n)
     a.   Cabinet department.
     b.   clientele agency.
     c.   government corporation.
     d.   executive agency.

9)   The Environmental Protection Agency (EPA) is an example of a(n)
     a.   independent executive agency.
     b.   government corporation.
     c.   clientele agency.
     d.   independent regulatory commission.

10) The relatively stable relationship and pattern of interaction that occurs among an agency, interest groups, and congressional committees is called a(n)
     a.   issue network.
     b.   implementation network.
     c.   policy circle.
     d.   iron triangle.

11) The bureaucracy has the ability to make choices about the best way to implement congressional or executive intentions, thus giving the bureaucracy tremendous leeway to carry out its assigned tasks. This ability is called
   a.   administrative adjudication.
   b.   administrative discretion.
   c.   regulatory authority.
   d.   legislative override.

12) Administrative discretion is exercised through two formal administrative procedures:
   a.   sunset review and administrative oversight.
   b.   rule-making and issue networking.
   c.   administrative adjudication and rule-making.
   d.   congressional review and oversight.

13) The president has the power to hold agencies accountable through
   a.   appointments to the bureaucracy.
   b.   reorganization of the bureaucracy.
   c.   issuing executive orders.
   d.   All of the above.

14) Congress can hold the bureaucracy accountable through
   a.   issuing executive orders.
   b.   appointment and removal of bureau heads.
   c.   investigation and appropriations.
   d.   All of the above.

15) The most commonly used and effective form of congressional oversight is
   a.   staff communication with agency personnel.
   b.   removal of agency heads.
   c.   fire alarm oversight.
   d.   police patrol oversight.

TRUE/FALSE

1) The bureaucracy consists of a set of complex, hierarchical departments, agencies, commissions, and their staffs that exist to help the president carry out the laws of the country.

2) The "spoils system" allowed each political party to "pack" the bureaucracy with its supporters when it won the presidency.

3) The passage of the Sixteenth Amendment significantly impeded the growth of the federal bureaucracy.

4) Governments exist for the public good, not to make money and, therefore, cannot be run like a business.

5) The graying of the federal workforce has not been of concern to many in governmental authority.

6) Bureaucrats make, as well as implement, policies.

7) The first president to act on the issue of bureaucratic accountability was Thomas Jefferson.

8) The bureaucracy is accountable to no one except the president.

9) An executive order is a presidential directive to an agency that provides the basis for carrying out laws or for establishing new policies.

10) Congress's power to control the bureaucracy is severely limited because Congress lacks the power of the purse.

SHORT ANSWER AND ESSAY QUESTIONS

1) Discuss the history of the bureaucracy in terms of presidential influence and needs. What historical issues affected the creation of, expansion, or contraction of the bureaucracy? Which president, in your estimation, was the most influential in expanding the size and power of the bureaucracy? Which president, in your estimation, was the most influential in contracting the size and power of the bureaucracy? Explain your reasoning in both situations.

2) What was the spoils system, and how did it lead to civil service reforms? What were those reforms?

3) What are iron triangles and are they as significant as they once were?

4) Does the bureaucracy make policy? Discuss two ways that it does or does not.

5) Discuss three methods by which the bureaucracy can be held accountable.

6) Discuss the roots and development of the federal bureaucracy.

7) What is the formal organization of the bureaucracy, and what are the main functions of each agency, commission, or department? Give examples.

8) Discuss the nature of bureaucratic policy making.

9) Discuss the checks and balances the president, Congress, and the judiciary have on the bureaucracy. Which techniques are used most often, and which are most effective and why?

10) What problems plague bureaucratic politics, and what reforms have been aimed at addressing them? How effective have these reform efforts been?

COMPARE AND CONTRAST

patronage, spoils system, and merit system

Cabinet departments, government corporations, independent executive agencies, and independent regulatory commissions

iron triangles and issue networks

administrative discretion and administrative adjudication

executive versus congressional versus judicial control of the bureaucracy

ANSWERS TO STUDY EXERCISES

MULTIPLE CHOICE ANSWERS

1) a
2) c
3) b
4) c
5) b
6) a
7) d
8) b
9) a
10) d
11) b
12) c
13) d
14) c
15) c

TRUE/FALSE ANSWERS

1) T
2) T
3) F

4) T
5) F
6) T
7) T
8) F
9) T
10) F

CHAPTER 10
THE JUDICIARY

Chapter Goals and Learning Objectives

The role of the federal judiciary today, particularly the U.S. Supreme Court, differs dramatically from its function early in the nation's history. The "least dangerous branch" gained prominence from the development of the doctrine of judicial review and, as well, from the growth in the size and reach of the federal government. The Framers never envisioned the ambit and authority of the Supreme Court and lower federal courts; of course, the Framers never envisioned the incredible growth of the federal government and its laws, laws adjudicated by the federal courts. The Supreme Court today, as arbiter of the Constitution, can, in a single decision, dramatically reshape the social and political structure of the country as evidenced, for example, by *Brown* v. *Board of Education, Roe* v. *Wade, Bush* v. *Gore* and *Lawrence* v. *Texas*. As our social and political beliefs change in the country, so do the interpretations of our laws by judges and justices on the federal bench. Who sits on the Supreme Court and in the federal courts across the nation truly matters. It is no wonder that many scholars believe the most lasting decision a president makes while in office is who he appoints to the Supreme Court and the federal bench.

This chapter is designed to give you an overview of the federal judicial system. The main topic headings in the chapter are:

- The Constitution and the Creation of the National Judiciary
- The American Legal System
- The Federal Court System
- How Federal Court Judges are Selected
- The Supreme Court Today
- Judicial Philosophy and Decision Making
- Judicial Policy Making and Implementation

In each section, there are certain facts and ideas that you should strive to understand. Many are in boldface type and appear in both the narrative and in the glossary at the end of the book. Other ideas, dates, facts, events, people, etc. are more difficult to pull out of the narrative. (Keep in mind that studying for objective tests [multiple choice, T/F] is different than studying for essay tests. See the Study Guide section on test taking for hints on study skills.)

In general, after you finish reading and studying this chapter, you should understand the following:

- the Constitution and the creation of the federal judiciary: the Supreme Court's explicit creation by Article III and creation of the lower federal courts by Congress under the authority of Article III and Article I
- the American legal system and the civil and criminal law
- the federal court system, its types, and jurisdiction
- how federal court judges are selected by presidential nomination and Senate review and confirmation
- the operation and function of the Supreme Court today
- judicial philosophy and decision making: how judicial decisions are reached based on legal and extra-legal factors
- how judicial policies are made and implemented

Chapter Outline and Key Points

In this section, you are provided with a basic outline of the chapter and key words/points you should know. Use this outline to develop a complete outline of the material. Write the definitions or further explanations for the terms. Use the space provided in this workbook or rewrite that material in your notebook. This will help you study and remember the material in preparation for your tests, assignments, and papers.

Hamdi, et. al. v. *Rumsfeld* (2004) and the separation of powers—

"the least dangerous branch"—

the physical location provided the Supreme Court in the early days of the country as a clue to the significance given it by the founders—

how the Supreme Court is referred to—

The Constitution and the Creation of the Federal Judiciary

the consideration given to the creation of a federal judiciary at the Constitutional Convention—

Federalist No. 78—

Article III—

Article III, section I—

judicial review—

Marbury v. *Madison* (1803)—

Martin v. *Hunter's Lessee* (1816)—

Article III, Congress and the lower federal courts—

life tenure—

independence of the judiciary—

The Judicial Power of the U.S. Supreme Court (Table 10.1)—

checks on the power of the judiciary—

"advice and consent" power of the Senate and judicial nominations—

The Judiciary Act of 1789 and the Creation of the Federal Judiciary

Judiciary Act of 1789—

federal district courts—

litigants—

circuit courts—

size of the Supreme Court—

first public session of the Supreme Court—

characteristics of the early Supreme Court that created problems of prestige and personnel—

the Supreme Court justices as circuit court jurists in the early days of the Court—

John Jay—

early Court's refusal to issue advisory opinions to Washington—

early Court's work advancing principles of nationalism and national supremacy—

Chisholm v. *Georgia* (1793)—

The Marshall Court: *Marbury* v. *Madison* (1803) and Judicial Review

John Marshall—

Marshall elimination of the practice of *seriatim*—

Marshall Court helps define federalism in series of decisions from 1810 to 1821—

concept of judicial review mentioned in *Federalist No. 78* but not in the U.S. Constitution—

judicial review—

Marbury v. *Madison* (1803)—

the facts and the politics of *Marbury*—

immediate and long-term effect of Court's decision in *Marbury*—

The American Legal System

the judicial system of the United States—

Dual Structure of the American Court System (Figure 10.1)—

trial courts—

appellate courts—

Jurisdiction

jurisdiction—

original jurisdiction—

where do more than 90 percent of all state and federal cases end?—

appellate jurisdiction—

Criminal and Civil Law

criminal law—

style of the case—

civil law—

settlements—

plaintiff—

defendant—

the state as plaintiff—

judges during trial—

juries—

historic exclusion of women and blacks—

peremptory challenges—

The Federal Court System

constitutional courts—

legislative courts—

District Courts

federal district courts—

number of federal district courts—

least number in each state and number in most populist states—

district court jurisdiction:

    1)

    2)

    3)

The Federal Court System (Figure 10.2)—

U.S. Attorney—

The Courts of Appeals

U.S. Courts of Appeals—

circuit courts of appeals—

intermediate level courts—

eleven numbered courts of appeals—

D.C. Court of Appeal—

U.S. Court of Appeals for the Federal Circuit—

number of sitting federal court of appeals active judges as of 2005—

chief judge—

three-judge panels—

en banc—

do courts of appeals have original jurisdiction?—

jurisdiction of courts of appeals—

right to appeal—

courts of last resort—

general purpose of appellate courts and procedures—

brief—

precedent—

stare decisis—

The Supreme Court

jurisdiction today—

membership number since 1869—

Supreme Court staff—

How Federal Court Judges are Selected

political process of selection—

senatorial courtesy—

nominations under Bill Clinton and George W. Bush—

How a President Affects the Federal Judiciary (Figure 10.3)—

Who are Federal Judges?

Characteristics of District Court Appointees from Carter to Bush (Table 10.2)—

The Supreme Court, 2006 (Table 10.3)—

political nature of appointments—

prior judicial experience—

Appointments to the U.S. Supreme Court

constitutional requirements—

importance to president—

instances where president was wrong in assumptions about nominees—

Eisenhower appointments—

Nomination Criteria

competence—

ideological or policy preference—

rewards—

pursuit of political support—

religion—

race, ethnicity, and gender—

The Supreme Court Confirmation Process

power of the Senate—

simple majority vote for confirmation—

Investigation

FBI—

ABA—

George W. Bush and ABA—

Federalist Society—

Senate Judiciary Committee—

Lobbying by Interest Groups

Interest Groups Appearing in Selected Senate Judiciary Committee Hearings (Table 10.4)—

Robert Bork—

lobbying for district and appellate court nominations—

The Senate Committee Hearings and Senate Vote

first nominee to testify in detail—

committee recommendation to full Senate—

The Supreme Court Today

public awareness of Court and members—

Don't Know Much About the Supreme Court (Table 10.5)—

"cult of the robe"—

comparison of how proceedings of the Supreme Court and Congress are conducted and covered—

Deciding to Hear a Case

petitions received and opinions issued in 2005-2006 term—

workload of Supreme Court from its inception until 1950—

Supreme Court Caseload, 1950-2005 Terms (Figure 10.4)—

significant role in policy making and politics—

significance of content of Supreme Court's docket—

increase in number of Bill of Rights cases since the 1950s—

The Roberts Court (picture and caption)—

How a Case Gets to the Supreme Court (Figure 10.5)—

two types of jurisdiction—

substantial federal questions—

writ of *certiorari*—

two requirements for meeting *certiorari*:

1)

2)

cert pool—

discuss list and percentage of cases that reach it—

Rule of Four—

the role of clerks—

What Do Supreme Court Clerks Do? (Table 10.6)—

How Does a Case Survive the Process?

criteria for Court accepting a case—

cues regarding the characteristics of cases the Court accepts—

solicitor general—

amicus curiae—

percentage of cases accepted where the U.S. government is the petitioning party—

conflict among the circuits—

interest group participation—

use of *amicus* briefs by interest groups—

Hearing and Deciding the Case

submission of legal briefs—

oral arguments—

tradition and ceremony of oral argument—

when do oral arguments take place?—

who participates in oral arguments?—

mechanics of oral arguments—

how do justices use oral arguments?—

the conference and the vote—

role of conferences—

role of least senior member of the Court in conferences—

how conferences highlight the power and importance of the Chief Justice—

majority vote wins—

writing opinions—

majority opinion—

who assigns task of writing majority opinion?—

importance of majority opinion—

concurring opinion—

plurality opinion—

dissenting opinion—

Judicial Philosophy and Decision Making

principles of *stare decisis*—

Judicial Philosophy, Original Intent, and Ideology

judicial restraint—

judicial activism—

strict constructionist—

judicial activism: liberal and conservative—

Models of Judicial Decision Making

behavioral characteristics—

the attitudinal model—

the strategic model—

Public Opinion

check on the power of the courts—

energizing factor—

Court as direct target of public opinion—

Court's effect on public opinion—

prestige of the Court—

public confidence in the Court—

The Supreme Court and the American Public (Table 10.8)—

Judicial Policy Making and Implementation

primary way federal judges and the Supreme Court, in particular, make policy—

democratic theorists on the power of the courts to make policy—

Policy Making

measures of the power of the Court—

declaring laws unconstitutional—

ability to overrule itself—

political questions—

Implementing Court Decisions

judicial implementation—

role played by well-crafted or popular decisions—

implementation populations—

consumer population—

three requirements for effective implementation:

1)

2)

3)

Research Ideas and Possible Paper Topics

1) Research the Court's current docket (see official Supreme Court Web site below). How many cases will it hear (or has heard)? What types of cases will the Court hear (or has heard)? What constitutional issues are (or were) at stake? Why do you think the Court has chosen to rule (or ruled) on these cases?

2) Research biographies on the current Supreme Court justices. What are their backgrounds? Why were they chosen for the Court and by whom? How are they perceived by court-watchers? (In other words, what do the experts think of them?)

Is there a definite majority on the Court for any single set of constitutional issues? The Warren Court was characterized as very activist, particularly regarding due process rights. Will the Rehnquist Court be so characterized as very activist (although in other areas)? If so, how? And what evidence can you find about activist trends on the Roberts Court?

3)   Choose two well-known Supreme Court cases of the past twenty years. Research to determine interest group activity and attempts at public persuasion on the Court during the cases. Using those examples and the text, write a paper (or prepare a short talk) about the impact of public opinion and lobbying on the Supreme Court.

4)   Research and analyze President Bush's judicial appointments to the Supreme Court and the federal bench. What type of judicial policy does Mr. Bush seek in a nominee? How have his nominees reflected the president's political opinions? How well have President Bush's nominees faired in the process of Senatorial confirmation?

5)   Constitutional law is taught textually. The language and nuance of what the Court says in its opinions is very important. Choose five cases and read the actual opinions. What types of language does the Court tend to use? Are rulings broad or narrow? Are precedents overturned? How does the Court use precedent generally? What did you learn about the Court from reading opinions?

Web sites

The official Web site of the **Supreme Court of the United States** offers transcripts of oral arguments before the Court, recent case decisions, a history of the Court, the Court's docket, and other information.
    www.supremecourtus.gov

Oyez-Oyez-Oyez is a comprehensive database of major constitutional cases featuring multimedia aspects such as audio of oral arguments.
    http://www.oyez.org/oyez/frontpage

The site of the **Supreme Court History Society** covers the basic history of the Court and has a gift catalog (for that special gift to your pre-law friends).
    www.supremecourthistory.org

SCOTUS Blog (Supreme Court of the United States—SCOTUS) was started several years ago by an attorney whose practice is exclusively devoted to appeals before the U.S. Supreme Court and who is one of the most prominent private lawyers in that field, Tom Goldstein. Goldstein manages the blog as well as contributes to it, along with other attorneys, scholars and journalists who are all ardent students of the Court. It is fascinating reading for anyone keenly interested in the Court.
    http://www.scotusblog.com/movabletype

Findlaw is a searchable database of S.C. decisions plus legal subjects, state courts, law schools, bar associations, and international law.
www.findlaw.com

Rominger Legal Services provides U.S. Supreme Court links, including history, pending cases, rules, bios, etc.
www.romingerlegal.com/supreme.htm

FLITE: Federal Legal Information Through Electronics offers a searchable database of Supreme Court decisions from 1937-1975.
www.fedworld.gov/supcourt/index.htm

U.S. Supreme Court Plus has decisions from the current term as well as legal research, bios, basic Supreme Court information, and more. Also offers a free e-mail notification service of Supreme Court rulings. While this is primarily a subscriber fee site, you can still find some good free information here.
www.usscplus.com

The Legal Information Institute offers Supreme Court opinions under the auspices of Project Hermes, the court's electronic-dissemination project. This archive contains (or will soon contain) all opinions of the court issued since May of 1990.
http://supct.law.cornell.edu/supct/

The **Federal Judiciary Homepage** offers a wide variety of information about the U.S. Federal Court system.
www.uscourts.gov

Law.com offers the latest Supreme Court news on its "United States Supreme Court Monitor" Web site. (Free registration is required.)
http://www.law.com/jsp/scm/news.jsp

The American Bar Association provides analysis of the issues, arguments, background and significance of every case slated for argument in the U.S. Supreme Court.
http://www.abanet.org/publiced/preview/home.html

C-SPAN also offers information about oral arguments before the U.S. Supreme Court.
http://www.c-span.org/courts/oralarguments.asp

MULTIPLE CHOICE QUESTIONS

1) Article III establishes
   a.   the Supreme Court.
   b.   inferior courts.
   c.   ten-year terms for federal judges.
   d.   All of the above.

2) The three-tiered structure of the federal court system was established by
   a.   Article III.
   b.   Article IV.
   c.   the Judiciary Act of 1789.
   d.   the Seventeenth Amendment.

3) The doctrine of judicial review was established by
   a.   the Judiciary Act of 1789.
   b.   Article III.
   c.   *Chisholm* v. *Georgia.*
   d.   *Marbury* v. *Madison.*

4) The Supreme Court in its early history met
   a.   in a small room in the basement of the U.S. Capitol building.
   b.   in the Supreme Court Building constructed across the street from the U.S. Capitol building.
   c.   in the county courthouse in Alexandria, Virginia
   d.   rarely because it had so little work to accomplish.

5) Federal district courts are courts of original jurisdiction, meaning that they hear
   a.   cases only involving federal questions.
   b.   appellate cases or trials.
   c.   appellate cases.
   d.   trials.

6) The court that handles most cases involving federal regulatory agencies is the
   a.   First Circuit Court of Appeals.
   b.   District Court.
   c.   D.C. Court of Appeals.
   d.   U.S. Court of Appeals for the Federal Circuit.

7)	The reliance on past decisions to reach decisions in new cases is based on the doctrine of
	a.	*stare decisis.*
	b.	*per curiam.*
	c.	*amicus curiae.*
	d.	*seriatim.*

8)	The size of the Supreme Court is
	a.	alterable only by constitutional amendment.
	b.	set by Congress.
	c.	set by the Constitution.
	d.	All of the above.

9)	Which of the following is a criterion for nomination to the U.S. Supreme Court?
	a.	must be over the age of 35
	b.	must be a native-born citizen
	c.	must have graduated from an accredited law school
	d.	None of the above.

10)	The original jurisdiction of the Supreme Court
	a.	includes disputes between states.
	b.	includes cases affecting ambassadors, public ministers, or a state.
	c.	includes territorial disputes among states.
	d.	All of the above.

11)	Nearly all Supreme Court cases arrive at the Court through
	a.	*in forma pauperis* petitions.
	b.	original jurisdiction cases.
	c.	writ of *certiorari.*
	d.	informal request for review by state courts.

12)	For the Court to grant a writ of *cert,* the case typically
	a.	involves a substantial federal question.
	b.	comes from a state court of last resort or the U.S. Court of Appeals.
	c.	must be approved by four justices of the Supreme Court for review.
	d.	All of the above.

13)	The person responsible for handling appeals on behalf of the U.S. government before the Supreme Court is the
	a.	solicitor general.
	b.	attorney general.
	c.	procurator.
	d.	U.S. prosecuting attorney for the District of Columbia.

14) When a justice disagrees with the ruling of a Court majority opinion, he/she may write a
   a.   concurring opinion.
   b.   dissenting opinion.
   c.   *per curiam* opinion.
   d.   plurality opinion.

15) The idea that judges should refrain from making policy is referred to as
   a.   democratic theory.
   b.   delegation.
   c.   judicial restraint.
   d.   judicial activism.

TRUE/FALSE QUESTIONS

1)   John Marshall was the first Chief Justice of the United States.

2)   The opinion by John Marshall in *Marbury* v. *Madison* (1803) dramatically increased the power and importance of the Supreme Court.

3)   In courts of original jurisdiction, judges are interested only in questions of law.

4)   The federal court structure is established in Article III.

5)   The Supreme Court has nine justices as stipulated in the Constitution.

6)   President Eisenhower was pleased with the work on the Court of his appointee as Chief Justice, Earl Warren.

7)   Politics permeates the selection process of federal court judges and Supreme Court Justices.

8)   The vetting of federal judicial nominees by the ABA remains a crucial element in the decision of the president in selecting a nominee to the Supreme Court under the administration of George W. Bush.

9)   The Chief Justice of the Supreme Court always assigns the writing of opinions.

10) The Supreme Court is in no way subject to public opinion or the lobbying of interest groups

COMPARE AND CONTRAST

original and appellate jurisdiction

Supreme Court's exercise of jurisdiction in its early days versus today

criminal and civil law

federal and state court systems

constitutional and legislative courts

common law and statutory (legislative) law

selection of federal and state judges

writ of *certiorari* and *in forma pauperis*

opinions: *seriatim*, majority, concurring, plurality, dissenting

judicial restraint and judicial activism

SHORT ANSWER AND ESSAY QUESTIONS

1) Discuss the facts and ruling in *Marbury* v. *Madison* and the significance of the case to American jurisprudence. Does opposition to the doctrine of judicial review still exist today? Research this latter question.

2) What impact did John Marshall have on the Court and the nation?

3) Define and discuss the concepts of jurisdiction and precedent.

4) What are briefs, and are they used by Supreme Court?

5) What kinds of opinions does the Supreme Court issue, and what are their effects?

6) Explain the basics of the American judicial system. How was it created, and what are its structures and rules?

7) How are federal judges and Supreme Court justices selected? Discuss fully the legal and political issues involved.

8) Discuss judicial philosophies of the Warren, Rehnquist and Roberts Courts.

9) What is the process by which the Supreme Court decides a case? Be sure to start at the process of getting on the docket and going through to the opinion stage.

10) What "extra-legal" factors shape judicial decision making?

ANSWERS TO STUDY EXERCISES

MULTIPLE CHOICE ANSWERS

1) a
2) c
3) d
4) a
5) d
6) c
7) a
8) b
9) d
10) d
11) c
12) d
13) a
14) b
15) c

TRUE/FALSE ANSWERS

1) F
2) T
3) F
4) F
5) F
6) F
7) T
8) F
9) F
10) F

CHAPTER 11
POLITICAL SOCIALIZATION AND PUBLIC OPINION

Chapter Goals and Learning Objectives

What do you think about politics and government? In other words, what are your beliefs and opinions about politics and government? Are they the same as your parents', your friends', of people in your community? Public opinion polls reveal that Americans are a diverse lot, but nonetheless, agree on many issues. Politicians and others who want to sway public opinion depend on public opinion polls to inform them of what Americans believe and want from their government and elected officials. This is nothing new. Politicians back in the time of the Framers did not have sophisticated public opinion polls to tell them what the citizens believed or wanted, nor did they have national news media to tell them the results of those polls, but they sought to mold public sentiment nevertheless. What opinions do people hold about government, politics, and issues? Why do they count to politicians? And, how are your opinions, beliefs, and values formed and how are they changed? These are vital questions in a democracy. We all want our opinion and our beliefs to mean something to others. We want our voices heard. Do polls effectively reflect our values and beliefs? Do they accurately predict trends, directions, and decisions?

This chapter is designed to give you a better understanding of polling and the nature of public opinion. It is also designed to help you better understand from whence your own opinions, and the opinions of others, have come. The main topic headings of the chapter are:

- What is Public Opinion?
- Public Opinion and Polling
- Why We Form and Express Political Opinions
- How Public Opinion Is Measured
- The Effects of Public Opinion and Polling on Government and Politics

In each section, there are certain facts and ideas that you should strive to understand. Many are in boldface type and appear in both the narrative and in the glossary at the end of the book. Other ideas, dates, facts, events, people, etc. are more difficult to pull out of the narrative. (Keep in mind that studying for objective tests [multiple choice, T/F] is different than studying for essay tests. See the Study Guide section on test taking for hints on study skills.)

In general, after you finish reading and studying this chapter, you should understand the following:

- political socialization and the panoply of factors that influence this process

- public opinion and polling, the role of political socialization in public opinion formation, and the role of public opinion polls in determining public perception of political issues
- why Americans form and express political opinions
- the effects of public opinion and polling on government and politics and how since the writing of *The Federalist Papers*, parties, candidates, and public officials have worked to sway as well as gauge public opinion for political purposes

Chapter Outline and Key Points

In this section, you are provided with a basic outline of the chapter and key concepts and terms you should know. Use this outline to develop a complete study guide for the chapter. Use the space provided in this workbook to write notes from your reading, defining the terms and explaining the concepts listed below. You may wish to rewrite the material in your notebook or computer. However you work up this outline, the effort and information will help you study and remember the material in preparation for your tests, assignments, and papers.

John Jay in *Federalist No. 2*—

homogeneous society in early America—

today's heterogeneous society—

Political Socialization

political socialization—

agents of political socialization—

The Family

communications and receptivity—

political socialization in early years up to age ten—

political socialization by age eleven—

1988 study of political socialization by family—

Ideological Self-Identification of First-Year College Student (Figure 11.1)—

School and Peers

elementary school influence—

Kids Voting USA—

Weekly Reader—

peers—

high school influence—

college influence—

ideological self-identification of first-year college students (Fig. 11.2)—

The Mass Media

growing role—

time in front of TV—

impact of TV—

impact of alternative sources of political information on TV—

2004 study of alternative TV sources for election information—

average time for sound bite—

role of Internet—

Religion

role of religion—

percentage of Americans who consider religion an important part of their lives—

faith-based political activity through much of twentieth century from the left—

leaders of civil rights movement—

1972 appearance of religious gap in voting and public opinion—

Nixon's "Silent Majority" strategy—

Jerry Falwell and the Moral Majority—

Pat Robertson and the Christian Coalition—

today' second largest predictor of the vote (after party identification)—

Ideological Self-Identification of Protestants, Catholics and Jews (Figure 11.2)—

shared religious attitudes tendency to affect voting and issue stances—

Race and Ethnicity

differences in political socialization between African Americans and whites from early age through adulthood—

Views of Whites and Blacks in Wake of Hurricane Katrina (Figure 11.3)—

importance of race and ethnicity as factors in elections and the study of public opinion—

Hispanics' response to issues—

Asian/Pacific Islanders' response to issues—

Native Americans' response to issues—

divisions in Hispanic community—

Racial and Ethnic Attitudes on Selected Issues—

Gender

Gender Differences on Political Issues (see Table 11.1)—

suggested reasons for women's more liberal attitudes on social welfare concerns—

women's opinions about war—

effect of terrorism and national security concerns on women's opinions—

Age

Comparing Four Age Cohorts on Issues, 2004 (Figure 11.4)—

causes of differences—

consequences of the graying of America—

fastest growing age group in the U.S. and their tendency to vote—

Region

effect of regional and sectional differences in developing and maintaining political beliefs since colonial times—

differences between the North and the South—

characteristics of the South—

characteristics of the West—

stark regional difference in candidate appeal in 2004 presidential election—

Impact of Events

role of key political events—

November 22, 1963—

effects of 9/11 attacks—

America's Collective Memory (Table 11.2)—

Nixon's resignation—

2006 study of Americans, age eighteen to twenty—

impact of events leading and the marked increase in distrust of government—

<u>Public Opinion and Polling</u>

public opinion—

public opinion polls—

George Gallup—

role of public opinion and governance—

The History of Public Opinion Research

efforts by newspapers in 1824 and 1833—

Walter Lippmann—

Public Opinion (1922)—

Literary Digest—

straw polls—

three errors in straw polling by *Literary Digest*:

    1)

    2)

    3)

Gallup and 1936 election—

The Success of the Gallup Poll in Presidential Elections, 1936-2004 (Figure 11.5)—

"Dewey Defeats Truman" headline—

Gallup Poll in presidential elections (Fig. 11.1)—

National Election Study—

Internet and polling—

Traditional Public Opinion Polls

how polls are used—

several key phrases of various polls—

Determining the Content and Phrasing of the Questions

wording of the question—

responses often tied to wording of a particular question—

Selecting the Sample

random sampling—

most common unrepresentative sampling used today—

quota sample—

stratified sampling—

nonstratified samples—

Contacting Respondents

telephone polls—

random-digit dialing surveys—

individual, in-person interviews—

Political Polls

Push Poll

push questions—

push polls—

do candidates use this poll method?—

effect of the Internet on push polls—

Tracking Polls

tracking polls—

A Daily Tracking Poll for the 2004 Presidential Election (Figure 11.6)—

Exit Polls

exit polls—

who uses exit polls?—

exit polls and 1980, 2000, and 2004 presidential elections—

Shortcomings of Polling

VNS—

networks form own polling pool—

Sampling Error

accuracy of poll depends on quality of what?—

small samples—

poor and homeless underrepresentation—

sampling error (or margin of error)—

all polls contain errors—

Limited Respondent Options

how it leads to inaccuracies—

Lack of Information

when respondents don't care about an issue or lack information—

filter question—

Difficulty Measuring Intensity

inability to measure intensity of feeling about particular issues—

<u>Why We Form and Express Political Opinions</u>

Personal Benefits

"I"-centered—

what effects attitudes on issues that do not affect someone individually—

issues that do not affect someone individually and do not involve moral issue—

Political Knowledge

reciprocal effect—

Americans' level of knowledge about history and politics—

Americans' Political Knowledge (Table 11.3)—

Americans' knowledge about foreign policy and geography—

gender differences on political knowledge—

Cues from Leaders

V.O. Key—

role political leaders play in influencing public opinion—

bully pulpit—

followers—

presidential efforts to drum up support for their programs—

George W. Bush and fall in public opinion polls over Iraq War—

Political Ideology

political ideology—

conservatives—

liberals—

Roper Center survey on Americans' political ideology—

<u>The Effects of Public Opinion and Polling on Government and Politicians</u>

Federalist Papers' comment on public opinion—

public opinion influences the actions of politicians and public officials—

political opinion and political capital—

studies on whether public policy is responsive to public opinion—

criticism of political polling—

bandwagon effect in New Hampshire primary—

underdog effect in New Hampshire primary—

effect of strong showing in New Hampshire primary—

Research Ideas and Possible Paper Topics

1) Use the library or Internet to find the content and results of a number of polls. Bring them to class and in discussion groups, analyze the quality and reliability of those polls. Be sure to discuss sampling, error rates, question wording, how respondents are contacted, and other factors that affect the results.

2) Write a paper based on your own political ideology and opinions. How were they formed? Consider those who have influenced these opinions and political views. Is the text correct in asserting what the dominant factors of political socialization are? Compare your experiences with those of your classmates.

3) Most people's opinions are affected by what can be called a "formative political event." For some people, this event was the assassination of JFK, for others, it was Watergate or the Iranian hostage crisis, and for still others, it was the Persian Gulf War, the Bill Clinton investigation, 9/11, or the Iraq invasion and occupation. Think about your "formative political event" or first political memory. How did that event shape your political ideas and worldview? What about your parents and grandparents? Ask them what major events affected their political perceptions. Compare notes with your classmates.

4) As a class project, choose an issue of interest and formulate your own poll. Then administer it on campus. Discuss the process, the results, and problems of your poll and extrapolate that to polling in general.

5) Examine the popularity polls of George W. Bush during his first and second term. Then stage a debate in class based on those results. One side should argue that public opinion polling is inherently problematic and should not be used to criticize a president and his actions. The other side should argue that polling is a valid way to determine the will of the people in a democracy and, thus, should be used to determine the efficacy of a president's actions in office. Each side should do research to flesh out their arguments.

The **Gallup Organization** is one of the best-known and most well-respected polling agencies. Their Web site offers access to reports, polling data, and more about a variety of issues.

www.gallup.com

The **American National Election Study** at the University of Michigan offers regular polls on elections, voting behavior, and electoral issues.

http://www.electionstudies.org

The **National Opinion Research Center (NORC)**, a research arm of the University of Chicago, offers surveys of American attitudes and opinions.

www.norc.org

Roper Center for Public Opinion Research, located at the University of Connecticut, is the largest library of public opinion data in the world. The Center's mission focuses on data preservation and access, education, and research. Includes the GSS—General Social Survey.

www.ropercenter.uconn.edu

The **Subject Guide to Political Socialization and Political Culture** is a Web site hosted by Appalachian State University.

http://www.library.appstate.edu/reference/subjectguides/polsoc.html

The **Washington Post Data Directory** is a guide to public opinion data published on the Internet by nonpartisan organizations.

www.washingtonpost.com/wp-srv/politics/polls/datadir.htm

The **Research Industry Coalition** is an organization promoting professionalism and quality in public opinion and marketing research. Their Web site includes an interesting article on the problems with the proliferation of "call in" polls and 900 number polls.

www.researchindustry.org/index.html

The **American Association for Public Opinion Research** is a professional association that publishes *Public Opinion Quarterly* whose tables of contents are available on this Web site.

www.aapor.org

The **Virtual Reference Desk at Binghamton University** offers a Web site devoted to polling and public opinion, including information on bad polls and techniques; also offers links to some opinion sites.

http://library.lib.binghamton.edu/vrd/polls.html

MULTIPLE CHOICE QUESTIONS

1) The founder of modern-day polling is
   a. Louis Harris.
   b. George Gallup.
   c. Steve Roper.
   d. Walter Lippman.

2) An unscientific survey used to gauge public opinion on issues and policies is called a
   a. deliberative poll.
   b. exit poll.
   c. straw poll.
   d. public opinion poll.

3) The popular magazine which from 1920 to 1932 correctly predicted the outcome of every presidential election based on unscientific surveys of public opinion was
   a. *The American Voter.*
   b. *The Voice of the People.*
   c. *Public Opinion and American Democracy.*
   d. *Literary Digest.*

4) Which of the following would be considered agents of political socialization?
   a. schools and peers
   b. families
   c. television, radio, newspapers and the Internet
   d. All of the above.

5) The influence of family on political socialization stems from
   a. communication.
   b. receptivity.
   c. time with parents.
   d. All of the above.

6) Most first-year college students identify themselves as being
   a. liberal.
   b. conservative.
   c. far right.
   d. middle of the road.

7) Based on public opinion polling, women tend to be
   a. more liberal about issues of social welfare concerns.
   b. more negative about war and military intervention.
   c. concerned about terrorism and national security at home.
   d. All of the above.

8) Which of the following groups tends to be the most liberal?
   a. those who attend church regularly
   b. Jews
   c. Catholics
   d. Protestants

9) What percentage of Americans today report that they consider religion an important part of their lives?
   a. 47
   b. 76
   c. 91
   d. 99

10) The single largest predictor of the vote today, following party identification, is
   a. age.
   b. gender.
   c. race.
   d. religion.

11) People can be influenced in forming political opinions by ideology, party affiliation and social grouping. They may also influenced by
   a. personal benefits.
   b. political knowledge.
   c. cues from leaders and opinion-makers.
   d. All of the above.

12) The political knowledge of Americans is quite low. In a 2002 survey, what percent of Americans could not identify the Chief Justice of the Supreme Court?
   a. 69
   b. 12
   c. 37
   d. 41

13) One reason politicians and the news media have regular opportunities to influence public opinion is because
   a. of the deep trust Americans place in the integrity and reliability of political and media sources.
   b. of the lack of deep conviction with which most Americans hold many of their political beliefs.
   c. of the deep conviction with which most Americans hold many of their political beliefs.
   d. All of the above.

14) One reason that polling results are often skewed, especially when interest groups want a poll to yield a particular result, is because
   a. most people lie on polls.
   b. of the wording of the questions.
   c. pollsters are often bribed by politicians.
   d. computer technology currently makes it difficult to accurately process the raw data.

15) Most national surveys and commercial polls use samples of _____ individuals to obtain fairly accurate polling results.
   a. 75 to 100
   b. 300 to 400
   c. 1,000 to 1,500
   d. at least 5,000

TRUE/FALSE QUESTIONS

1) In elementary schools, children are not taught respect for their nation and its symbols.

2) Straw polls, such as those used on local television newscasts, are scientifically based and accurate.

3) Polls predicting the outcome of presidential races proved embarrassingly inaccurate in 1948 when Governor Thomas E. Dewey defeated incumbent President Harry S Truman.

4) The average television news sound bite for a presidential candidate has increased significantly in length since the 1960s and 1970s, thus giving the electorate a greater chance to evaluate the candidates.

5) In the last two presidential elections, all of the major candidates used the Internet in an attempt to inform and sway voters.

6) Events can have a very strong effect on political attitudes and values.

7) Most Americans, in response to polling, indicate that they are politically moderate.

8) Noted political scientist V.O. Key argued in his 1966 *The Irresponsible Electorate* that most voters "are fools and idiots."

9) American society is far more heterogeneous today than in the early days of the country.

10) Polls clearly can distort the presidential election process, particularly in the early stages such as the New Hampshire primary, by creating a "bandwagon" effect.

COMPARE AND CONTRAST

agents of political socialization: family, mass media, school and peers, events, social groups, and political ideology

random sampling, nonstratified sampling, and stratified sampling

telephone polls and in-person polls

tracking polls, exit polls, straw polls, and deliberative polls

sampling error and margin of error

SHORT ANSWER AND ESSAY QUESTIONS

1) Discuss early efforts to measure public opinion.

2) What is political socialization?

3) What is political ideology?

4) Compare and contrast the various ways of sampling used in polls.

5) Discuss deliberative polling. What are the costs and benefits of this method of polling?

6) What is public opinion? How do we measure it, and how accurate are those measurements?

7) Discuss the various processes of political socialization. What factors affect our opinion formation and how do these factors affect the broader political system?

8)   How do we form political opinions and ideologies? What is the relationship
      between opinion and ideology?

9)   How do we measure public opinion? Discuss methods of sampling, polling, and
      their shortcomings.

10)   How do politicians and the media use polls? What are the implications of these
      uses?

ANSWERS TO STUDY EXERCISES

Multiple Choice Answers

1) b
2) c
3) d
4) d
5) d
6) d
7) d
8) b
9) b
10) d
11) d
12) a
13) b
14) b
15) c

True/False Answers

1) F
2) F
3) F
4) F
5) T
6) T
7) T
8) F
9) T
10) T

CHAPTER 12
POLITICAL PARTIES

Chapter Goals and Learning Objectives

Much attention was given to the 2006 midterm election and the resultant political shift in power from Republican control of the U.S. Congress to Democratic Party control in both houses. This shift in political party control is significant to politicians and political activists and does have a significant effect on the making of public policy. But was it significant to you? To determine that answer, you might ask yourself the following: Are you a Democrat, or are you a Republican? If you are a Democrat or a Republican, you would say the change can dramatically affect your life. If you identify with neither party, you would say, probably, that it was no bid deal. If you are in this latter category, you probably spurn party labels and vote for a candidate based upon his or her qualifications, record, platform or even how he or she looks on television rather than vote for a candidate based upon her political party membership. To many Americans, party affiliation is not a significant factor in their political lives. Yet to many other Americans, party affiliation, or allegiance to the issues a party espouses, is important. For instance, the 2004 election saw a revitalized Democratic Party attacking particularly the presidency of George W. Bush, and a Republican Party energized to defend and reelect its president. And the 2006 midterm election infused new life and new hope into the Democratic Party nationally. We have entered a new, more fluid era of party politics. While many voters take their party allegiance seriously, some observers maintain that our two-party system should be replaced by a chaotic multiparty system in which presidential and congressional hopefuls bypass party nominations altogether and compete on their own. However, it is important to understand that the two major parties control the power structure in Congress and in all 50 states. Since Democrats and Republicans write the laws, including the election laws across the country, the rumors of and proposals of demise of the two-party system in this country are, at best, as Mark Twain said of reports of his own death, greatly exaggerated. In one form or another, political parties have been staples of American political life since the late 1700s and they will continue to be. In essence, political parties are the engines which run the machinery of government. While you need not become a mechanic, you should look under the hood and develop an understanding of how these engines operate.

This chapter is designed to give you an overview of political parties and how they have changed over time. The main topic headings of the chapter are:

- What is a Political Party?
- The Evolution of American Party Democracy
- The Functions of the American Party
- The Party Organization
- The Party in Government
- The Party in the Electorate

- Is the Party Over or Has It Just Begun?

In each section, there are certain facts and ideas that you should strive to understand. Many are in boldface type and appear in both the narrative and in the glossary at the end of the book. Other ideas, dates, facts, events, people, etc. are more difficult to pull out of the narrative. (Keep in mind that studying for objective tests [multiple choice, T/F] is different than studying for essay tests. See the Study Guide section on test taking for hints on study skills.)

In general, after you finish reading and studying this chapter, you should understand the following:

- what a political party is
- how the American party system evolved
- the functions of the American party system
- the formal structure of American political party organization
- the party in government—office holders and candidates who campaign and govern under their party's banners
- the party in the electorate—how the parties tenuously hold onto the electorate
- the likely future of party influence in the United States and whether "the party is over has just begun?"

Chapter Outline and Key Points

In this section, you are provided with a basic outline of the chapter and key words/points you should know. Use this outline to develop a complete outline of the material. Write the definitions or further explanations for the terms. Use the space provided in this workbook or rewrite that material in your notebook. This will help you study and remember the material in preparation for your tests, assignments, and papers.

President Bush and the implementations of his party's platform—

Party Platforms: Moderate But Different (Table 12.1)—

2006 midterm election and the political parties—

What is a Political Party?

political party—

governmental party—

organizational party—

party-in-the-electorate—

The Evolution of American Party System

George Washington's farewell warning—

end of the brief era of partyless politics in the U.S.—

American Party History at a Glance (Figure 12.1)—

Hamilton's Federalists—

Jefferson Democratic-Republicans—

Jefferson's attitude toward the party system—

The Early Parties Fade

Era of Good Feelings—

fuel for the growth of political parties—

popular election of Electoral College delegates—

party membership broadens—

Democratic Party and Andrew Jackson—

Whigs—

Henry Clay and the Whig Party—

Republican Party and Abraham Lincoln—

Democrats and Republicans: The Golden Age

central traits of the "Golden Age"—

machines—

population's desire for important services—

"Boss" Tweed—

The Modern Era

government's gradual assumption of key functions of parties—

Franklin Roosevelt's New Deal—

direct primary—

civil service laws—

issue-oriented politics—

ticket-split—

candidate-centered politics—

population shift from urban to suburban—

Realignment

party realignment—

critical elections—

three tumultuous eras producing significant critical elections (see, Figure 12.2):

1)

2)

3)

dominant outcome of elections since World War II—

recent research suggests partisanship is responsive to—

Secular Realignment

secular realignment—

prospects of a national realignment—

Democratic Party shift toward civil rights and social spending—

The Functions of the American Party System

two-party system over the past 150 years—

Mobilizing Support and Gathering Power

how party affiliation is helpful to elected leaders—

coalition—

GOTV—

signals of partisan resurgence—

A Force for Stability and Moderation

mechanisms for organizing and containing political change—

FDR's New Deal coalition—

white southerners leave the Democratic Party for the GOP in the South—

more partisan in Congress—

Unity, Linkage, and Accountability

why parties are the glue holding together fragmented U.S. governmental and political apparatus—

division in government by design of the Federalists—

basis for mediation and negotiation laterally among the branches of government—

basis for mediation and negotiation vertically among national, state, and local layers of government—

party-linkage function—

how parties dampen sectionalism—

The Electioneering Function

how political parties assist in the "great function" of elections—

elections in a democracy can only have meaning if what?—

Party as a Voting and Issue Cue

party identification as a perceptual screen—

party identification as filter for information—

Policy Formulation and Promotion

national party platform—

impact and influence of platform—

Crashing the Party: Minor Parties in the American Two-Party System

proportional representation—

winner-take-all-system—

effect of the adaptive nature of the two-party system on the growth of third parties in the United States—

impact of minor parties on American politics—

roots in sectionalism—

Dixiecrats—

Populists—

Green Party—

ideology and third parties—

Bull Moose Party—

George Wallace and the American Independent Party in 1968—

Ross Perot in 1992—

Third Parties: Good or Bad for the American Political System?—

minor parties in congressional elections—

when third parties do best—

two major parties co-opt third party popular issues—

Party Organization

Political Party Organization in America: From Base to Pinnacle (see Figure 12.3)—

National Committees

Democratic National Committee (DNC)—

Republican National Committee (RNC)—

National Republican Congressional Committee (NRCC)—

National Democratic Congressional Committee (NDCC)—

Seventeenth Amendment and creation of Senate campaign committees for both parties—

Leadership

role of chairperson of the national committee—

role of the president—

post-campaign, out-of-power party committee and chairperson—

National Conventions

national convention—

television coverage of national conventions—

ultimate governing body for the party—

Howard Dean—

States and Localities

where are the parties structurally based?—

what level of government is responsible for virtually all regulation of political parties?—

party leadership comes from what level of government?—

precinct—

precinct committee members—

state central (or executive) committee—

national party and state party organizations division of powers—

New Hampshire resists DNC in 2006—

effect of Bipartisan Campaign Reform Act—

527 groups—

Informal Groups

groups affiliated with the parties—

supportive interest groups and associations—

think tanks—

The Transformation of Party Organization

Republican versus Democratic fund-raising efforts—

soft money—

hard money—

Republican versus Democratic fund-raising in 2006 midterm elections—

Political Party Finances (Figure 12.4)—

network of donors—

technology and the parties—

money spent on surveys and data accumulation—

technological and fund-raising modernization by the Democratic Party—

The Party in Government

The Congressional Party

political parties most visible in Congress; why?—

party caucus at beginning of each congressional session—

party leadership selection in Congress—

party discipline—

Senate majority leader—

pork barrel projects—

limits to coordinated, cohesive party action in Congress—

the most powerful predictor of congressional roll-call voting—

Congressional Party Unity Scores, 1959-2005 (Figure 12.5)—

reasons for recent growth of congressional party unity—

The Presidential Party

significance of political party of the president—

nonpartisan presidents—

presidential neglect and personal use of the their party—

pro-party presidents—

The Parties and the Judiciary

party affiliation influence on judicial decisions—

areas where party affiliation is a moderately good predictor of judicial decisions—

partisanship and elected judges as opposed to appointed judges—

The Parties and State Government

parties and governors—

governor's influence over state party—

significance of line-item veto for governor—
parties and state legislatures—

the state with a nonpartisan legislature—

comparison of effects and powers of party affiliation in legislatures versus
Congress—

The Party-in-the-Electorate

party-in-the-electorate—

party identification as indicator of likely voting choices—

Party Identification

party identification—

aspects and influences of party identification—

Party Identification, 1952-2004—

loyalty generated by party label—

A Purple Electorate?—

legal institutionalization of the major parties and party identification—

single greatest influence in establishing a person's first party
identification—

aspects of adult life that influence party identity—

Group Affiliation

Party Identification by Group Affiliation (Table 12.2)—

geographic region—

gender—

race and ethnicity—

Gender Gap: Men and Women's Vote Choices in the 2004 Presidential Election (Figure 12.6)—

race and ethnicity—

age—

Party Affiliation Among College Students (page 454)—

social and economic factors—

religion—

marital status—

ideology—

Is the Party Over or Has It Just Begun?

dealignment—

rise of independents—

self-identified Democratic and Republican partisans—

the two stages pollsters go through when asking for party identification information—

how independent "learners" vote much like real partisans—

importance of partisan affiliation in the community in the past—

reasons for anti-party attitudes today—

how voter-admitted partisanship has dropped (despite the underlying partisanship of the American people)—

has the decline of the parties been exaggerated?—

strengths of parties in the broad sweep of American parties:

1)

2)

3)

4)

5)

Research Ideas and Possible Paper Topics

1) As the textbook points out, the Republican Party has developed an extensive public relations and campaign training organization, as well as a highly efficient fund-raising effort. The Democratic Party has, in the 2004 presidential election and the 2006 midterm election, exploited the Internet as a dynamic new communications and fund-raising tool. How have the various Democratic campaigns in 2004 and 2006 used the Internet successfully for fundraising, information dissemination, voter involvement, and GOTV? Give examples.

2) Using the Internet or the library, look up state party organizations in three different states (for example, a Southern state, a New England state, and a Western state). Compare the Democratic and Republican parties from those states on a variety of indicators, including issue positions, platforms, and organization. Are they different? How and why?

3) Talk with, or invite to class, some local party activists. Ask them to talk to you about what they do in the party, why and how they got involved in politics, and the issues that they consider important. Does the information you learn ring true with what you have read in the text?

4) Congress currently has several independent members. Do some research to determine whether their independent status truly makes them different from the Democrats and Republicans. What kinds of compromises must an independent member of Congress make? How is the Congress controlled by party affiliation both formally and informally?

5) Research the 2004 and 2006 national platforms for the Democratic and Republican parties. Compare them on a variety of issues. Then, look at public opinion polls to see how the party positions correspond to those of average Americans. What do you find? Why do you think that is the case?

Web sites

The National Political Index features a Web page titled "Contacting Political Parties" with scores of links to the two major parties, third parties and minor parties, along with associated links.

> http://www.politicalindex.com/sect8.htm

University of Michigan Documents Center offers links to political parties; includes national and state parties, as well as links to congressional party leadership and platforms.

> http://www.lib.umich.edu/govdocs/polisci.html

EdGate, a service of **USAToday**, offers an illustrated history of political parties in the United States.

> http://www.edgate.com/elections/inactive/the_parties

Third Party Central offers links to third parties.

> www.3pc.net/index.html

Politics 1 offers links to political parties, campaign information, candidate information, and more. They also offer a free e-mail newsletter.

> www.politics1.com/parties.htm

The **American Library Association** hosts an Internet Resources page on political parties and elections with links to a wide range of related information.

> http://www.ala.org/ala/acrl/acrlpubs/crlnews/backissues2004/july04/elections.htm

Major Parties

The **Democratic National Committee** site.

> www.democrats.org

The **Republican National Committee** site.

> www.gop.org

Third Parties

The **Reform Party**.

> www.reformparty.org

The **Libertarian Party**.

> www.lp.org

The **Green Party.**

> www.greenparty.org

MULTIPLE CHOICE

1) The farewell address of which early president, in which he warned the nation against political parties, ironically marked the effective end of the brief era of partyless politics in the United States?
   a. George Washington
   b. John Adams
   c. Andrew Jackson
   d. Abraham Lincoln

2) Party politics was nearly nonexistent on the national level during the
   a. Gilded Age.
   b. Era of Good Feelings.
   c. Populist Era.
   d. Progressive Era.

3) The first President of the United States elected as the nominee of a truly national, popularly based political party was
   a. Thomas Jefferson.
   b. John Adams.
   c. Andrew Jackson.
   d. Theodore Roosevelt.

4) The power of political parties was undercut by the government assuming a number of services previously performed by the parties, including
   a. printing ballots.
   b. conducting elections.
   c. providing social welfare services.
   d. All of the above.

5) The utopian hopes of the Founders for the avoidance of partisan factionalism proved inevitable, as feared and warned by which Founding Father?
   a. James Madison
   b. Alexander Hamilton
   c. John Jay
   d. Thomas Jefferson

6) In Congress, parties perform a number of functions, including
   a. enforcing absolute party discipline through the use of sanctions.
   b. providing leadership and organization.
   c. decentralizing power in Congress.
   d. All of the above.

7) Political parties are most visible and important in the
   a.   legislative branch.
   b.   executive branch.
   c.   judiciary.
   d.   state governments.

8) Among the most party-oriented, party-building presidents was
   a.   Dwight Eisenhower.
   b.   Richard Nixon.
   c.   Ronald Reagan.
   d.   Jimmy Carter.

9) Among the most nonpartisan of presidents was
   a.   Dwight Eisenhower.
   b.   Gerald Ford.
   c.   Franklin Roosevelt.
   d.   Woodrow Wilson.

10) One state, _____, has a nonpartisan legislature.
   a.   Utah
   b.   Nebraska
   c.   Rhode Island
   d.   Vermont

11) Republicans surpass Democrats in fund-raising more than two to one. Most Republican fund-raising comes from
   a.   large, private donations.
   b.   wealthy corporations.
   c.   direct mail solicitation.
   d.   conservative interest groups.

12) While the Democratic Party still trails the Republican Party in most measures of party organization and activity, the Democratic Party shows as its greatest strength
   a.   the number of rich, corporate donors who faithfully contribute to the party.
   b.   campaign schools.
   c.   media manipulation and corporate public relations expertise.
   d.   its high number of party activists.

13) Self-professed independents (including those leaning in that direction) increased from about one-fifth of the electorate in the 1950s to _____ during the last three decades.
   a.   one-fourth
   b.   one-third
   c.   one-half
   d.   two-thirds

14) The American Independent Party enjoyed a modicum of success because of
    a.   a dynamic leader, George Wallace.
    b.   a firm geographic base, the South.
    c.   an emotional issue, civil rights.
    d.   All of the above.

15) Third parties often find their roots in
    a.   economic protest.
    b.   sectionalism.
    c.   issues and charismatic personalities.
    d.   All of the above.

TRUE/FALSE

1) A political party is a group of office holders, candidates, activists, and voters who identify with a group label and seek to elect people to public office who run under that label.

2) George Washington advocated the formation of parties because they perform a useful organizational function in Congress.

3) By the 1820s, all the states in the Union except South Carolina had switched from state legislative selection of presidential electors to popular election of Electoral College delegates from their state.

4) The slavery issue exacerbated many divisive issues within the Whig Party, leading to its gradual dissolution and replacement by the new Democratic Party.

5) Because it emphasizes personalities rather than abstract concepts, television has been a major factor in preventing the decline of political parties in the electorate.

6) Few political party platform promises ever get implemented by a party when elected to power in government.

7) The Democratic and Republican Parties are structurally based in Washington, D.C., and are primarily organized and operated by their national organizations.

8) American judges are completely nonpartisan.

9) Most American voters identify with a party but do not belong to it.

10) Third parties tend to remain minor due to ballot access laws, laws that provide public funding to campaigns, news coverage, and efforts by the major parties.

COMPARE AND CONTRAST

roots and development of the Democratic Party and the Republican Party

modern era and Golden Age

civil service laws, patronage, and spoils system

evidence of party decline and evidence of endurance of the two-party system

Democratic platform and Republican platform

proportional representation and single-member plurality electoral systems

congressional party and presidential party

pro-party and nonpartisan presidents

Republican strengths and Democratic strengths

advantages given to two main parties versus third parties

ESSAY AND SHORT ANSWER QUESTIONS

1) Discuss the political machines of the "Golden Age" of parties.

2) The significance of political party among the electorate has diminished over the past several decades, yet the significance of the two parties in operating the government remains strong. Discuss the factors that contributed to overall party loyalty among the electorate and why party affiliation remains important for most office holders.

3) What is the role of the national platform, and how is the platform treated by office holders once elected?

4) What are one-partyism and third-partyism? Why are they important in our system?

5) Discuss the party-in-the-electorate.

6) What are the roles of political parties in the U.S. political and governmental system?

7) What is a third party, and why do they tend to remain peripheral to the political system?

8)   Discuss the basic structure of American political parties on the state and local level.

9)   Discuss the meaning of the term "party-in-government."

10)   Compare and contrast the strengths and strategies of the Republican and Democratic parties.

ANSWERS TO STUDY EXERCISES

Multiple Choice Answers

1) a
2) b
3) c
4) d
5) a
6) b
7) a
8) c
9) a
10) b
11) c
12) d
13) b
14) d
15) d

True/False Answers

1) T
2) F
3) T
4) F
5) F
6) F
7) F
8) F
9) T
10) T

CHAPTER 13
VOTING AND ELECTIONS

Chapter Goals and Learning Objectives

Do you vote? Do your friends and family vote? Probably, you know people who consider voting meaningless. Or they consider the process of voting too cumbersome for so little impact. Of course, ask Al Gore if a handful of votes matter. A few more people showing up at the polls across Florida in November of 2000 and the presidential election would not have produced such a questionable and controversial outcome. And had a minor percentage of the total votes cast in the 2004 election in key states shifted because of increased voter turnout, George W. Bush would have moved back to Texas and John Kerry would have moved into the White House in 2005 rather than back to the Senate.

Elections in America allow a peaceful and legitimate transfer of power. The United States has more elections more often than any other country in the world. We also have the lowest turnout of the industrialized countries—fewer than half of our eligible voters vote on a regular basis. There are a wide variety of explanations for nonvoting. There are even those who claim that having a low voter turnout is a good thing and increases stability in the political system. Others argue that reform is necessary to increase voter turnout. After the 2000 presidential election, where some argue the votes of five Republican members of the U.S. Supreme Court rather than the votes of the people of Florida were the final arbiter of who would be president, calls for reform of the Electoral College system were widespread. This chapter will look at those arguments and others related to voting and elections.

This chapter is designed to give you an overview of voting and elections in the United States. The main topic headings of the chapter are:

- Voting Behavior
- Elections in the United States
- Presidential Elections
- Congressional Elections
- The 2006 Midterm Elections
- Reforming the Electoral Process

In each section, there are certain facts and ideas that you should strive to understand. Many are in boldface type and appear in both the narrative and in the glossary at the end of the book. Other ideas, dates, facts, events, people, etc. are more difficult to pull out of the narrative. (Keep in mind that studying for objective tests [multiple choice, T/F] is different than studying for essay tests. See the Study Guide section on test taking for hints on study skills.)

In general, after you finish reading and studying this chapter, you should understand the following:

- voting behavior and distinct patterns in voter turnout and vote choice
- purposes and types of elections and how elections at all levels confer a legitimacy on regimes better than any other method of change
- how presidential elections work, including the primaries, national conventions, and the Electoral College
- how congressional elections work and how they differ from presidential elections (even though they share many similarities)
- the 2006 midterm election and its similarities and differences with other midterm elections
- arguments for reforming the electoral process as well as the potential benefits and unintended consequences of electoral change

Chapter Outline and Key Points

In this section, you are provided with a basic outline of the chapter and key words/points you should know. Use this outline to develop a complete outline of the material. Write the definitions or further explanations for the terms. Use the space provided in this workbook or rewrite that material in your notebook. This will help you study and remember the material in preparation for your tests, assignments, and papers.

Tuesday following the first Monday in November every odd numbered year—

the increase in the size of the electorate and the number of elections—

Voting Behavior

conventional political participation—

unconventional political participation—

Cindy Sheehan—

Voting Behavior

Patterns in Voter Turnout

turnout—

why turnout is so important in American elections—

2004 presidential election and the power of a single vote—

factors known to influence voter turnout:

Education—

Income—

Age—

Gender—

Race and Ethnicity—

    turnout in 2004 presidential election for minorities—

    The South Versus the Non-South for Presidential Voter Turnout (Figure 13.1)—

    Voting Rights Act of 1965—

    Hispanic vote—

    Hispanics elected to office in 2004 and 2006—

Interest in Politics—

Why is Voter Turnout So Low?

percentage of U.S. voter participation—

Why People Don't Vote (Figure 13.2)—

contributing factors for low voter participation rates:

    Too Busy—

    Difficulty of Registration—

        reasons for low U.S. registration rate—

        National Voter Registration Act of 1993 (Motor Voter Act)—

    Difficulty of Absentee Voting—

    Number of Elections—

Voter Attitudes—

Weaken Influence of Political Parties—

Efforts to Improve Voter Turnout

Easier Registration and Absentee Voting—

proposals—

Oregon's all-mail balloting—

success of motor voter law—

Make Election Day a Holiday—

Strengthen Parties—

Patterns in Vote Choice

Ticket-Splitting—

effect of party affiliation intensity on ticket-splitting—

potential explanations for ticket-splitting—

Race and Ethnicity—

African Americans—

Hispanics—

Chinese Americans and Vietnamese Americans—

Gender—

Income—

Ideology—

liberals—

conservatives—

Issues—

retrospective judgment—

prospective judgment—

how voters retrospectively and prospectively judged recent presidential administrations in reaching their voting decisions:

1992—

1996—

2000—

2004—

two major campaign-specific issues of the 2004 presidential election—

how voters responded to the two major campaign-specific issues of the 2004 presidential election—

Elections in the United States

The Purposes of Elections

popular sovereignty and elections—

authoritarian systems—

"referenda" in authoritarian systems—

elections in a democratic society—

electorate—

elections and policies—

mandate—

claims to a mandate by presidents—

mandates in midterm elections:

Contract with America in 1994—

Iraq War and Bush in 2006—

Types of Elections

Primary Elections—

closed primary—

open primary—

crossover voting—

raiding—

runoff primary—

General Elections—

Initiative, Referendum, and Recall—

ballot measures—

initiative—

referendum—

recall—

1990 California election and referenda and initiatives—

2003 California gubernatorial recall and election—

<u>**Presidential Elections**</u>

sequential events in the presidential election process—

methods state party organizations use to elect national convention delegates and ultimately select the candidate who will run in the general election:

winner-take-all primary—

proportional representation primary—

caucus—

Primaries Versus Caucuses

trend from caucuses to primary elections—

which states use primaries and which use caucuses to select presidential delegates—

Methods of Selecting Democratic Party Presidential Delegates (Figure 13.4)—

characteristics of caucuses—

characteristics of primaries—

"sophisticated voting"—

critics of presidential primaries—

earliest primary—

front-loading—

important effects of front-loading on the nomination process—

2004 and Internet fund-raising's effect of softening fund-raising advantages of front-loading—

2008 addition of Nevada's caucus between the contests in Iowa and New Hampshire by Democratic Party—

The Party Conventions

which party traditionally holds its national convention first?—

characteristics of the national conventions—

three ways national party conventions are different today—

1)

2)

3)

delegate selection—

unit rule—

Democratic Party rule regarding state delegates selection in proportion of votes cast in primary or caucus, the effect and consequence—

before 1972, most delegates to Democratic National Convention were not bound by primary results to support a particular candidate for nomination and the effect of this freedom to maneuver at the convention—

superdelegates—

percentage of minorities and women at 2004 national Democratic convention—

contrast in the delegation make-up at the Democratic and Republican national conventions—

Historic Moments for Women at the Conventions (Table 13.1)—

National Candidates and Issues—

News Media and National Conventions—

how television has shaped the business of the convention—

pros and cons of extensive media coverage of the convention—

The Electoral College: How Presidents Are Elected

Electoral College—

electors—

number of electors—

magic number for winning the Electoral College vote—

Electoral College was result of compromise between two groups—

three essentials reasons why the Framers constructed the Electoral College—

        1)

        2)

        3)

complex nature of Elector College as originally designed and implemented by the Framers—

system was designed by Framers for the America they (erroneously) foresaw lasting in perpetuity—

why Electoral College worked well when elections were nonpartisan—

Electoral College in the Nineteenth Century

Twelfth Amendment (1804)—

1876 race between Hayes and Tilden—

The Electoral College Today

1976 presidential election—

2000 presidential election—

Bush v. *Gore* (2000)—

reapportionment—

implications of reapportionment after 2000 census—

The States Drawn in Proportion to their Electoral College Votes (Figure 13.5)—

recent reapportionment favored which party?—

The Electoral College Reconsidered—

    1) Popular Vote—

    2) Congressional District Plan—

3) Keep the College, Abolish the Electors—

Congressional Elections

attention given congressional elections compared to presidential elections—

celebrity nominees for Congress—

the vast majority of party nominees for Congress—

The Incumbency Advantage

incumbency—

congressional reelection rates—

Staff Support—

size of staffs—

free mass mailings—

constituency services—

Media and Travel—

The "Scare-off" Effect—

Redistricting—

how used by the majority party in the state—

Texas redistricting in 2003 and protests of Texas Democratic legislators—

gerrymandering—

U.S. Census—

Supreme Court rulings on redistricting:

1)

2)

3)

4)

dominant party's use of redistricting to make incumbents safer—

effect of Supreme Court's consideration of political redistricting based on partisan consideration as a political question and not a judicial question—

Countervailing Forces to the Incumbency Advantage

four major reasons the few incumbent members of Congress lose their election bids—

Redistricting—

Scandals—

2006 midterm election results and impact of scandals—

Presidential Coattails—

Midterm Elections

midterm elections—

why the president's party usually loses seats in Congress during midterm elections—

Congressional Election Results, 1948-2006 (Table 13.2)—

sixth year of a two-term presidency—

six year itch and the second term of George W. Bush—

Senate elections and off-year patterns—

Voter Turnout in Presidential and Midterm Elections (page 498)—

The 2006 Midterm Elections

results in the fourteen midterm elections before 2002—

2002 midterm election—

2006 midterm election—

scandals and Bush Iraq policy in 2006 midterm elections—

Results of Selected Elections, 2006 (Table 13.3)—

Democratic Party control of Congress—

Reforming the Electoral Process

legitimacy of the electoral outcomes—

Protecting the Electoral Process—

effects of Electoral College's ability to distort public input—

least likely reforms to succeed—

Regional Primaries

regional primaries—

twofold goal of this reform—

Campaign Finance Reform

McCain-Feingold Campaign Finance Reform of 2002—

soft money donations—

Online Voting

quest for a secure, reliable, fraud-free voting mechanism—

state boards of election—

use of voting machines—

Internet voting and instant democracy—

2000 experiment in Arizona with Internet voting—

2004 Michigan attempt with presidential caucus—

2004 U.S. military attempt at Internet voting—

Voting by Mail

mail-in ballots—

Oregon's entirely mail-in election vote—

absentee balloting—

late reporting of mail-in votes and other concerns—

Modernizing the Ballot

electronic voting machine use—

Percentage of Voters Using Electronic Voting Machines, 2000-2006 (Figure 13.7)—

beliefs of supporters of electronic voting—

beliefs of opponents of electronic voting—

Research Ideas and Possible Paper Topics

1) Many reform proposals argue that the U.S. should adopt proportional representation. In this method of election, voters choose a party list as opposed to an individual candidate. This method strengthens parties and tends to increase voter turnout and the number of parties in the political system. Among those countries that use PR are: Holland, Poland, and others. Research the nature of PR and how it might work, or why it would not work, in the United States.

2) Accusations of voter irregularities in Ohio and Florida surfaced soon after the November 2004 presidential election, some of which were tied to the new electronic voting technologies which critics claimed lacked sufficient verification procedures for recount and accuracy. What were some of the allegations of fraud in Ohio and with regard to electronic voting? What measures, if any, do you think should be taken to secure the integrity of electronic voting procedures? What measures should be taken to assure voters that their votes count in an election?

3) Many scholars argue that low voter turnout is due to electoral rules, frequency of elections, apathy, etc. Discuss how you would change these impediments to voting and discuss the impact increased voter turnout would have on the electoral process.

4)   Look at several sources discussing the Electoral College. What reforms have been proposed? How useful is the Electoral College now? Would you advocate a different approach? Does it matter that a presidential candidate can lose the popular vote and still become president as in the 2000 election? Hold a debate in class on the merits of the various routes to reform.

5)   The recall of Governor Grey Davis of California in 2003 and the subsequent election of Arnold Schwarzenegger as the new governor was an unprecedented example of the use of voter recall in recent times. What is a recall election? What precipitated this recall in California and what were the partisan factors involved? Was this a harbinger for the future of elections or a unique event politically? What impact has this had on electoral politics?

Web sites

BlackBoxVoting.Org is a nonpartisan, nonprofit, 501c(3) organization which states that it is "the official consumer protection group for elections, funded by citizen donations." It focuses on information about irregularities in electronic voting technology.
         http://www.blackboxvoting.org

Project Vote-Smart is a nonpartisan information service funded by members and nonpartisan foundations. It offers "a wealth of facts on your political leaders, including biographies and addresses, issue positions, voting records, campaign finances, evaluations by special interests." It also offers "CongressTrack," a way for citizens to track the status of legislation, members and committees, sponsors, voting records, clear descriptions, full text, and weekly floor schedules, as well as access to information on elections, federal and state governments, the issues, and politics. Includes thousands of links to the most important sites on the Internet.
         www.vote-smart.org

The **American National Election Studies** Web site is a key source of data on voting behavior.
         http://www.electionstudies.org

Campaigns and Elections magazine's Web site is oriented toward campaign professionals but is also useful to teachers and students. It offers articles, their table of contents from the print version, job opportunities, and more.
         www.campaignline.com

The **Federal Election Commission (FEC)** website offers campaign finance information, a citizens' guide to political contributions, news and information about elections and voting. Includes data about state regulations on voting (registration and residency rules, etc.) as well as elections data from a variety of elections.
         www.fec.gov

Rock-the-Vote is an organization dedicated to getting young people involved in politics.
www.rockthevote.org

The **League of Women Voters** provides information to voters across the country on state, federal, and local elections and works to encourage election reform and campaign finance reform. Their Web site offers an interactive section on election information.
www.lwv.org

The **Office of the Federal Register** coordinates the functions of the Electoral College on behalf of the Archivist of the United States, the States, the Congress and the American people. This site assembles a variety of information and statistics on the Electoral College, past and present.
http://www.archives.gov/federal_register/electoral_college/index.html

The **Census Bureau** has information on voter registration and turnout statistics.
www.census.gov/population/www/socdemo/voting.html

The Electronic Freedom Foundation is a donor-supported non-profit agency and activist group working to defend free speech, privacy, innovation, and consumer rights today by championing the public interest in every critical battle affecting digital rights. Their **E-Voting** page provides extensive information about this issue and the EEF's efforts in this area.
http://www.eff.org/Activism/E-voting

Practice Tests

MULTIPLE CHOICE

1) Which of the following is not a requirement for voters to engage in prospective voting?
   a. voters must have an opinion on an issue
   b. voters must have an idea of what action, if any, the government is taking on an issue
   c. voters must have a personal, immediate, and direct stake in the outcome of the election
   d. voters must see a difference between the two parties on the issue

2) A primary election that is held to choose a party's candidate and that allows only registered party members to vote is called a
   a. simple primary.
   b. closed primary.
   c. blanket primary.
   d. open primary.

3) In the 2003 California gubernatorial recall election, Arnold Schwarzenegger was elected to replace who as the Governor of California?
a. Grey Davis
b. Bill Simon
c. Gary Coleman
d. Kenny Guinn

4) Many people favor the use of caucuses to select party nominees because
a. caucus participants tend to be knowledgeable party stalwarts.
b. caucuses reduce the influence of the media.
c. the quality of participation in caucuses is higher than in primaries.
d. All of the above.

5) The Electoral College encountered problems in the election of 1800. In order to remedy the problem of selecting a president of one party and a vice president of another, Congress passed the
a. Law on Presidential Elections.
b. Law on the Electoral College.
c. Twelfth Amendment.
d. Eleventh Amendment.

6) If there is no majority in the Electoral College for a candidate, the election is decided by the
a. popular vote.
b. House of Representatives.
c. Senate.
d. Congress as a whole.

7) The representation of states in the Electoral College is altered to reflect population shifts
a. at the start of each new Congress.
b. every four years at the start of a new presidential term.
c. every ten years.
d. whenever Congress deems it necessary.

8) If an incumbent member of Congress loses a reelection bid, the change is likely to be the result of
a. redistricting.
b. a high-spending challenger.
c. advertising by well-financed interest groups.
d. racism.

9)   About _____ percent of eligible adults vote regularly.
        a.   65
        b.   55
        c.   40
        d.   30

10)   In 1971, the voting age was lowered to 18 by the _____ Amendment.
        a.   Nineteenth
        b.   Twenty-Second
        c.   Twenty-Fourth
        d.   Twenty-Sixth

11)   Which of the following is most likely to vote in an election?
        a   a lower-income citizen
        b.   a wealthy, well-educated citizen
        c.   a citizen age 18-24
        d.   a citizen with little education

12)   Which of the following is not a reason why people who are more highly educated
        tend to vote more so than people who are less educated?
        a.   people with more education tend to be more patriotic
        b.   people with more education tend to learn more about politics
        c.   people with more education are less hindered by registration requirements
        d.   people with more education are more self-confident about their ability to
                influence public life

13)   Voter turnout in this country is low due to the
        a.   difficulty of registration.
        b.   difficulty of absentee voting.
        c.   frequency of elections.
        d.   All of the above.

14)   In 1993, Congress and President Clinton passed a law designed to increase voter
        turnout called the
        a.   Election Law of 1993.
        b.   Law on Participation.
        c.   Motor Voter Law.
        d.   Voting Rights Act.

15)   In the 2004 election, the percentage of people who vote a split ticket in that
        presidential election year was
        a.   75 percent.
        b.   60 percent.
        c.   48 percent.
        d.   26 percent.

TRUE/FALSE

1)   Regular elections are a mechanism to keep office holders accountable.

2)   General elections are elections in which only the party faithful may vote.

3)   Caucuses are more democratic than primaries.

4)   The first national party convention was held in 1831.

5)   People who vote are usually more highly educated than nonvoters.

6)   Incumbency advantage in congressional elections is quite high due to name recognition, media access, opportunities to help constituents, and free mailing privileges.

7)   In midterm or off-year elections, members of the president's party tend to gain a significant number of seats.

8)   The results of the 2006 midterm elections, President George W. Bush's second midterm election, was consistent with the trends of most midterm elections.

9)   Less than half of eligible citizens ages 18 to 24 are even registered to vote.

10)   Nonvoters tend to be low-income, younger, blue collar, less educated, and more heavily minority.

COMPARE AND CONTRAST

electorate and mandate

retrospective and prospective judgment

primary elections: open, closed, blanket, runoff

primary and general elections

initiative, referendum, and recall

primaries vs. caucuses

presidential and congressional elections

Democratic and Republican convention delegate selection process party realignment and critical election

presidential year and off-year/midterm elections

midterm elections in 2002 and 2006

participation: turnout, income, age, gender, race, interest

ticket-splitting and straight ticket voting

ESSAY AND SHORT ANSWER QUESTIONS

1) Explain the various types of primaries. How are they similar, how are they different, and why would a state choose one variant over another?

2) Discuss initiative, referendum, and recall. Why and where do we have them? How pervasive are they? What are some examples of recent uses of each?

3) What impact could regional primaries and front-loading have on the process of nominating a president?

4) What is the Electoral College? Why is it often the subject of reform proposals? What problems did it present in the 2000 election? Where there historical precedents to the problems in 2000 with the Electoral College? Explain.

5) What are the incumbency advantages for members Congress, and what events serve to lessen them?

6) Compare and contrast the nature of primary and general elections for both congressional and presidential candidates.

7) Discuss the changing nature of the party conventions and how the Republican and Democratic conventions are similar and different.

8) Discuss the role of parties in presidential elections and the nature of party alignments.

9) Analyze the nature of congressional elections from 1994 to the present. Detail and discuss the nature and impact of the congressional elections of 2006.

10) Discuss voting behavior and voter turnout. Who votes and why? What voting patterns exist? Why is voter turnout so low? Does low turnout matter?

ANSWERS TO STUDY EXERCISES

Multiple Choice Answers

1) d
2) b
3) a
4) d
5) c
6) b
7) c
8) a
9) c
10) d
11) b
12) a
13) d
14) c
15) d

True/False Answers

1) T
2) F
3) F
4) T
5) T
6) T
7) F
8) T
9) T
10) T

CHAPTER 14
THE CAMPAIGN PROCESS

Chapter Goals and Learning Objectives

It is an election year and you know that for sure because your government professor keeps yapping about it in class. You come home from school or work, flop down on the sofa, click on the TV to relax and what do you see? Those annoying political commercials. They seem to go on and on for months before an election. And usually it's one guy trashing another. Irritating, right? But for most Americans, the TV ad is where they get most of their information about political candidates running for office. Isn't there a better way of doing this?

American political campaigns are long and expensive. We have more elections than most other countries and they last longer, too. Our campaigns also seem to turn a large number of voters off the process entirely. People say they hate negative campaigning, but negative campaign ads work. Many Americans believe that wealthy donors and political action committees have a disproportionate influence on the process. Do candidates sell themselves on TV like advertisers sell toothpaste or soap, processed and packaged like products for sale? Indeed, the art of electioneering has seemingly merged with the science of marketing and advertising. Yet the goals of campaigning remain the same: Get voters' attention and get their votes. How candidates pursue these goals is the subject of this chapter.

This chapter is designed to give you a basic understanding of the campaign process from how candidates are chosen to who wins and loses. The main topic headings of the chapter are:

- The Nature of Modern Political Campaigns
- The Key Players: The Candidate and the Campaign Staff
- Coverage of the Game: The Media's Role in Defining the Playing Field
- The Rules of the Game: Campaign Finance
- The Main Event: The 2004 Presidential Campaign

In each section, there are certain facts and ideas that you should strive to understand. Many are in boldface type and appear in both the narrative and in the glossary at the end of the book. Other ideas, dates, facts, events, people, etc. are more difficult to pull out of the narrative. (Keep in mind that studying for objective tests [multiple choice, T/F] is different than studying for essay tests. See the Study Guide section on test taking for hints on study skills.)

In general, after you finish reading and studying this chapter, you should understand the following:

- the nature of modern campaign structure, generally segmented into nomination and general election campaigns, and often reported and discussed in military and sports metaphors
- the key players in the modern campaign, the campaign managers, and the paid and volunteer staff who make up the campaign organization
- the coverage of the game by the media—the media's role in defining the playing field, and how tradition and new media depict the political battlefield and how campaigns try to manage media coverage
- the rules of the game—campaign finance, and the effect of the Bipartisan Campaign Reform Act of 2002
- the main event—the 2004 presidential campaign and the lessons learned on the battlefield

Chapter Outline and Key Points

In this section, you are provided with a basic outline of the chapter and key words/points you should know. Use this outline to develop a complete outline of the material. Write the definitions or further explanations for the terms. Use the space provided in this workbook or rewrite that material in your notebook. This will help you study and remember the material in preparation for your tests, assignments, and papers.

the art of modern campaigning—

what campaigning involves—

The Nature of Modern Political Campaigns

the language of campaigns: the military and sports metaphors—

The Elements of a Political Campaign (Figure 14.1)—

Nomination Campaign

nominating campaign—

how candidates use the nominating campaign—

danger of moving too far to the extremes in the nominating campaign—

General Election Campaign

general election campaign—

courting interest groups—

brief theme or slogan—

deciding on issues—

defining a stance on topics of interest to voters—

factors influencing candidate's positions and core issues—

public opinion polls—

The Key Players: The Candidate and the Campaign Staff

most important aspect of any campaign—

in the hands of the candidate—

the work of the campaign staff—

requiring the combined efforts of staff and candidate—

The Candidate

reasons candidates run for office—

what a candidate must do to be successful—

symbolic efforts—

importance of visiting numerous localities—

candidate's schedule in a typical campaign—

The Campaign Staff

staff—

collective work of the staff—

working on candidate's needs—

size and nature of the organizational staff—

Volunteer Campaign Staff—

    lifeblood of every campaign—

    work done by unpaid volunteers—

    voter canvass—

    get out the vote (GOTV)—

The Candidate's Professional Staff—

    campaign manager—

    finance chair—

    pollster—

    direct mailer—

    communications director—

    press secretary—

    Internet team—

The Candidate's Hired Guns—

    campaign consultants—

    the specialized consultants candidates hire—

    media consultants—

    who works with the media consultants?—

The Candidate's Personal Advisers—

    Bush Campaign Organizational Staff (Figure 14.2)—

    Ken Mehlman—

    Karl Rove—

Covering the Game: The Media's Role in Defining the Playing Field

paid media—

free media—

new media—

Paid Media

who decided on use of paid media?—

positive ads—

negative ads—

contrast ads—

spot ads—

Federalists' negative portrait of Thomas Jefferson in 1796—

how well-known incumbents handled negative ads before the 1980s—

the new rule of politics regarding negative ads—

inoculation ads—

news media analysis of accuracy of candidate's ads—

Free Media

control of free versus paid media—

how the new media cover campaigns—

news media regard candidates with suspicion—

effect of media's expectations on how public views a candidate—

superficial coverage—

The New Media

candidate-centered campaigns and the new media—

new array of weapons available to campaign—

"rapid-response" technique—

recorded phone messages—

first widespread use of the Internet in national campaigning—

blogs and the candidate's Web site—

how Kerry kept base after 2004 loss—

Campaign Strategies to Control Media Coverage

campaign strategies to influence news coverage:

1)

2)

3)

4)

candidate debates—

what candidates can control and what they can't control regarding debates—

how candidates must prepare for debates—

Ford's costly error in October 1976 presidential debate—

George H.W. Bush's error in 1992 presidential debate—

importance of debates demonstrated in 2004 presidential debates—

confirmation of public preconceptions of candidates in the debates—

Kennedy-Nixon debate—

The Rules of the Game: Campaign Finance

campaign funds raised in various elections—

The Road to Reform

civil service reform and campaign finance, 1883—

Tillman Act, 1907, and campaign finance—

Federal Election Campaign Act of 1971—

Federal Elections Commission—

Bipartisan Campaign Reform Act of 2002 (BCRA)—

BCRA and soft money—

McConnell v. *FEC* (2003)—

Current Rules

BRRA of 2002—

Individual Contribution Limits Per Election Cycle Before and After Bipartisan Campaign Reform Act of 2002 (Table 14.1)—

Individual Contributions—

current maximum allowable contribution under federal law for congressional and presidential elections—

limit on an individual's gifts to all candidates, PACs, and parties combined in each calendar year—

most candidates received majority of all funds directly from individuals—

strict disclosure law for individuals who spend over $10,000 to air "electioneering communications"—

Political Action Committee (PAC) Contributions

PACs—

current limits on PAC contributions—

PACs registered with FEC—

PAC contributions in 2004 election cycle—

why corporate PACs give primarily to incumbents—

which PACs more likely to support challengers—

disproportionate influence of PACs over individual contributors—

BCRA attempts to control PACs—

why PACs remain controversial—

PACs began in the 1970s—

PAC contributions in 2006—

Growth in Total Contributions by PACs to House and Senate Candidates (Figure 14.3)—

Expenditure by PACs in the 2004 Election Cycle (Figure 14.4)—

special interest money of all types made it into politics well before PACs—

Political Party Contributions—

parties can give substantial contributions to their congressional nominees—

current limits on contributions by political parties—

political party contributions in 2006—

percentage of total campaign war chest from parties in contested races—

Member-to-Candidate Contributions—

contributions from electorally secure incumbents—

done in one of two ways:

1)

2)

Barbara Boxer (D-Ca) contributions in 2006 to regain control of the House and Senate—

Candidates' Personal Contributions—

contributions from candidates and their families—

Buckley v. *Valeo* (1976)—

the meaning for wealthy candidates—

self-contributing candidates expenditures in 2006—

most self-contribution candidates spend less than $100,000—

Public Funds—

only federal candidates to receive public funds—

a few local and state candidates—

FECA controls—

how a presidential candidate qualifies to receive public funds during the nominating contest—

matching funds—

Presidential Election Fund—

how it is funded—

percentage of taxpayers who participate in contributing to the fund—

procedures for general election funding of the two major-party presidential nominees—

third-party candidate funding in general election—

The Fall of the Soft-Money Loophole and the Rise of the 527 Loophole

soft money—

1978 FEC advisory opinion—

245

1979 amendment passed by Congress—

line separating expenditures that influence federal elections from those that do not—

controversy over political advertising—

hard money and advocacy ads—

parties produced political ads that skirted the hard money rule, allowing them to be paid for with unregulated soft money—

soft money contributions now prohibited by BCRA—

current rules for third-party issue ads—

soft money raised by Republican and Democrats during 2001-2002 (the last election cycle for the parties to use soft money)—

reformers hoped-for result of soft money ban—

loophole found in 2004 to go through BRCA—

527 political committees—

The Ten Most Active 527 Groups in 2004—

IRS Code and 527s—

sham issue ads—

BRCA now forbids 527 funded ads thirty days before a primary and sixty days before a general—

Media Fund and America Coming Together (ACT)—

Texas developer Bob Perry—

Most Active Contributors to 527 Groups, 2004 (Table 14.2)—

contributions and spending by 527 groups in 2006 election—

likelihood of abolishing 527s—

The Main Event: The 2004 Presidential Campaign

The Party Nomination Battle

no significant opposition to Bush in Republican primary—

heated Democratic primary—

2004 Democratic Candidates and Their Strategies (Table 14.3)—

Howard Dean—

John Edwards—

John Kerry—

"anything but Bush"—

The Democratic Convention

Bush v. Kerry immediately before and after the convention—

Barack Obama—

overarching theme—

testimonials from Kerry's Vietnam swiftboat crewmates—

Kerry's speech—

small post-convention bounce—

The Republican Convention

New York City and 9/11 theme—

moderate Republicans showcased—

Georgia Democratic Senator Zell Miller—

protests outside Madison Square Garden—

The Presidential Debates

first debate, high ratings—

questions on foreign policy elicited clashes—

Kerry considered winner of first debate—

second debate, town-hall format—

Bush energetic, unlike first debate—

Kerry generally considered winner of second debate—

The Fall Campaign and General Election

public opinion in final days of campaign—

particularly close in six states—

Iraq in campaign—

Kerry charges against Bush—

Bush charges against Kerry—

Election Results

2004 Election Results (Popular Vote Percentage) (Table 14.4)—

Ohio in dispute—

Kerry concedes Wednesday afternoon—

Analyzing the Outcome of the 2004 Election

voter turnout—

reason for high turnout—

Group-Identified Voting Patterns in the 2004 Presidential Election (Figure 14.5)—

similarities to 2000 election—

continuation of modern trends—

Research Ideas and Possible Paper Topics

1) Write a campaign plan. Call your local political parties and ask for copies of their electioneering materials or candidate training course materials. Using those materials, write up a campaign plan for a U.S. House or Senate candidate. Be sure you can explain why you chose your tactics and strategies.

2) Research and analyze the campaign for president in the 2004 election. Examine the campaign organization for the Kerry campaign and the Bush campaign. Place yourself in the position of the campaign managers for both campaigns. What where the plans developed and implemented for media, issues, polling, fundraising, scheduling, travel, get out the vote, and other aspects of the campaign and how did they change during the course of the general election campaign? What would you have done differently if you were the campaign manger for the Kerry campaign? For the Bush campaign?

3) Write an essay designed to prepare your candidate for an upcoming presidential debate in the 2008 campaign. Choose a strategy and a message for your campaign. What tactics, etc. will help you win the debate?

4) Go to the library or Internet and find a cache of campaign commercials and free media coverage of one of the last few elections. Compare tactics, strategies, and content of the ads. How would you classify them? How effective is each ad? To whom are they targeted? Discuss what these ads tell you about the political process and the candidates.

5) Research the current campaign finance laws and the reform measures recently passed by Congress and interpreted by the courts. Once you understand the nature of the laws and their purpose, devise a reform plan of your own. And consider how you would sell it to the people, the incumbents in the House and Senate, the president, and other interested parties.

Web sites

Project Vote-Smart is a nonpartisan information service funded by members and nonpartisan foundations. It offers "a wealth of facts on your political leaders, including biographies and addresses, issue positions, voting records, campaign finances, evaluations by special interests." It also offers "CongressTrack" a way for citizens to track the status of legislation, members & committees, sponsors, voting records, clear descriptions, full text, and weekly floor schedules, as well as access to information on elections, federal & state governments, the issues, and politics. Includes thousands of links to the most important sites on the Internet.

www.vote-smart.org

The **Democracy Project of PBS** offers a Web site called "**Dissect the Ad**" that features a changing set of campaign ads that visitors are asked to criticize, dissect, and discuss. The point is to determine how the message is constructed—what images, tones, music, etc. and how it is designed to sway us. There are numerous current and past ads on which to practice from all ends of the political spectrum. You can read the content of the ads or, by downloading a player, you can view them. Following each ad are commentaries on both sides discussing the ad and you get the chance to post your comments, if you are so inclined, and read the comments of others.

> http://www.pbs.org/elections/savvydissect.html

The **30-Second Candidate** PBS Web site provides information about campaign television ads including historical timelines, "from idea to ad," questions and answers and a transcript of the 1999 Emmy Award winning program.

> www.pbs.org/30secondcandidate

Campaigns and Elections magazine's Web site is oriented toward campaign professionals but is also useful to teachers and students. It offers articles, their table of contents from the print version, job opportunities, and more.

> www.campaignline.com

Federal Election Commission Web site on campaign finance laws.

> http://www.fec.gov/law/law.shtml

Democratic Congressional Campaign Committee-DCCC

> www.dccc.org

Democratic Senatorial Campaign Committee-DSCC

> www.dscc.org

National Republican Congressional Committee-NRCC

> www.nrcc.org

National Republican Senatorial Committee-NRSC

> www.nrsc.org

The **Washington Post OnPolitics** Web page reports on campaigns and elections. (Will require free registration with *The Washington Post*.)

> www.washingtonpost.com/wp-dyn/politics/elections

Brookings Institution's Campaign Finance Web page

> http://www.brookings.org/gs/cf/cf_hp.htm

Common Cause offers information on soft money donations, PAC contributions, and voting records on campaign finance issues as well as other information.

> www.commoncause.org

The Public Campaign offers articles on campaign finance reform at the state and national levels as well as numerous links.

www.publicampaign.org

Open Secrets, the Web site for The Center for Responsive Politics, documents the money raised and spent by congressional candidates, individual donors, and PACs. It includes information on large soft money donations and the financial disclosure reports of members of Congress.

www.opensecrets.org

The Center for Public Integrity, which conducts investigative research and reporting on public policy issues, hosts a Web page featuring news and information about 527 political nonprofits.

http://www.publicintegrity.org/527

The **American Association of Political Consultants** provides information for and about political campaign consultants.

www.theaapc.org

Practice Tests

MULTIPLE CHOICE QUESTIONS

1) An early danger for a candidate in the nomination campaign is
   a. extremism.
   b. corruption.
   c. having too much money.
   d. All of the above.

2) The public part of the campaign in which the candidate makes appearances and meets voters, in part to stimulate local activists, is called the
   a. general election campaign.
   b. nomination campaign.
   c. personal campaign.
   d. media campaign.

3) Perhaps the most significant political adviser to President George W. Bush, both in the 2000 and 2004 presidential campaigns, is an individual who was not even listed on the Bush-Cheney 2004 campaign organization chart. That key adviser is
   a. Marc Racicot.
   b. Karl Rove.
   c. Ken Mehlman.
   d. Mary Cheney.

4)   Advertising that attempts to counteract an anticipated attack from the opposition before the attack is launched is called an
        a.   attack ad.
        b.   innuendo ad.
        c.   inoculation ad
        d.   immunization ad.

5)   The first president or presidential candidate to make effective use of the electronic media was
        a.   Franklin Roosevelt.
        b.   John F. Kennedy.
        c.   Bob Dole.
        d.   Howard Dean.

6)   One of the most significant pieces of legislation dealing with campaign finance reform, a law which has altered the campaign finance landscape in ways we may have yet to discover, is called the
        a.   Federal Election Campaign Act.
        b.   Bipartisan Campaign Reform Act.
        c.   Federal Election Commission Act.
        d.   Political Action Committee Act.

7)   Citizens often contribute money to political campaigns because
        a.   they like the candidate or party or a particular stand on issues they care about.
        b.   they want to feel involved in the political process.
        c.   they want access to the candidate.
        d.   All of the above.

8)   Individuals are allowed to contribute _____ to a single federal candidate in each of the primary and general elections.
        a. $5,000
        b. $3,000
        c. $2,500
        d. $2,000

9)   There are approximately ____ PACs in the U.S.
        a.   6,500
        b.   4,000
        c.   2,400
        d.   1, 500

10) The U.S Supreme Court in 1976 ruled that no limit could be placed on a candidate's personal spending in his or her own election campaign due to free speech guarantees in the case of
   a. *U.S.* v. *Nixon.*
   b. *Rockefeller* v. *U.S.*
   c. *Buckley* v. *Valeo.*
   d. *Perot* v. *Mitchell.*

11) The only federal political campaigns that receive public funds are
   a. presidential campaigns.
   b. House campaigns.
   c. Senate campaigns.
   d. All of the above

12) The 2002 Bipartisan Campaign Finance Reform Act
   a. banned soft money contributions.
   b. allowed the growth of 527 political committees.
   c. had no effect on overall spending in the 2004 campaigns.
   d. All of the above.

13) One of the more controversial campaign finance issues to evolve in the 2004 presidential election centered around the use of
   a. soft money.
   b. PAC contributions.
   c. 527 political committees.
   d. All of the above.

14) What effect did third parties play in the 2004 presidential election?
   a. Ralph Nader once again played the role of the spoiler.
   b. The Green Party nearly won presidential electors in several Northeastern states.
   c. The Reform Party nearly won presidential electors in several upper-Midwestern states.
   d. Third parties played an insignificant role in the 2004 election.

15) Former general and Supreme Allied Commander in Europe who ran unsuccessfully for the Democratic nomination for president in 2004 was
   a. Howard Dean.
   b. Richard Gephardt.
   c. Bob Graham.
   d. Wesley Clark.

TRUE/FALSE QUESTIONS

1) Negative advertising is a new phenomenon.

2) The news media usually regard political candidates with suspicion.

3) Candidate debates are entirely staged and scripted.

4) Knowing they cannot be successful in doing so, modern candidates rarely attempt to manipulate press coverage.

5) Political action committees can give unlimited amounts of money to candidates.

6) Candidates can spend as much of their own money as they wish on their own campaigns.

7) Third-party candidates for president, by federal law, are not allowed to receive public funds for their campaigns.

8) PACs are the primary source of election funding and threaten to destroy the legitimacy of the election process.

9) The Republicans were the first to vigorously pursue the use of 527s in 2004.

10) The factor that significantly undermined the campaign of Howard Dean for the Democratic nomination for president in 2004 was his reputed temper.

COMPARE AND CONTRAST

campaign types: nomination, general election, personal, organizational, and media

free and paid media

positive, negative, contrast, and spot ads

campaign finance: individual v. member v. party v. PAC contributions

public funds, matching funds, personal funds, voluntary contributions

soft money and hard money

express advocacy and issue advocacy advertisements

campaign finance reform and 527s

ESSAY AND SHORT ANSWER QUESTIONS

1)   What are the personal and organizational aspects of a campaign?

2)   What are the pressures and hazards of the nomination campaign?

3)   What are independent expenditures? What are the constitutional issues and concerns surrounding them?

4)   Discuss candidate debates. How effective are they? Are they truly debates? How might they be changed to make them more effective and useful?

5)   Can the press be manipulated by candidates? Does spin work? How do the media cover political campaigns?

6)   Discuss the structure of a political campaign and the personnel involved.

7)   Discuss the types of media and advertising a candidate may choose to use.

8)   What are the rules regarding campaign finance for presidential elections? Do they work? Why or why not?

9)   What are PACs and how do they affect the election process?

10)   Discuss the 2004 presidential campaign and election.

ANSWERS TO STUDY EXERCISES

Multiple Choice Answers

1) a
2) c
3) b
4) c
5) a
6) b
7) d
8) d
9) c
10) b
11) a
12) d
13) c
14) d
15) d

True/False Answers

1) F
2) T
3) F
4) F
5) F
6) T
7) F
8) F
9) F
10) T

CHAPTER 15
THE MEDIA

Chapter Goals and Learning Objectives

Journalism acts as the eyes and ears of democracy in this country. Have you ever sat down with George W. Bush or Condoleezza Rice over coffee to talk about the threat of terrorism and what to do about it? When did you last visit a congressional hearing to learn how the proposed new federal budget will affect your student loans? Probably never. You're busy at home working and going to school and don't have the time or resources to go to Washington and learn firsthand about what's happening with your government.

That's why the news media is so important in our democracy. An essential function of the press is to report to the American people on what your elected representatives are doing in Washington. That is why the news business is the only private business protected directly by the U.S. Constitution. The First Amendment protects the freedom of the press to report on the activities of our government. The manner in which they do it and how effectively they do it is another matter entirely.

The news media—the aggregate of electronic and print journalism—has the potential to exert enormous influence over Americans. The news media is crucial in facilitating public awareness of and discourse on politics necessary for the maintenance of a free country. The First Amendment grants the media broad rights. But is there a corresponding responsibility? Do citizens get the information from the news media we need to make educated decisions about elections? Does the news media provide complete, objective, issue-based coverage of politicians and public policy or does it focus on the trivial, entertaining, and sensational? In this chapter, we look at these questions as well as the historical development and evolving nature of journalism in America.

This chapter is designed to give you a basic understanding of the opportunities, challenges, and problems posed by the news media today as well as the effects of our (the citizenry's) unthinking consumption of the media's messages. The main topic headings of the chapter are:

- The Evolution of News Media in the United States
- Current Media Trends
- Rules Governing the Media
- How the Media Cover Politics
- The Media's Influence on the Public

In each section, there are certain facts and ideas that you should strive to understand. Many are in boldface type and appear in both the narrative and in the glossary at the end of the book. Other ideas, dates, facts, events, people, etc. are more difficult to pull out of the narrative. (Keep in mind that studying for objective tests [multiple choice, T/F] is different than studying for essay tests. See the Study Guide section on test taking for hints on study skills.)

In general, after you finish reading and studying this chapter, you should understand the following:

- the evolution of the news media in this country from the founding to today
- current media trends
- rules governing the media, both self-imposed rules of conduct and government regulations affecting radio, television, and the Internet
- how the media cover politics
- the media's influence on the public, including media bias

Chapter Outline and Key Points

In this section, you are provided with a basic outline of the chapter and key words/points you should know. Use this outline to develop a complete outline of the material. Write the definitions or further explanations for the terms. Use the space provided in this workbook or rewrite that material in your notebook. This will help you study and remember the material in preparation for your tests, assignments, and papers.

Thomas Jefferson's opinions about the press—

First Amendment—

role of a free press—

The Evolution of News Media in the United States

mass media—

news media—

various outlets that make up the news media—

Print Media

growth of newspapers in the 1700s—

Anti-Federalists and the press—

early partisan press—

Landmarks of the American News Media (Table 15.1)—

penny press—

the sensational and the scandalous—

yellow journalism—

muckraking—

role of corporate profit—

electronic media supplants newspapers and magazines—

Radio News

advent of radio in early part of Twentieth Century—

most Americans had never heard the voice of a president—

Franklin Roosevelt and "fireside chats" (first president to make effective use of electronic media)—

radio news surpassed by television news in 1950s—

rise of right-wing radio in mid-1980s—

Television News

television first demonstrated publicly in U.S. at 1939 Worlds Fair—

importance of television—

in early 1960s, 15 minute evening newscast—

TV versus print—

role of cable television—

C-SPAN—

comedy news programming—

The Daily Show—

The Colbert Report parodies *The O'Reilly Factor*—

The New Media

the Internet—

ARPANET—

use of Internet in 2000 and 2005—

rise of Internet as source of news and information—

traditional news media on Internet—

heavy users of online news sites and newspaper readership—

U.S. government on Internet—

foreign news media on Internet—

Al-Jazerra—

The News Generation Gap (Table 15.2)—

Current Media Trends

print media—

broadcast media—

new media—

The Influence of Media Giants

Great Britain's national newspapers—

United States' national newspapers—

networks—

affiliates—

wire services—

national news magazines—

Web-based magazines—

Media Consolidation

private ownership of the media in the United States—

monopolies—

potential risks of media consolidation—

competition—

competing daily newspapers in 1923 and 2005—

independence and networks—

Clear Channel—

Increasing Use of Experts

what influences use of experts—

what impact experts have on shaping American's views—

fairness and reliability of experts?—

Narrowcasting

narrowcasting—

FOX News—

Main Source of Campaign News by Party Affiliation (Table 15.3)—

minority news programming—

Christian conservative news programming—

news to confirm preexisting views—

polarization—

Public Discontent with the Media

political bias—

perception of political bias by party affiliation—

261

2005 survey by Pew Research Center for the People and the Press—

credibility of broadcast news outlets—

trusted news anchors—

9/11 and shifts in public's attitude toward the media—

watchdog role—

majority's belief regarding media's influence—

Technological Innovation

technology's effect on the flow and dispersal of news—

information misers—

information misers and the news—

blogs—

mainstream media's use of blogs—

Blogs Versus Mainstream Media Internet Links (Figure 15.2)—

various blogs—

future of new media—

<u>Rules Governing the Media</u>

First Amendment

Journalistic Standards

Society of Professional Journalists' "Code of Ethics"—

unscrupulous actors—

less obvious ethical dilemmas—

pressure to get the story right versus to get the story first—

twenty-four hour news cycle—

media critics hired by some major newspapers—

Center for Media and Public Affairs—

conservative Accuracy in Media (AIM)—

liberal Fairness and Accuracy in Reporting (FAIR)—

Government Regulation of the Electronic Media

two reasons for unequal treatment of print and broadcast media—

1996 Telecommunications Act—

FCC and 2003 regulation changes—

     1)

     2)

     3)

     4)

2003 changes by FCC allowed media corporations to own more of different kinds of media in a given market—

many in Congress opposed FCC changes, arguing more, not less, media diversification needed—

opposition to deregulation by FCC—

Congress passes a compromise measure in July, 2003—

Content Regulation

content regulation—

equal time rule—

2000 FCC rules and court decision on requiring broadcasts to give candidates chance to respond to personal attacks and political endorsements by a station—

fairness doctrine—

Red Lion Broadcasting Co. v. *FCC* (1969)—

Reagan's FCC abolishes fairness doctrine in 1985—

Reagan veto of fairness doctrine bill—

proponents and opponents arguments regarding fairness doctrine—

Communications Act of 1934—

Internet Service Providers (ISP)—

net neutrality—

Efforts to Regulate Media Practices

prior restraint—

New York Times v. *U.S.* (1971)—

Pentagon Papers—

1991 Gulf War and military's isolation of reporters—

"Vietnam Syndrome"—

2003 Iraq invasion and "embedded" journalists—

embedded journalists—

regulation of broadcasters in Britain—

Official Secrets Act of 1911 (Great Britain)—

D-notice—

How Much Freedom Should the Press Be Allowed?—

How the Media Cover Politics

print reporters—

increase in number of print reporters accredited at U.S. Capitol since 1983—

increase in coverage of presidential campaigns—

journalists accredited as daily White House correspondents—

How the Press and Public Figures Interact

press release—

press briefing—

press conference—

on background—

deep background—

off the record—

on the record—

protecting confidentiality of sources—

Judith Miller in 2005—

media manipulation by politicians—

campaign consultants hired by politicians and media research—

politicians by-passing national news media—

libel—

New York Times v. *Sullivan* (1964)—

actual malice—

effect of actual malice rule—

Covering the Presidency

first among the three equal branches of government in coverage—

reasons for focus on president over Congress and the courts—

Franklin D. Roosevelt, press conferences, and the bully pulpit—

Presidential Press Conferences (Figure 15.3)—

role and history of presidential press secretary—

conflict between reporters and White House over what becomes news—

Tony Snow—

negative coverage of presidency—

George W. Bush and reluctance to face the press—

George W. Bush tries to control his image—

"Mission Accomplished" image symbolizing Bush failures—

Covering Congress

why it is difficult for news media to survey and cover Congress—

size of congressional press corps—

news media focuses on three groups in covering Congress—

    1)

    2)

    3)

negative coverage of Congress—

C-SPAN coverage of Congress—

coverage of investigative committee hearings:

    McCarthy—

    Enron and WorldCom—

    Abu Ghraib—

Covering the Supreme Court

media vacuum surrounding Court—

television in the Court—

reasons for Court's reticence to allow cameras in—

audio recordings—

number of reporters covering the Court full-time—

reasons the amount of coverage of Court-related stories diminishing—

American's knowledge about the Court—

The Media's Influence on the Public

Media Effects

effect of media on the public—

what limits ability of news media to sway public opinion?—

as party identification declined, media influence increased—

when media especially affects public opinion—

media effects—

how media-influenced changes might occur:

1)

2)

3)

4)

5)

Media Bias

"biased reporting"—

research suggests why candidates might charge media with bias—

why are journalists biased?—

claims of liberal bias in 1980s and 1990s—

corporate bias—

corporate interests and corporate broadcast ownership—

lack of news media skepticism over Iraq—

one-sided media—

"fair and balanced" self-applied slogan versus FOX News obvious conservatism—

audience aware of news bias and seek out their biases—

Objective Versus Biased Reporting—

Democrats more likely to watch CNN—

Republicans twice as likely to watch FOX News—

Democrats and Republicans habits regarding network news, cable news, AM talk radio, NPR, newspapers—

Partisan Bias in Media Reporting?—

ideological fragmentation of media—

political journalists desire for a good campaign story (usually negative)—

news media prefers covering horse-race components of campaigns rather than public policy issues—

effect of journalists' personal feelings about a candidate—

celebrity status of news reporters—

revolving door between politics and news media—

Research Ideas and Possible Paper Topics

1) For several days, tape each of the major broadcast network's newscasts (ABC, CBS, NBC) and the two largest cable networks' (FOX and CNN). View at least two days of each broadcast. Pay attention to the order and length of each story, the tone of the report, and the graphics/images used. How are these broadcasts similar or different? Which reports seem most objective and why? What kinds of information are they offering? Is it the type of information you need to make educated decisions about politics and world affairs? Why or why not?

2) Choose a current event and compare the coverage in local press, national press, network news, and cable news. How and why do the ways each of these types of media cover the issues differ? How are they similar? What media outlets do you find most useful?

3) Locate several blogs on the Internet which focus on news and current events. What types of information are you finding there? Does it differ from more traditional types of media? How and why?

4) Using a major national newspaper (*The New York Times, The Washington Post*, or *The Wall Street Journal*), analyze the way in which the president is treated. Is he treated well or poorly? Why? Do you perceive an obvious bias? What is it? Is he treated similarly or differently than other major political figures? Why?

5) Examine the history of corporate consolidation of broadcast news media outlets over the past several decades. Examine examples of how the corporatization of the news industry diminishes diversity in news coverage and, thus, hinders your ability to get different viewpoints on critical issues. Discuss how this would hinder the free exchange of ideas in a democracy and undermine personal freedoms.

Web sites

Fairness and Accuracy in Reporting (FAIR) is a liberal watchdog group looking for media bias. In their own words: "FAIR believes that independent, aggressive, and critical media are essential to an informed democracy. But mainstream media are increasingly cozy with the economic and political powers they should be reporting on critically. Mergers in the news industry have accelerated, further limiting the spectrum of viewpoints that have access to mass media. With U.S. media outlets overwhelmingly owned by for-profit conglomerates and supported by corporate advertisers, independent journalism is compromised." The Web site offers examples of bias and more.
www.fair.org

Media Research Center is a right-wing organization that claims the media have a liberal bias. Offers links to conservative media and political sites.

www.mediaresearch.org

Media Matters for America is an extensive, comprehensive Internet site reporting on corporate and conservative bias in the news media. **Media Matters** was created by former conservative journalist David Brock. Updated daily with reportage and video clips.

http://mediamatters.org

The Pew Center for People and the Press is an independent opinion research group that studies attitudes toward the press, politics, and public policy issues. Its Web site offers the results of numerous surveys including those of public attitudes toward the media's coverage of politics and offers information trends in values and fundamental political and social attitudes.

www.people-press.org

The **Annenberg Public Policy Center** at the University of Pennsylvania conducts content analysis on TV coverage of politics.

http://www.annenbergpublicpolicycenter.org

The Pew Center for Civic Journalism works to encourage "good journalism." The institute is trying to battle cynicism and re-engage citizens in the political process.

www.pewcenter.org

The Project for Excellence in Journalism is sponsored by Pew, Columbia School of Journalism, and the Committee of Concerned Journalists. They are trying to raise the standards of journalism and are running several projects, including one on local TV news and the state of newspapers in America. This and more are available through their Web site.

www.journalism.org

Center for Media and Public Affairs conducts studies of new news media and politics.

www.cmpa.com

The Center for Media Literacy encourages critical thinking about the news media including media values.

www.medialit.org

Freedom Forum is an organization that champions freedom of the press under the First Amendment. This Web site provides a significant amount of full-text information (journal articles, press releases, study reports) about press freedom issues.

www.freedomforum.org

J-Lab, a Web site hosted by the **Institute for Interactive Journalism** at the University of Maryland, uses new technologies to engage visitors in critical public policy issues covered by the press.

http://www.j-lab.org

The Organization of News Ombudsmen hosts a Web site linking to newspapers and broadcasting outlets across the country which have hired ombudsmen. The ONO defines a news ombudsman on its Web site: "A news ombudsman receives and investigates complaints from newspaper readers or listeners or viewers of radio and television stations about accuracy, fairness, balance and good taste in news coverage. He or she recommends appropriate remedies or responses to correct or clarify news reports."

http://www.newsombudsmen.org/what.htm

Law and the Media in Texas: Handbook for Journalists is a compact and marvelous examination of issues journalists face in covering the courts and in dealing with libel issues. It is written by David McHam, longtime professor of journalism at Baylor University and SMU. McHam is the recipient of the Society of Professional Journalists national award for excellence in teaching reporting. Although the handbook is written about Texas courts, it does cover the federal courts and its state content is applicable in general to most states.

http://www.texaspress.com/Lawpress/LawPress.html

Practice Tests

MULTIPLE CHOICE QUESTIONS

1) Inclusion of a provision to protect the freedom of the press in the final version of the Constitution was demanded by
   a. George Washington.
   b. the Anti-Federalists.
   c. the Federalists.
   d. Thomas Jefferson.

2) The Founders placed such importance in the value of a free exchange of ideas in a democratic society that, despite the written assaults many received from the press, the Founders guaranteed freedom of the press in
   a. the Preamble to the Constitution.
   b. Article I of the Constitution.
   c. the First Amendment of the Constitution.
   d. the Fifth Amendment of the Constitution.

271

3) Approximately _____ percent of adult Americans read a daily newspaper.
   a. 10
   b. 25
   c. 50
   d. 90

4) Most newspapers today are owned by chains, which
   a. reduces the diversity of editorial opinion available.
   b. results in the homogenization of the news.
   c. caused a drop in the overall level of competition.
   d. All of the above.

5) The first president to make effective use of the electronic media to push his programs and assuage the fears of the American people during a time of national crisis was
   a. Franklin D. Roosevelt.
   b. Harry S Truman.
   c. Dwight D. Eisenhower.
   d. John F. Kennedy.

6) According to researchers, which one of the following age groups is the least likely to have read a newspaper yesterday?
   a. 18-29
   b. 30-49
   c. 50-64
   d. 65+

7) If you talk to a reporter and want not to be quoted or used as a source, yet you want the reporter to use the material you give her, you need to tell the reporter up front that you are talking
   a. off the record.
   b. on shallow background.
   c. on background.
   d. on the record.

8) The first president to have a press secretary was
   a. Herbert Hoover.
   b. Franklin D. Roosevelt.
   c. Dwight Eisenhower.
   d. John F. Kennedy.

9) The branch of the federal government receiving the most coverage by the news media is the
    a.   judiciary.
    b.   Congress.
    c.   presidency
    d.   bureaucracy.

10) The Internet began as a project for
    a.   the Department of Defense.
    b.   the Time-Warner Corporation.
    c.   the Postal Service.
    d.   AT&T.

11) In what 1964 case did the Supreme Court rule that for public figures to claim libel there must not only be a defamatory falsehood but also actual malice, making it much harder for public figures to prove libel?
    a.   *Burnett* v. *National Enquirer.*
    b.   *New York Times* v. *Sullivan.*
    c.   *Hamilton* v. *Graber.*
    d.   *Newman* v. *The Globe.*

12) The inception of the actual malice proof requirement in libel cases involving public figures had the effect of
    a.   enhancing First Amendment press protection.
    b.   reducing the expense of defending libel claims.
    c.   allowing editors and reporters to expend more time and energy on libel claims.
    d.   increasing the number of libel suits filed.

13) Journalists, being people, reflect bias. The bias(es) most commonly exhibited by the news media is/are
    a.   personal biases against or for individuals.
    b.   competition—fear of missing a good story.
    c.   corporate bias.
    d.   All of the above.

14) The fairness doctrine required broadcasters to cover events and present contrasting views on important government issues. The fairness doctrine
    a.   is still in effect.
    b.   is also called the equal time rule.
    c.   was in effect from 1949-1985, but eliminated during the Reagan administration.
    d.   was proposed by Congress but never passed.

15) In the 1971 case of *New York Times* v. *United States*, the U.S. Supreme Court held that prior restraint
   a. could not be imposed by newspaper editors.
   b. could be applied against broadcast media but not the print media.
   c. could be imposed on the publication of the Pentagon Papers.
   d. could not be imposed by the government except under extremely rare and confined circumstances.

TRUE/FALSE QUESTIONS

1) The first U.S. president to condemn the press for its coverage of his presidency was Franklin D. Roosevelt.

2) Television was first demonstrated in the United States in Washington, D.C., in January of 1953 at the inaugural of President Dwight D. Eisenhower.

3) William Randolph Hearst and Joseph Pulitzer were known for championing sensationalized, oversimplified news coverage.

4) The modern press is less partisan and more concerned with corporate profit than the press in the eighteenth and nineteenth centuries.

5) Television is the most popular source for news today.

6) Coverage by C-SPAN of congressional proceedings and major political events is far more glitzy and filtered than coverage offered by broadcast and cable networks.

7) Politicians have found that they have little ability to influence or manipulate the news media.

8) More men than women seek political content online.

9) The news media affects the public more by what events it chooses to cover as opposed to how it covers events.

10) The U.S. Constitution prohibits all regulation of the news media.

COMPARE AND CONTRAST

yellow journalism and muckraking

American and international approaches to the mass media

print press and electronic media

broadcast news networks and cable news networks

media coverage of the president, Congress, and judiciary

on background, deep background, off-the-record and on-the-record statements

broadcasting under the fairness doctrine and broadcasting without the fairness doctrine

ESSAY AND SHORT ANSWER QUESTIONS

1) Discuss the functioning of the U.S. press from its establishment in 1690 through the nineteenth century.

2) Discuss the impact of media mergers on the diversity of information available to American citizens.

3) When covering Congress, which figures do the news media tend to cover and why?

4) What effect did the repeal of the fairness doctrine in the mid-1980s have on broadcasting and on American politics?

5) What kind of influence do the news media have on the public's attitudes and opinions?

6) The news media today consists of a number of types of media. What are they and how do they differ? How are they similar? What incentives do they operate under and how do they decide what to use and what not to use?

7) Compare and contrast the ways in which the media cover the Congress versus the presidency.

8) Are the media biased? How? Discuss fully and give examples.

9) Discuss the ways in which government regulates and censors the media.

10) How have the news media changed in the last two decades? What have been the impacts of these changes?

ANSWERS TO STUDY EXERCISES

Multiple Choice Answers

1) b
2) c
3) c
4) d
5) a
6) a
7) b
8) a
9) c
10) a
11) b
12) a
13) d
14) c
15) d

True/False Answers

1) F
2) F
3) T
4) T
5) T
6) F
7) F
8) T
9) T
10) F

CHAPTER 16
INTEREST GROUPS

One of the most influential men in Washington during the late 1990s and through much of the first term of George W. Bush was a Washington, D.C. lobbyist named Jack Abramoff. As a former President of the College National Republican Committee, Abramoff used his long-standing college political alliances to advance his career, eventually joining a prominent law firm's Washington, D.C. office as a lobbyist after the Republican take over of the U.S. House in the mid-1990s. He developed friendships with such Republican luminaries as Ralph Reed and House Majority Leader Tom DeLay. Abramoff's influence grew with the Republican controlled Congress and the new administration of President George W. Bush, even serving on the 2001 Bush Administration's Transition Team. However, in January of 2006, Abramoff pled guilty to several felony criminal counts in a Washington, D.C., federal court on fraud and corruption of public officials charges. In March of 2006, he was sentenced to over five years in prison and ordered to pay restitution of more than $21 million.

Abramoff's case was exceptional. Most lobbyists in Washington go about their business of representing clients in the halls of Congress and before federal agencies without committing fraud or bribery. Yet the Abramoff scandal caused an intense focus on the business of lobbying and the role of special interest groups in American politics and government. Special interest groups spend incredible amounts of money in an attempt to sway the votes of members of Congress and decision-makers in the executive branch. One must question, however, whether the interests of the working man and woman, the student, the poor, the mid-level executive, the elementary teacher and other Americans without the wherewithal to hire million-dollar lobbyists are being forgotten in Washington thanks to the power and influence of wealthy corporate special interest groups.

James Madison in the *Federalist Papers* warned against "a number of citizens, whether amounting to a majority or minority of the whole, who are united and actuated by some common impulse of passion, or of interest, adverse to the rights of other citizens or to the permanent and aggregate interest of the community." Madison called these groups "factions." Today we might call them interest groups.

Thomas Hobbes and other early political philosophers discussed the designs of self-interest among men in society—beasts in competition. Some Americans today fault interest groups as "selfish interest groups," seeking benefits for the few at the expense of the many. Yet, as a society that has its roots in the concept of individual freedom, do we not want individuals and groups to seek support for their unique, individual interests? What is the role of interest groups in American government? Participation in the political process is necessary for a democracy to flourish. Is it necessary and beneficial that individuals and groups pressure policy makers at all levels of government? What are interest groups today? What do they seek and how do they operate? Do they supplement and complement political parties? Do they enhance representation? Or are they vehicles for powerful and wealthy interests to take over policy making? Do you have interests that could be served by participating in an interest group? This chapter addresses these questions and others about the nature of interest groups and participation in America.

This chapter is designed to give you some ideas about the nature and desirability of interest groups. The main topic headings of the chapter are:

- What Are Interest Groups?
- The Origins and Development of American Interest Groups
- What Do Interest Groups Do?
- What Makes an Interest Group Successful?

In each section, there are certain facts and ideas that you should strive to understand. Many are in boldface type and appear in both the narrative and in the glossary at the end of the book. Other ideas, dates, facts, events, people, etc. are more difficult to pull out of the narrative. (Keep in mind that studying for objective tests [multiple choice, T/F] is different than studying for essay tests. See the Study Guide section on test taking for hints on study skills.)

In general, after you finish reading and studying this chapter, you should understand the following:

- what interest groups are
- the historical roots and the development of interest groups in America
- what interest groups do, their strategies and tactics to further their agendas
- what makes an interest group successful

Chapter Outline and Key Points

In this section, you are provided with a basic outline of the chapter and key words/points you should know. Use this outline to develop a complete outline of the material. Write the definitions or further explanations for the terms. Use the space provided in this workbook or rewrite that material in your notebook. This will help you study and remember the material in preparation for your tests, assignments, and papers.

importance of citizen participation in political or civic interest groups—

the changing face of interest group politics in the U.S.—

"bowling alone"—

social capital—

civic virtue—

What Are Interest Groups?

interest groups—

disturbance theory—

Kinds of Organized Interests

Public Interest Groups—

Common Cause—

MoveOn.org—

Economic Interest Groups—

business groups (including trade and professional groups)—

labor organizations—

most fully and effectively organized of all types of interest
groups—

reason for existence—

Governmental Units—

state and local interests—

federal earmarks—

Political Action Committees—

1974 amendments to the federal Election Campaign Act—

PACs—

nature and characteristics of PACs—

Multi-Issue Versus Single-Issue Interest Groups—

multi-issue groups (and examples)—

279

single-issue groups (and examples)—

Profiles of Selected Interest Groups (Table 16.1)—

The Origins and Development of American Interest Groups

James Madison and factions—

concern over any one individual or group of individuals becoming too influential—

role of decentralizing power—

National Groups Emerge (1830-1889)

effect of the improvement of communications networks—

Women's Christian Temperance Union—

The Grange—

larger role of business interest after the civil war—

oil, steel, and sugar industries—

railroad industry—

lobbyist—

Progressive Era (1890-1920)

changes by the 1890s—

Progressive movement—

national government begins to regulate business—

Organized Labor—

American Federation of Labor—

open shop laws—

1914 Clayton Act—

Business Groups—

> National Association of Manufacturers (NAM)—
>
> President Wilson denounces NAM's tactics—
>
> trade associations—
>
> U.S. Chamber of Commerce—
>
> 1928 FTC investigation of lobbying tactics of business groups—

The Rise of the Interest Group State

rise of the Progressive spirit in the 1960s and 1970s—

ACLU—

NAACP—

AARP—

Common Cause—

Public Citizen, Inc.—

Ralph Nader—

Unsafe at Any Speed—

"Nader Network"—

AARP—

Conservative Response: Religious and Ideological Groups

conservative response to Progressive groups of the 1960s and 1970s—

1978, Jerry Falwell and the "Moral Majority"—

1990, Pat Robertson and the Christian Coalition—

Bush and his Office of Faith-Based and Community Initiatives—

National Rifle Association (NRA)—

Focus on the American Family—

Students for Academic Freedom—

Business Groups, Corporations, and Associations

    some business people dissatisfied with NAM or Chamber of Commerce—

    Business Roundtable—

    Kyoto Protocol—

    corporations with their own government affairs departments also hire D.C.-based lobbyists—

    527 groups—

    527 groups' 2004 contributions—

    congressional family members as well as former members of Congress work as lobbyists—

Organized Labor

    Labor Union Membership (Figure 16.2)—

    American Federation of Labor (AFL) merges with Congress of Industrial Organizations (CIO) in 1955—

    AFL-CIO—

    labor members (and clout) diminishes—

    electoral weaknesses evident in 2004 presidential primaries—

    split at 2005 annual AFL-CIO meeting—

    Service Employees International Union (SEIU)—

    Change to Win Coalition—

    Andrew Stern—

    James Hoffa—

What Do Interest Groups Do?

what interests groups do—

working for their members' interests—

NAACP efforts for its members—

downside to interest groups—

interest groups play important role in U.S. politics—

Lobbying

lobbying—

how term came about—

hiring lobbying firms—

Groups and Lobbyists Using Each Lobbying Technique (Table 16.2)—

Lobbying Congress—

efforts to reform lobbying—

wide variety of lobbying techniques—

outright payment of money (bribery)—

former members and staff as lobbyists—

skills of lobbyists—

developing close relations with members of Congress—

symbiotic relations—

lobbyists and representatives who share interests—

lobbyists reputation for fair play and accurate information—

Leaving Congress for Lobbying Careers (Figure 16.4)—

Tom DeLay's K Street Project—

283

Lobbying the Executive Branch—

        importance and frequency of lobbying executive branch increasing because of what?—

        many potential access points—

        influencing policy decisions at formulation and implementation stages—

        importance of ability to provide decision makers with important information and sense of public opinion—

        interest groups and regulatory agencies—

        monitoring the implementation of laws or policies—

Lobbying the Courts—

        types of efforts to lobby the courts—

        amicus curiae briefs—

        influencing nominations to federal courts—

        paying for "informational conferences"—

        Scalia, golf, and the Federalist Society—

Grassroots Lobbying—

        grassroots lobbying—

        efforts as early as 1840s—

        efforts to persuade ordinary voters to serve as advocates—

        expensive, carefully targeted television ads—

Protests and Radical Activism—

        Boston Tea Party—

        Shays's Rebellion—

        anti-war protestors—

other protests—

People for the Ethical Treatment of Animals (PETA)—

Operation Rescue—

Regulating Lobbying Practices—

lobbying unregulated for first 150 years of U.S. history—

Federal Regulation of Lobbying Act of 1946—

ACLU blocks expansion of lobbying in courts on First Amendment grounds—

Lobbying Disclosure Act of 1996:

1)

2)

3)

4)

how many lobbyists registered as of June 2005?—

how much money spent on lobbying for every member of Congress?—

Jack Abramoff—

"GOP culture of corruption"—

1978 Ethics in Government Act (Table 16.3)—

restrictions on executive branch employees becoming lobbyists—

Election Activities

Candidate Recruitment and Endorsements—

EMILY's List—

WISH List—

Nancy Pelosi—

Getting Out the Vote—

Rating the Candidates or Office Holders—

Political Action Committees—

what PACs allow—

role of PAC money—

significance of PACs for congressional incumbents—

What Makes an Interest Group Successful?

pressure politics—

what all the groups have in common—

shaping the public agenda—

groups claim credit—

getting leaders of groups elected—

phenomena that contribute to interest groups' successes:

1) leaders

2) patrons and funding

3) members

Leaders—

role of leaders—

Patrons and Funding—

patron—

expense of activities of interest groups—

Members—

three kinds of members in interest groups:

1)

2)

3)

"upper-class bias"—

characteristics of interest group members—

Potential Versus Actual Interest Groups Members (Table 16.4)—

overlapping memberships—

collective good—

free rider problem—

factors that overcome the free rider problem—

why members join groups—

importance of alliances—

organizational advantage of small group—

Research Ideas and Possible Paper Topics

1)   Research the role interest groups played in the 2004 and 2006 elections for both the presidency and the Congress. Which groups made what levels of contributions to which candidates? What do you believe were the goals of the groups in making those contributions? Which party's candidates benefited the most from what interest groups?

2)   Call, write, or visit the Web sites of a number of interest groups. What are they doing? What are their key issues and tactics? Who are their members? How many members do they have? How does this information correlate with what you have learned in this chapter?

3)   Interview your member of Congress or their staff members about their views of interest groups and lobbyists (or have your professor invite them to class to

discuss the issue). What do they say? How much access do lobbyists actually have? How much influence? What kinds of tactics work best with Congress?

4)   Interview several lobbyists (or ask your professor to invite several lobbyists to talk to your class). Discuss how they see their job and what tactics work and which ones don't. What issues do they deal with and what do they offer to politicians? How do they define a successful lobbyist? After talking with the professional lobbyists, what do you think about lobbying now? Does it seem less "unsavory"? Do the media do lobbyists justice in their coverage?

5)   As a class project, form an interest group. Decide what issue(s) you will promote and how you would promote them. What strategies and tactics would you use? How would you attract members? How would you ensure the success of your group?

Web sites

Open Secrets, sponsored by the Center for Responsive Politics, maintains a searchable Washington lobbyist database.
        http://www.opensecrets.org/lobbyists/index.asp

Public Citizen, a nonprofit, nonpartisan consumer advocacy group, maintains a special interests reports page listed by industry group.
        http://www.citizen.org/congress/special_intr/index.cfm

The University of Michigan Document Center Web site on the 2004 elections offers a wide-ranging list of links on subjects relating to the election including campaign contributions and interest groups. Click, under the heading "Campaign," the "Lobby Groups," and "Lobby Group Ratings" links in particular.
        http://www.lib.umich.edu/govdocs/elec2004.html#activ

American Association of Retired Persons (AARP) is an interest and advocacy group devoted to the interests of those over 50.
        www.aarp.org

American Civil Liberties Union (ACLU) offers information on the entire Bill of Rights, including racial profiling, women's rights, privacy issues, prisons, drugs, etc. Includes links to other sites dealing with the same issues.
        www.aclu.org

AFL-CIO is the largest trade union organization in America. Their Web site offers policy statements, news, workplace issues, and labor strategies.
        www.aflcio.org

The United States **Chamber of Commerce** is a business-oriented interest group whose Web site offers articles of interest, policy information, and membership info.

    www.uschamber.org

The **American Trial Lawyers Association** is an interest group for trial lawyers who support access for citizens to civil courts and oppose business groups working to limit these rights. The Web site offers news and information for the reporters and citizens.

    www.atla.org

Common Cause, founded by Ralph Nader, was one of the first public interest groups. They promote responsible government.

    www.commoncause.org

Mexican American Legal Defense and Education Fund (MALDEF) Web site offers information on Census 2000, scholarships, job opportunities, legal programs, regional offices information, and more.

    www.maldef.org

Native American Rights Fund (NARF) Web site offers profiles of issues, an archive, resources, a tribal directory, and treaty information, as well as a lot of other information.

    www.narf.org

The **National Association for the Advancement of Colored People** (NAACP) website offers information about the organization, membership, and issues of interest to proponents of civil rights. Has sections on the Supreme Court, Census 2000, the Education Summit and includes links to other Web sites.

    www.naacp.org

The **National Rifle Association (NRA)** is a highly effective interest group on behalf of its members. Its Web site offers information on gun ownership, gun laws, and coverage of legislation on associated issues.

    www.nra.org

National Organization of Women (NOW) Web site offers information on the organization and its issues/activities including women in the military, economic equity, reproductive rights, and so on. They offer an email action list and the ability to join NOW online. Also has links to related sites.

    www.now.org

Public Interest Research Group (PIRG) is a public interest group that promotes issues such as the environment, anti-tobacco, and so on.

    www.pirg.org

MULTIPLE CHOICE QUESTIONS

1) Political scientist David Truman argues that interest groups form to counteract other groups that already exist. This theory is called
   a. patron theory.
   b. disturbance theory.
   c. potential group theory.
   d. group formation

2) Groups such as Common Cause are often categorized as a
   a. public interest group.
   b. single issue group.
   c. economic issue group.
   d. All of the above.

3) An example of a multi-issue group is the
   a. Christian Coalition.
   b. NAACP.
   c. NOW.
   d. All of the above.

4) During the 1960s and 70s, interest groups often formed around issues important to groups, such as
   a. religious groups and economic organizations.
   b. minorities, the elderly, the poor, and consumers.
   c. elites, activists, and party regulars.
   d. economic, foreign policy advocates, and conservatives.

5) After developing close ties to George W. Bush before the 2000 election, a vice president of an interest group boasted: "We'll have a president...where we work out of their office...[and have] unbelievably friendly relations." This interest group contributed $20 million for the reelection of President George W. Bush in 2004. Its primary purpose is the protection and advancement of the Second Amendment to the U.S. Constitution, the "right to bear arms." Which interest group is this?
   a. Christian Coalition
   b. U.S. Chamber of Commerce
   c. National Rifle Association
   d. American Civil Liberties Union

6)   Labor unions were formed beginning in the 1900s and membership held steady through the middle of the century. In 2000, approximately what percent of workers were unionized?
  a.   50
  b.   35
  c.   25
  d.   14

7)   Almost all lobbyists and interest groups use _____ as lobbying techniques.
  a.   testimony at legislative hearings and personal contacts
  b.   the endorsement of candidates and working on elections
  c.   filing suit or otherwise engaging in litigation
  d.   protest and demonstrations

8)   In order to be effective, a lobbyist depends on
  a.   a reputation for winning on behalf of his client, no matter what the cost or by whatever means possible.
  b.   a reputation for providing accurate information and playing fair.
  c.   a limited financial base in the interest group's PAC in order to fund campaigns of those legislators who support the lobbyists' goals
  d.   All of the above.

9)   The Ethics in Government Act requires that executive branch employees must
  a.   disclose the source and amount of their income.
  b.   reveal any positions held in business, labor, or nonprofit groups.
  c.   not represent anyone before their agency for one year after leaving office.
  d.   All of the above.

10)   Interest groups have a particularly strong link with
  a.   Congress.
  b.   the president.
  c.   regulatory agencies.
  d.   the courts.

11)   Today, grassroots lobbying efforts by interest groups often use
  a.   faxes, e-mail, and the Internet.
  b.   carefully targeted television advertising.
  c.   radio talk shows to stir up listeners to contact their representatives in Congress.
  d.   All of the above.

12) A federally registered group that raises funds to donate to the political process is known as a(n)
   a. political action committee.
   b. interest group.
   c. political party.
   d. special interest.

13) Successful interest groups rely in varying degrees, on
   a. leaders.
   b. patrons.
   c. rank and file members.
   d. All of the above.

14) People who belong to an interest group often belong to more than one group. This overlapping membership can have the effect of
   a. increasing member activity in both groups.
   b. increasing the cohesiveness of the groups.
   c. reducing the cohesiveness of the groups.
   d. enhance the activity level of members.

15) Something of value, such as a clean environment, that cannot be withheld from a noninterest group member can reduce the number of paying members an interest group can attract. This is known as
   a. a collective good.
   b. the potential membership problem.
   c. the overlapping interest problem.
   d. cost of membership.

TRUE/FALSE QUESTIONS

1) The American Medical Association is an example of a public interest group.

2) Political Action Committees were first permitted by amendments in 1974 to the Federal Election Campaign Act.

3) Thomas Jefferson, from his days in the Virginia Assembly, warned of the development of factions in American politics.

4) As a result of intense lobbying by American business groups, corporations, and associations, President George W. Bush, early in his first administration, rejected U.S. participation in the Kyoto Protocol on Climate Change.

5) Few politically active groups use lobbying to make their interests heard by those in a position to influence or change governmental policies.

6) Interest groups often lobby the courts by filing *amicus* briefs in cases that go before the U.S. Supreme Court.

7) The Ethics in Government Act requires former executive branch employees to refrain from representing anyone before a federal agency for nine years after leaving government service on matters that came within the former employees' sphere or responsibility.

8) Some 35 million people over the age of 50 belong to the AMA, which lobbies Congress on such issues as Social Security and Medicare.

9) People with low incomes are just as likely to join interest groups as those with low incomes.

10) Jack Abramoff's felony conviction and prison sentence led to a promise by Congress to re-examine the role of lobbying in the legislative process.

COMPARE AND CONTRAST

potential vs. actual group membership

collective goods and free riders

multi-issue and single-issue groups

kinds of interest groups: economic, public, governmental

business groups, trade, and professional organizations

election activities of interest groups: endorsements, ratings, creating parties, PACs

ESSAY AND SHORT ANSWER QUESTIONS

1) Define interest groups and discuss their functions.

2) Why do interest groups form? Discuss a number of theories and their rationales for group formation.

3) Compare and contrast potential vs. actual interest group membership.

4) What is lobbying, and why is it important? Is it "good" or "bad" or neither?

5) How do interest groups lobby the courts?

6) Discuss the effect of campaign contributions by interest groups on the democratic process.

7) What makes interest groups successful?

8) Discuss the changes in the nature and outlook of interest groups from the 1950s and 60s to the 1970s and 80s.

9) Discuss the right-wing backlash to the rise of the interest groups 1960s.

10) Discuss the various reforms attempted in lobbying practices.

ANSWERS TO STUDY EXERCISES

Multiple Choice Answers

1) b
2) a
3) d
4) b
5) c
6) d
7) a
8) b
9) d
10) c
11) d
12) a
13) d
14) c
15) a

True/False Answers

1) F
2) T
3) F
4) T
5) F
6) T
7) F
8) F
9) F
10) T

CHAPTER 17
SOCIAL WELFARE POLICY

Chapter Goals and Learning Objectives

Intended to improve the quality of life for all segments of society, especially the less fortunate, social welfare policies involve a broad and varied range of government programs. These policies and programs are designed to provide people with protection against want and deprivation, to enhance their health and physical well-being, to provide educational and employment opportunities, and otherwise to enable them to lead more satisfactory, productive, and meaningful lives. These social policies are meant to benefit all members of society, but especially the less fortunate. Social welfare policy focuses on issues such as public education, income security, medical care, sanitation and disease prevention, public housing, employment training, children's protective services, and improvements in human nutrition. The idea behind these policies is that these services are so worthy to society as a whole that the government should provide the services regardless of the ability of the recipients to pay. The question of where the line should be drawn between government and individual responsibility for these services and goods is the essence and scope of social welfare policy development. The question that is asked is, "In a civilized society, what obligation does the government (in other words, the community or nation as a whole) owe to promoting the social welfare of its people?"

This chapter is designed to give you a basic understanding of the broad range of programs called social welfare. The main topic headings of the chapter are:

- The Policy-Making Process
- The Origins of Social Welfare Policy
- Social Welfare Policies Today

In each section, there are certain facts and ideas that you should strive to understand. Many are in boldface type and appear in both the narrative and in the glossary at the end of the book. Other ideas, dates, facts, events, people, etc. are more difficult to pull out of the narrative. (Keep in mind that studying for objective tests [multiple choice, T/F] is different than studying for essay tests. See the Study Guide section on test taking for hints on study skills.)

In general, after you finish reading and studying this chapter, you should understand the following:

- the nature of the policy-making process, including a model that presents a manageable way of disassembling the policy-making process and examining its components
- the genesis of social welfare policy and the twentieth century expansion of the government's commitment

- social welfare policies today, including income security, health care, and public education

---

Chapter Outline and Key Points

In this section, you are provided with a basic outline of the chapter and key words/points you should know. Use this outline to develop a complete outline of the material. Write the definitions or further explanations for the terms. Use the space provided in this workbook or rewrite that material in your notebook. This will help you study and remember the material in preparation for your tests, assignments, and papers.

social welfare policy—

The Policy-Making Process

public policy—

"course of action"—

Theories of Public Policy

elite theory—

elites—

masses—

bureaucratic theory—

interest group theory—

pluralist perspective—

A Model of the Policy-Making Process

policy-making process model—

Stages of the Public Policy Process (Fig. 17.1)—

policy making as a process of sequential steps—

Problem Recognition and Definition

a necessary criterion—

FEMA and Katrina—

effects of perceptions on government—

definitions of the problem—

problems differ in their definition but also in the difficulty of resolving them—

public policies seen as problems or causes of other problems—

Agenda Setting

Defining Agendas—

agenda—

systemic agenda—

governmental or institutional agenda—

problems or issues may move onto an institutional agenda—

issues emerge when?—

Getting on the Congressional Agenda—

agenda setting—

president as agenda-setter for Congress—

a recalcitrant Congress—

Dubai Port deal in 2006—

interest groups in the agenda-setting process—

securing agenda setting by crisis, disaster, extraordinary event—

9/11—

cost of prescription drugs for the elderly—

individual private citizens, member of Congress, and other officials as policy entrepreneurs—

Unsafe at Any Speed and *Silent Spring*—

permanent food stamp program—

Michael J. Fox and Christopher Reed—

importance of media coverage—

political changes—

Policy Formulation

policy formulation—

political aspect of policy formulation—

technical aspect of policy formulation—

routine formulation—

analogous formulation—

creative formulation—

policy formulation by various players in the policy process—

partnerships between elected officials and nongovernmental organizations in policy formulation—

Policy Adoption

policy adoption—

what's needed to achieve policy adoption—

congressional policy adoption consequences:

1)

2)

3)

unilateral presidential decision-making—

veto threat—

Budgeting

budgetary process—

effect of refusal to fund—

2006 decision by Bush administration not to seek funds for HOPE VI—

effect of inadequate funding—

policy and program review—

Policy Implementation

policy implementation—

use of the courts—

authorized techniques by administrative agencies to implement public policies within their jurisdictions:

authoritative techniques—

incentive techniques—

capacity techniques—

hortatory techniques—

effective administration of public policy depends on what?—

Policy Evaluation

policy evaluation—

possible players in policy evaluation—

GAO—

role of evaluation research and studies—

demise of programs, and underfunded, undersupported programs—

policy-maker judgments and anecdotal and fragmentary evidence—

The Origins of Social Welfare Policy

attitude of Americans in early history of country—

gradual change in late nineteenth century—

Coxey's Army—

product of twentieth century—

effect of social changes here and abroad on social welfare policy—

Great Depression of 1930s—

Income Security

market crash of 1929—

Republican "hands off" economic policy—

election of Franklin D. Roosevelt in 1932—

CWA and FERA—

WPA—

Social Security Act of 1935—

three major component of 1935 Social Security Act:

1)

2)

3)

core of the Social Security Act—

"sacred trust" rather than welfare—

critics of Social Security—

unemployment and Social Security—

expansion of Social Security—

Health Care

how governments in the U.S. had been active in health care—

National Marine Service (established in 1789)—

national health insurance proposed with Social Security Act of 1935—

opposition of AMA—

Harry Truman proposed national health insurance in 1945—

opposition to President Truman's national health insurance plan—

later national health care plans proposed—

Medicare—

Medicaid-

dramatic expanse of national government's role in health care—

Public Education

exclusive province of state and local governments until twentieth century—

Tenth Amendment—

Northwest Ordinance of 1785—

history of public education in U.S.—

G.I. Bill in 1945—

Cold War and Sputnik—

Lyndon Johnson's Great Society—

Pell Grants—

increase in student loans over the past decade—

reliance on local property taxes—

equalization formulas—

local control of schools and the federal government—

Social Welfare Policies Today

Income Security Programs

income security programs—

nonmeans-based program—

means-tested program—

Social Insurance: Nonmeans-Based Programs—

how social insurance programs work—

Old Age, Survivors, and Disability Insurance—

Social Security tax—

not a pension plan—

employee tax and payment by employer—

regressive tax—

age when retirement benefits available—

unearned income—

Trustees of the Social Security Trust Fund 2006 report—

pressures on the Social Security Trust Fund—

George W. Bush and privatization plans—

public and congressional rejection of Bush privatization plans—

Bush's "Commission to Strengthen Social Security"—

how the report of the "Commission to Strengthen Social Security" disappointed privatization proponents:

1)

2)

3)

Recipients of Social Insurance Programs, 2004 (Table 17.1)—

Social Security Costs and Revenues, 1970-2080 (Figure 17.2)—

Unemployment Insurance—

how Social Security unemployment insurance works—

state programs—

Social Insurance: Means-Tested Programs—

means tested security programs—

Supplemental Security Income (SSI)—

started as a grant-in-aid program under the Social Security Act—

SSI program created in 1974—

1996, access to SSI and other programs limited by legislation—

Family and Child Support—

Aid to Families with Dependent Children (AFDC)—

criticisms of AFDC—

Family and Child Support Act of 1988—

state operation "JOBS" programs—

welfare reform of 1996—

TANF—

key provisions of the Personal Responsibility and Work
Opportunity Reconciliation Act of 1996:

    1)

    2)

    3)

    4)

    5)

    6)

    7)

    George W. Bush and TANF programs—

Earned Income Tax Credit (EITC)—

    designed to serve the working poor—

    intent and objectives of EITC—

    claiming EITC on tax returns—

Food Stamp Program

    initial purpose of food stamp program (1939-1943)—

    later food stamp program—

    nationwide food stamp program in 1974—

    food stamp program since 1977—

    calls for food stamp program reforms in mid-1990s—

    program in 2005—

    WIC—

school breakfast and lunch program—

The Effectiveness of Income Security Programs—

entitlement programs—

effectiveness of the programs—

Health Care

heath care for veterans and Indians—

federal expenditures in 2004 and 2006—

National Institution of Health—

other government-funded research facilities—

increases in funding for Medicare and Medicaid—

reasons for funding increases for public health care—

U.S. Health Care Spending, 1994-2004 (Figure 17.3)—

factors behind dramatic increase in health care costs:

1)

2)

3)

projected increases for Medicare and Medicaid—

Rising Cost of Entitlement and Other Programs (Table 17.2)—

Medicare—

Medicare Part A—

Medicare Part B—

2006 Medicare drug program—

criticism of new Medicare drug programs from liberals and conservatives—

Medicaid—

    what Medicaid covers that Medicare doesn't—

    1986 extension of Medicaid—

    states and Medicaid—

    how Medicaid funded—

    medically indigent—

Public Health—

    various programs—

    tools employed by the government—

    immunizing a nation—

    AIDS programs—

    obesity—

    Centers for Disease Control (CDC)—

    public opinion polls on public satisfaction with health care—

Public Education

Elementary and Secondary School Revenue Sources, 2002-2003 (Figure 17.4)—

variants of public education funding—

Federal Aid to Education—

    little federal assistance until mid-twentieth century—

    problems following World War II—

    Goals 2000—

    2002, "No Child left Behind"—

Individuals with Disabilities Education Act—

Inequality in Spending Among School Districts—

    property taxes—

    1973 U.S. Supreme Court decision on inequality in education—

    state administrative procedures usually decide most conflicts regarding school districts—

    other U.S. Supreme Court decisions involving school districts—

    New Jersey and state court forcing an income tax to support state schools—

Voucher Plans and Charter Schools—

    claims by supporters of vouchers—

    arguments of opponents of vouchers—

    1988 voucher program in Milwaukee and Cleveland—

    voucher plans popular among minorities—

    NAACP and teachers' unions oppositions to vouchers—

    Democratic Party opposition to vouchers—

    Clinton veto of vouchers plan in 1998—

    2002 U.S. Supreme Court decision upholding voucher plan in Cleveland—

    George W. Bush support of vouchers—

    charter schools—

    concerns about charter schools—

    Arizona charter school problems—

    Washington, D.C., charter school problems—
    hybrid versions of charter schools—

Research Ideas and Possible Paper Topics

1) Go to the Web site of the United States House of Representatives or call your local representative's office. Find out what social welfare laws are on the agenda for this session of Congress. Choose one and follow it over the course of the semester. Pay attention to partisan issues, which interest groups get involved and how, which members of Congress sponsor the bill, and how this bill fits the policy process you have learned about in this chapter.

2) Go to the library or the Internet and find out what the official poverty level is in your state and county and the demographics of poor people and people who receive federal assistance. How was it determined, and how appropriate is this figure today? Can a family of four really live on it? In addition, do some additional research about the policies designed to help the poor. Discuss what the country and your state is doing for the poor. Is it enough? Why or why not?

3) Do some research on President Bush's plan to privatize Social Security. Based on what you have learned about the policy process, discuss what was successful and unsuccessful about his plan. What tactics and strategies did he use to promote this policy? How effective were they? What tactics and strategies have been used by the opponents of privatization to what success?

4) Over the past several years, many of the responsibilities for social welfare policies have been delegated to the states. Choose three states and find out what they are doing regarding social welfare. Are the states different or similar in their approach? Why?

5) Interview your grandparents or older people in your neighborhood about the impact of the GI Bill on their lives and education. Find out whether their parents ever went to college and whether they think they would have been able to go without the GI Bill. You may also want to ask them about what they learned in high school and college, including asking them if they still have their old textbooks. Use that information to evaluate the current state of education in the country. Do they have different ideas than you do? Why do you think that might be?

Web sites

The Social Security Administration (SSA) Web site has information rules, regulations, and policies of the federal government on social security, both active and proposed. It offers information for citizens, scholars, and recipients. The Web site also offers historical perspectives on social security and its funding.

www.ssa.gov

The Social Security Network was a project started in 1997 as a resource for information and research on the Social Security program and the debate about its future by **The Century Foundation**. Its panel of researchers and scholars publish original research and other information about Social Security on its Web site.

http://www.socsec.org

The **U.S. Department of Education** "mission is to ensure equal access to education and to promote educational excellence for all Americans." The Education Department's Web site provides information about its offices, programs, information and assistance services, as well as funding opportunities, education statistics and publications.

www.ed.gov

GPO Access offers the full text of many Government Printing Office publications on the web, including the Federal Register, the Congressional Record, congressional bills, United States Code, Economic Indicators and GAO Reports. You can use this site to track legislation and laws pertaining to social policy and other issues.

http://www.gpoaccess.gov/index.html

The **Concord Coalition** is a nonpartisan, grassroots organization dedicated to eliminating federal budget deficits and ensuring Social Security, Medicare, and Medicaid are secure for all generations; founded by Senators Paul Tsongas (D) and Warren Rudman (R). The Coalition Website offers information about the debt and deficit, as well as some social policy issues. It also offers email newsletters, grassroots initiatives, statistics, and more.

http://www.concordcoalition.org

Northwestern University hosts a Web site about its **Poverty, Race and Inequality Program,** which features information about social welfare programs and policy.

http://www.northwestern.edu/ipr/research/socialwelfare.html

The **Cato Institute** is a libertarian think tank promoting free market ideas. Their Web site offers a variety of articles and links including information on Social Security and welfare.

www.cato.org

The **American Enterprise Institute** is a conservative think tank that addresses a variety of issues including social welfare policy. Their Web site offers information on their calendar of events, a variety of articles, and links.

www.aei.org

The **Brookings Institution** is the oldest think tank in America and has a moderate to liberal reputation. Their research and publications range across all public policy areas including social welfare policy. Their Web site offers policy briefings, articles, books, *The Brookings Review*, discussion groups, and links.

www.brook.edu

The **Children's Defense Fund** Web site has many articles and links of interest to advocates for issues affecting children and families. They offer a listserv and publications.

www.childrensdefense.org

The **Institution for Research on Poverty** of the University of Wisconsin studies social inequity and poverty. The IRP develops and tests social policy alternatives. Reports are available on this website.

www.ssc.wisc.edu/irp

The **Center on Budget and Policy Priorities** is a nonprofit research and policy institute devoted to studying governmental policies and programs, particularly those affecting low- and moderate-income people.

www.cbpp.org

The **Cato Institute** promotes private school vouchers on this Web site titled "School Choices."

http://www.schoolchoices.org/roo/vouchers.htm

The **National Education Association** has long opposed educational vouchers. This Web page explains their arguments against vouchers from an educators' standpoint.

http://www.nea.org/vouchers/index.html

Americans United for Separation of Church and State offers a "Myth v. Fact" page on private school vouchers.

http://www.au.org/site/DocServer/Private_School_Vouchers.pdf?docID=155

The **Anti-Defamation League** Web site presents information on how private school vouchers would undermine the public school system and threaten religious freedom and tolerance in the United States.

http://www.au.org/site/DocServer/Private_School_Vouchers.pdf?docID=155

Practice Tests

MULTIPLE CHOICE QUESTIONS

1)   All public issues that are viewed as requiring governmental attention are referred to as the
   a.   systemic agenda.
   b.   governmental agenda.
   c.   institutional agenda.
   d.   defining agenda.

2) Among those who might set the policy agenda for Congress are
   a. interest groups.
   b. political changes or events.
   c. individual private citizens.
   d. All of the above.

3) The crafting of appropriate and acceptable proposed courses of action to ameliorate or resolve public problems is called
   a. agenda setting.
   b. policy formulation.
   c. policy implementation.
   d. problem resolution.

4) In order for a policy to be adopted, it must
   a. be the subject of negotiation, bargaining, and compromise.
   b. clear the House Rules Committee.
   c. win a series of majority votes in subcommittee and committee.
   d. all of the above.

5) Providing people with information, education, resources, and training as a technique of policy implementation is called a(n) _____ technique.
   a. hortatory
   b. incentive
   c. capacity
   d. authoritative

6) The process of determining whether a course of action is achieving its intended goals is called
   a. policy evaluation.
   b. problem recognition.
   c. policy implementation.
   d. policy adoption.

7) Social insurance programs that provide cash assistance to qualified beneficiaries regardless of their income or means are called
   a. security assistance programs.
   b. grant-in-aid programs.
   c. nonmeans-based programs.
   d. means-based programs.

8) The poverty line for an urban family of four in 2006 was _____ per year.
   a. $19,307
   b. $27,649
   c. $36,136
   d. $49,371

9)   The federal educational aid that paid for college for many World War II veterans was provided by
     a.   Great Society programs.
     b.   Pell Grants.
     c.   the National Guard.
     d.   the GI Bill.

10) Unemployment insurance is funded through a
     a.   payroll tax paid by individuals.
     b.   payroll tax paid by employers.
     c.   general revenue funds.
     d.   state tax on employers.

11) The Earned Income Tax Credit was designed to help
     a.   the middle class.
     b.   very poor families without work.
     c.   working poor people.
     d.   all of the above.

12) The average food stamp recipient in 2005 received approximately _____ of food stamps per month.
     a. $970
     b. $730
     c. $411
     d. $93

13) Which of the follow programs pays for long-term nursing home care?
     a.   Medicaid
     b.   Medicare Part A
     c.   Medicare Part B
     d.   All of the above.

14) In 2003, the federal government provided _____ percent of public school funding.
     a.   8.3
     b.   27.9
     c.   47.0
     d.   57.1

15) Most school revenues come from
     a.   the federal budget.
     b.   the U.S. Department of Education.
     c.   state and local property taxes.
     d.   income taxes.

TRUE/FALSE QUESTIONS

1) Critics of Social Security have labeled it as "a sacred trust."

2) The national government has provided at least some form of health care for some citizens since 1798.

3) National health insurance was first considered during the Clinton Administration in the 1990s.

4) Responsibility for public education has historically been vested in the hands of the local community.

5) Social Security is a pension program that collects contributions from workers, invests them, and then returns them with interest to beneficiaries.

6) Eligible individuals are entitled to Social Security benefits regardless of how much unearned income they receive.

7) The biggest shift in social policy since the Great Depression came in the form of a new welfare reform bill in 1996.

8) The initial federal food stamp program was primarily an effort to expand domestic markets for farm commodities.

9) Most education funding comes from the national government.

10) Opponents of voucher programs argue that such programs would undermine public education by taking money away from public schools to give to private schools.

COMPARE AND CONTRAST

the phases of policy formation: problem recognition, agenda setting, formulation, policy adoption, budgeting, policy implementation, policy evaluation

systemic agenda, government agenda, and congressional agenda

means-tested and nonmeans-tested programs

Social Security and Supplemental Security Income (SSI)

Social Security and privatization agendas

entitlement programs and regular budget items

Medicare and Medicaid

vouchers and charter schools

ESSAY AND SHORT ANSWER QUESTIONS

1) Define and characterize public policy and social welfare policy.

2) What is a policy problem, and how is it identified?

3) What is an entitlement program? Give examples.

4) What is the historical role of government in education policy?

5) Compare and contrast voucher plans and charter schools. How does each proposal affect public schools?

6) Fully explain the stages of the policy process.

7) What are the techniques of policy implementation? Discuss how each one works using examples.

8) Detail and discuss policies designed to increase income security.

9) What policies has the U.S. followed regarding health care? Which ones have been enacted, and which ones have been defeated and why?

10) What is the national government's role in education? Be sure to discuss the various reform proposals on this issue.

ANSWERS TO STUDY EXERCISES

Multiple Choice Answers

1) a
2) d
3) b
4) d
5) c
6) a
7) c
8) a

9) d
10) b
11) c
12) d
13) a
14) a
15) c

True/False Answers

1) F
2) T
3) F
4) T
5) F
6) T
7) T
8) T
9) F
10) T

CHAPTER 18
ECONOMIC POLICY

Chapter Goals and Learning Objectives

The projected federal surpluses at the end of Bill Clinton's term have now turned to a projected federal deficit of $2.3 trillion over the next 10 years, due in part to President George W. Bush's large tax cuts, massive increases in federal spending (including the costs for the occupation of Iraq), and weaknesses in the economy.

Critics of the President say the Bush tax cuts were a failure because they cost Americans more on the local level to compensate for lost services, while the federal deficit sent jitters through the financial markets. Supporters of President Bush claim that tax cuts will impact the economy positively over the long-term.

The Iraq occupation costs Americans $200 million per day. Total direct and indirect costs to U.S. taxpayers will likely by more than $400 billion, and one estimate puts the total economic impact at up to $2 trillion, far greater than projections made by the Bush Administration at the outset of the controversial war. Supporters of President Bush claim the costs are necessary to protect American interests. Critics claim the war has done far more to undermine than protect American security interests.

Americans tend to measure their quality of life by their relative economic well-being. Americans vote with their pocketbooks and impact the economy by their faith in their leaders' economic policies, as reflected in measures of consumer confidence. Americans intrinsically know that politics and economics are two sides of the same coin.

The government and economy are, indeed, closely intertwined. The government defines and protects property rights, provides a common monetary system, grants corporate charters, issues patents and copyrights, handles bankruptcies, maintains law and order, and protects the environment, as well as many other economic tasks. In the early years of the republic, the federal government did little to regulate the economy. Following the era of large trusts and monopolies, the government substantially regulated business. Since the 1970s, deregulation has become the dominant buzzword of economic policy. This chapter will cover these historical processes and help you come to an understanding of why the role of government in the economy changes over time, where we are now, and where we might be going.

This chapter is designed to give you a basic understanding of the economic policies of the United States. The main topic headings of the chapter are:

- The Origins of Government Involvement in the Economy
- Stabilizing the Economy
- The Economics of Environmental Regulation

In each section, there are certain facts and ideas that you should strive to understand. Many are in boldface type and appear in both the narrative and in the glossary at the end of the book. Other ideas, dates, facts, events, people, etc. are more difficult to pull out of the narrative. (Keep in mind that studying for objective tests [multiple choice, T/F] is different than studying for essay tests. See the Study Guide section on test taking for hints on study skills.)

In general, after you finish reading and studying this chapter, you should understand the following:

- the roots of government involvement in the economy
- the role of the government in stabilizing the economy, sometimes called "macroeconomic regulation"
- the economics of government environmental regulation as an example of "microeconomic regulation"

Chapter Outline and Key Points

In this section, you are provided with a basic outline of the chapter and key words/points you should know. Use this outline to develop a complete outline of the material. Write the definitions or further explanations for the terms. Use the space provided in this workbook or rewrite that material in your notebook. This will help you study and remember the material in preparation for your tests, assignments, and papers.

The Roots of Government Intervention in the Economy

The Nineteenth Century

mixed free-enterprise economic system—

state regulation and promotion of economy—

economic growth after the Civil War—

business cycles—

Adam Smith's *The Wealth of Nations*—

laissez-faire—

governmental involvement favored by business—

public works projects such as the construction of the Erie Canal—

Interstate Commerce Act of 1887—

"trusts"—

Sherman Antitrust Act of 1890—

governmental influence in agriculture in nineteenth century—

The Progressive Era

Progressive movement—

regulatory actions of the Progressive administrations of Theodore Roosevelt and Woodrow Wilson—

Pure Food and Drug Act and the Meat Inspection Act in 1906—

three actions by Congress to control banking and regulate business:

1)

2)

3)

Sixteenth Amendment and expansion of federal revenue—

The Great Depression and the New Deal

end of Progressive era—

conservative administrations of Harding, Coolidge, and Hoover—

Great Depression—

Franklin D. Roosevelt and New Deal—

interventionist state—

Financial Reforms—

Roosevelt's banking holiday—

Glass-Steagall Act of 1933—

Federal Deposit Insurance Corporation (FDIC)—

Securities Act (1933)—

Securities Exchange Act of 1934—

Securities and Exchange Commission (SEC)—

stocks bought on margin—

Agriculture—

Agricultural Adjustment Act of 1933—

Soil Conservation and Domestic Allotment Act—

Agricultural Adjustment Act of 1938—

Labor—

National Labor Relations Act of 1935 (Wagner Act)—

unfair labor practices—

National Labor Relations Board (NLRB)—

Fair Labor Standards Act of 1938—

Industry Regulations—

Federal Communications Commission (FCC)—

Civil Aeronautics Board (CAB)—

Motor Carrier Act of 1935—

Legacy of the New Deal Era—

The Social Regulation Era

economic regulation—

social regulation—

regulatory programs and legislation of the 1950s, 1960s and 1970s—

regulatory agencies setup to implement new social regulations—

various forms of social regulatory statutes—

consequence of new social regulations on industry—

four reasons for surge in social regulation:

    1)

    2)

    3)

    4)

Deregulation

deregulation—

perceived defects in economic regulatory programs in 1950s and 60s—

claims of advocates of deregulation—

example of airline industry—

Gerald Ford and deregulation—

expansion under Carter of deregulation—

Airline Deregulation Act of 1978—

Telecommunications Act of 1996—

further deregulation of the media by FCC in 2003—

concern over concentrated corporate ownership of the media industry—

changes in agricultural regulation—

G.W. Bush's 2002 agriculture bill—

corporate scandals—

economic deregulation and politics—

Stabilizing the Economy

Harding, Hoover and Roosevelt and depression—

John Maynard Keynes—

economic stability—

inflation—

recession—

Monetary Policy: Controlling the Money Supply

monetary policy—

money—

Federal Reserve Board of Governors—

Federal Reserve System—

Federal Reserve Board (FRB)—

The Federal Reserve System (Figure 18.1)—

presidential appointment of the Fed—

Benjamin Bernake—

independence of FRB from the executive branch—

Alan Greenspan—

Federal Reserve Banks ("bankers banks")—

reserve requirements—

discount rate—

open market operations—

Federal Open Market Committee—

"moral suasion"—

The FRB and the Executive and Legislative Branches

the president and the economy—

the president and the FRB—

Fiscal Policy: Taxing and Spending

fiscal policy—

total spending—

discretionary fiscal policy—

first significant application of fiscal policy theory—

Revenue Act of 1964—

"commercial Keynesianism"—

tax cuts and the economy—

Clinton veto of Republican tax-cut proposal in 1999—

George W. Bush and tax cuts, May 2006—

The Effects of Globalization

the international economy—

free trade and globalization—

2001 recession and "jobless recovery"—

between July 2000 and January 2004, U.S. manufacturing sector loses 3 million jobs—

labor unions and free trade—

dumping low-priced goods onto American markets and opening other nations to more American goods—

minimum wage—

loss of real media American household income from 2000 to 2004—

323

only gain in real income from 2003-2004 was in the top 5 percent of households—

5.4 million Americans fell into poverty between 2000 and 2004—

Growth in the Minimum Wage Over Time (Figure 18.2)—

warning of impact of globalization on income distribution—

erosion of income of average workers—

outsourcing and the negative impact on American jobs—

Republican opponents of outsourcing and workers' concerns—

The Budgetary Process

purposes of federal budget—

budget planning and implementation—

How the Federal Government Raises and Spends Money—

    variety of sources of federal income—

    most money raised by federal government from what?—

    Receipts and Outlays of the Federal Government (Figure 18.3)—

    social insurance and retirement receipts—

    individual income taxes between 1991 and 2001—

    decrease in amount of federal income derived from income taxes during Bush Administration and resultant increasing in borrowing as a means of federal income during Bush Administration—

    most government spending directed toward what?—

    human resources includes what?—

    increase in human resource expenditures, 1991-2006—

Congress and the Budget Process—

Budget and Accounting Act of 1921—

Office of Management and Budget (OMB)—

fiscal year—

when does president send a budget to Congress?—

Federal Budget Process (Table 18.1)—

Article I of the Constitution and the budget—

who authorizes sending on programs?—

who actually provides the funding for programs?—

backdoor spending—

Budget and Impoundment Control Act of 1974—

Congressional Budget Office (CBO)—

reconciliation legislation—

Entitlements and Discretionary Spending, 1963-2007 (Figure 18.4)—

October 1 and action on appropriation bills—

continuing resolution—

Major Budget Conflicts—

conflicts between Congress and the president over what?—

budget conflicts during the 1980s—

Clinton 1993 budget reduction plan—

conflicts between Bill Clinton and Newt Gingrich—

three Clinton vetoes of appropriations bills—

Budget Initiatives of the George W. Bush Administration—

2001 Economic Growth and Tax Relief Reconciliation Act—

problems with the bill—

what the bill called for—

2003, a stagnant economy and Bush tax cuts—

2002 supplemental request of $27.1 billion for Defense and Homeland Security—

short-term and long-term effects of 2001 and 2003 Bush tax cuts—

soaring deficits—

2006 Bush budget deficit of $423 billion, 3.2 percent of GDP—

Bush 2007 budget proposals—

low Bush approval numbers and concern over the budget deficits—

The Budget Deficit and the Debt

national debt—

federal budget deficit—

factors contributing to annual budget deficits and burgeoning national debt from early 1980s to early 1990s—

gross domestic product (GDP)—

national debt tripled in 1980s (Reagan Administration)—

deficits and impact on economy and national debt—

staggering national debt of $8.37 trillion in May, 2006—

Americans paid $352 billion in interest on the national debt in 2005—

Deficit Reduction Legislation—

budget surpluses—

Gramm-Rudman-Hollings Act of 1985—

Budget Enforcement Act of 1990—

Omnibus Budget Reconciliation Act of 1993—

Budget Surplus and Renewed Deficits—

Clinton budgets and significant declines in deficit—

return to deficits under George W. Bush—

Greenspan warnings against Bush return to large deficits—

Deficit Reduction Act of 2005—

The Economics of Environmental Regulation

federal involvement in environmental controls until the late 1960s—

growth of environmental problems in 1960s—

extensive pollution control legislation of the 1970s—

The Environmental Protection Agency

EPA—

role of the EPA—

Clean Air Act—

four major eras in political life of EPA—

    1)

    2)

    3)

    4)

George W. Bush and Artic National Wildlife Refuge—

Environmental Protections: Two Examples

disposal of hazardous and toxic wastes, and transboundary atmospheric pollution and its impact on global warming—

economic costs of the problems—

health threats of the problems—

environmental threats of the problems—

Hazardous and Toxic Wastes—

> increase in the production and use of chemicals—
>
> prevention, safe disposal, and cleanup—
>
> Toxic Substances Control Act (1976)—
>
> Resources Conservation and Recovery Act (1976)—
>
> "cradle to grave" regulation—
>
> "midnight dumping"—
>
> Comprehensive Environmental Response, Compensation, and Liability Act of 1980 (also known as "the Superfund")—
>
> Love Canal—
>
> National Priority List—
>
> litigation—
>
> environmental civil rights—
>
> Third Circuit Court of Appeals in 2001 limits citizens' rights to sue for environmental rights—
>
> Superfund funding dwindling (Bush cuts fund in 2003 budget and beyond)—

Atmospheric Pollution, Acid Rain, and Climate Change—

> pollution from power plants—
>
> acid rain—
>
> Clean Air Act of 1970—

Reagan administration delayed action on acid rain—

President George H.W. Bush calls for major amendments to the Clean Air Act in early 1989 and Clean Air Amendments of 1990—

Clinton Administration crack-down on acid rain—

George W. Bush eases up on enforcement against acid rain—

global warming—

Kyoto Protocol of 1997—

George W. Bush refuses to join Kyoto accord—

Bush proposes "Clear Skies" initiative in 2002, allowing greater pollution and weakening major provisions of the Clean Air Act—

some Republicans join Democratic members of Congress to kill the "Clear Skies" legislation—

Bush implements key aspect of "Clear Skies" degradation of pollution controls administratively through EPA—

George W. Bush decision not to regulate deadly carbon dioxide pollution has been met by legal action from states and environmental protection groups—

some states work to address global warming threats despite Bush administration—

Research Ideas and Possible Paper Topics

1) Given the corporate scandals and convictions of recent years, such as with Enron, does the deregulation of business fostered by Republicans at the behest of corporate business interests seem effective and useful for Americans? Has deregulation hurt or helped the American middle class? Who does deregulation help the most—consumers or corporate owners? Research some key areas such as energy deregulation and deregulation of the broadcast media and discuss.

2) The Chairman of the Federal Reserve Bank is often described as the most powerful man in America. Do some research to determine why he is considered so powerful, who he is, and what his policies are. What are some arguments for and against the power vested in the hands of the Fed Chairman?

3)   There has been a debate in the past couple of decades over the pros and cons of a constitutional amendment requiring a balanced budget. Do some research on this topic. Be prepared to give the arguments of all sides in the discussion. If passed and ratified, what would happen? Who would decide what to cut if the president and Congress couldn't propose a balanced budget regularly? Republicans in the 1980s supported such an amendment, but many now (with dramatically increased budget deficits created under the Bush Administration) oppose one, while many Democrats, who previously opposed an amendment, now support an amendment or other deficit reduction measures. What are the politics of deficit reduction? Would the current Bush Administration support a balanced budget amendment, do you believe, considering the massive deficits of the George W. Bush era of government?

4)   A major concern of the nineteenth century was the business cycle. Monetary and fiscal policies have minimized these swings to some extent. Test the truth of these statements by looking at historical economic trends.

5)   The Environmental Protection Agency is the largest regulatory agency in the U.S. government. It has also been attacked for a variety of reasons by Republicans and Democrats. Using the information in this chapter as a starting point, do some research about the EPA. How effective is it? What does it do? What impact does it have on business? What effect has the rejection of the Kyoto Protocols by George W. Bush had on environmental policy in this country and the world? Do young Americans, who generally have a greater concern about the environment than most age groups, have confidence in this Administration's claims of environmental concern? What is the Bush Administration's real record on the environment?

Web sites

Federal Reserve Board Web site has basic information about the FRB, its structure, and purpose. Also has publications, announcements, lists of related Web sites, biographies of members, reports, and statistics.
      www.federalreserve.gov

Office of Management and Budget (OMB) Web site offers budget information, reports, testimony, regulatory policies, and more from the perspective of the administration.
      www.whitehouse.gov/OMB

Congressional Budget Office (CBO) Web site offers Congress' opinions on budget matters including statistics, reports, budget reviews, testimony, and more.
      www.cbo.gov

The **Council of Economic Advisors** Web site offers the Economic Report of the President and CEA publications, as well as basic information about the CEA and its members.

www.whitehouse.gov/cea

The **National Debt Clock** offers a running account of the public debt and offers links to a variety of groups and organizations interested in the debt and/or deficit and why and how it should be reduced.

www.brillig.com/debt_clock

GPO Access offers the full text of many Government Printing Office publications on the Web, including the economic indicators prepared for the Joint Economic Committee by the Council of Economic Advisors; updated monthly. Among the growing list of titles available are the Federal Register, the Congressional Record, Congressional Bills, United States Code, Economic Indicators and GAO Reports.

http://www.gpoaccess.gov/index.html

The **Concord Coalition** is a nonpartisan, grassroots organization dedicated to eliminating federal budget deficits and ensuring Social Security, Medicare, and Medicaid are secure for all generations; founded by Paul Tsongas (D) and Warren Rudman (R). The Coalition Web site offers lots of information about the debt and deficit, as well as some social policy issues. They offer e-mail newsletters, grassroots initiatives, statistics, and more.

www.concordcoalition.org

The **Economic Policy Institute (EPI)** is a nonpartisan think tank devoted to economic issues. This Web site offers a variety of reports on economic issues and a monthly newsletter delivered by e-mail. Despite their self-classification as nonpartisan, their board of directors is predominantly left-leaning (liberal).

www.epinet.org

The **Cato Institute** is a libertarian think tank promoting an unregulated free market. Their Web site offers a variety of articles and links. Deregulation is a favorite topic on the Cato Web site.

www.cato.org

The **American Enterprise Institute** is a conservative think tank that addresses a variety of issues including the government and the economy. Their Web site offers information on their calendar of events, a variety of articles, and links. On the left side of the Web page, click on "Joint Center for Regulatory Studies."

www.aei.org

Moving Ideas hosts policy, politics, and news from progressive and liberal research organizations and advocacy groups. Click on "The Economy" link at the left side of the Web page for information on the budget and the economy.

www.movingideas.org

The **Brookings Institution** is the oldest think tank in America and has the reputation of being fairly moderate. Their Web site offers policy briefings, articles, books, *The Brookings Review*, discussion groups, and links. On the left side of the Web page, click on "Research Topics" then on "Economic, U.S" for information on the budget and economy.

www.brook.edu

Bush Greenwatch is a Web site reporting on President George W. Bush's record and policies on environmental regulation from an environmentalist perspective.

http://www.bushgreenwatch.org

Practice Tests

MULTIPLE CHOICE QUESTIONS

1) The doctrine of *laissez-faire* is based on the theories of
   a. Adam Smith.
   b. Alexander Hamilton.
   c. John Maynard Keynes.
   d. Milton Friedman.

2) State "land grant" colleges were established by the
   a. Homestead Act.
   b. Morrill Land Grant Act.
   c. Clayton Act.
   d. Wagner Act.

3) Congress passed the Federal Reserve Act in
   a. 1961.
   b. 1948.
   c. 1935.
   d. 1913.

4) The income tax was made possible by the
   a. Clayton Act.
   b. law Congress passed on income taxes.
   c. Sixteenth Amendment.
   d. Hatch Act.

5) The law that created the New Deal government program called the Federal Deposit Insurance Corporation was the
   a. Taft-Hartley Act.
   b. Glass-Steagall Act.
   c. Securities Act.
   d. Federal Reserve Act.

6)   The first acts of the New Deal were directed at
     a.   the financial system.
     b.   the country's food and agricultural problems.
     c.   labor problems.
     d.   poverty problems.

7)   Workers' rights to organize and bargain collectively through unions of their own
     choosing were codified in the
     a.   Taft-Hartley Act.
     b.   Glass-Steagall Act.
     c.   Taylor Act.
     d.   Wagner Act.

8)   The radio, telephone, and telegraph industries became subject in 1934 to federal
     regulatory controls by the
     a.   Federal Broadcasting Act.
     b.   Federal Communications Commission.
     c.   Telecommunications Act.
     d.   Multimedia Act.

9)   Deregulation first became a serious part of the national policy agenda due to the
     efforts in the 1970s of
     a.   President Richard Nixon.
     b.   President Gerald Ford and Senator Edward Kennedy.
     c.   President Jimmy Carter.
     d.   President Ronald Reagan.

10) The landmark federal legislation that deregulated radio, which benefited
     corporate profits but caused a decline in minority ownership and diversity of
     content, was
     a.   the Communications Act of 1934.
     b.   instituted by President Ronald Reagan.
     c.   the Telecommunications Act of 1996.
     d.   All of the above.

11) The idea that government spending could offset a decline in private spending and
     thus help maintain high levels of spending, production, and employment was
     advocated by
     a.   David Ricardo.
     b.   John Maynard Keynes.
     c.   Herbert Hoover.
     d.   Franklin Roosevelt.

12) What seven-member federal agency has the responsibility for the formulation and implementation of monetary policy in the United States?
    a.   Federal Reserve Board
    b.   Office of Management and Budget
    c.   Council of Economic Advisors
    d.   None of the above.

13) Federal government policies on taxes, spending, and debt management are referred to as
    a.   aggregate policy.
    b.   economic policy.
    c.   fiscal policy.
    d.   monetary policy.

14) The president began preparing and submitting a budget to Congress under the authority given him by Congress in the
    a.   Revenue Act of 1964.
    b.   Budget and Accounting Act of 1921.
    c.   Budget Enforcement Act of 1990.
    d.   Budget and Impoundment Control Act of 1974.

15) President George W. Bush's plan to replace provisions of the Clean Air Act with voluntary reductions in carbon dioxide emissions is known as
    a.   Clear Skies.
    b.   Silent Spring.
    c.   Toxic Substances Control Act.
    d.   All of the above.

TRUE/FALSE QUESTIONS

1)   The Progressive movement sought to bring corporate power under the control of the government.

2)   The Wagner Act increased the power of labor unions.

3)   As a result of social regulation, many industries that previously had limited dealings with the federal government found they now had to comply with government regulation of their operations.

4)   Financial scandals of several large U.S. corporations have lead to calls for renewed oversight, accountability, and re-regulation.

5)   The first significant application of fiscal policy theory occurred in 1964 with the Revenue Act of 1964.

6)   The Congressional Budget Office is a professional staff of technical experts to advise Congress with budgetary information so Congress can be more independent of the president's budgetary influence.

7)   President George W. Bush's series of tax cuts early in his administration dramatically revitalized the economy, provided substantive tax cuts for the middle class, and led to years of low budget deficits.

8)   Following the Clinton budget and the Reconciliation Act of 1993, significant declines in the federal deficit were attained.

9)   The EPA is now confronting issues of environmental civil rights because many polluting industries are located in poor black neighborhoods.

10)   Acid rain has been an important environmental problem for over half a century.

COMPARE AND CONTRAST

laissez-faire vs. interventionist state

Wagner Act, the Fair Labor Standards Act, and Taft-Hartley

economic regulation, social regulation, and deregulation

economic stability and inflation

recession and depression

reserve requirements, discount rate, and open market operations

monetary and fiscal policies

OMB and CBO

budget deficit and national debt

ESSAY AND SHORT ANSWER QUESTIONS

1)   Discuss the American economic system, its roots and its interaction with political forces within the country.

2)   Discuss the Interstate Commerce Act and the Sherman Anti-Trust Act.

3)   What is the Taft-Hartley Act, and what was its significance to American labor?

4)   Compare and contrast economic and social legislation.

5)   Briefly explain the Federal Reserve System.

6)   Explain the process that America went through in its evolution from a *laissez-faire* state to an interventionist state.

7)   Discuss the nature of economic and social regulation in the nineteenth and twentieth centuries.

8)   How does the government use fiscal and monetary policy to stabilize the economy?

9)   Discuss the economics of regulating environmental pollution.

10)   The huge national debt has led many people to suggest a number of reforms in economic policy. Discuss the problem of the debt and deficit as well as the reforms that have been proposed. Discuss the positions Democrats and Republicans have taken and flip-flopped over in recent years.

ANSWERS TO STUDY EXERCISES

Multiple Choice Answers

1) a
2) b
3) d
4) c
5) b
6) a
7) d
8) b
9) b
10) c
11) b
12) a
13) c
14) b
15) a

True/False Answers

1) T
2) T
3) T
4) T
5) T
6) T
7) F
8) T
9) T
10) F

CHAPTER 19
FOREIGN AND DEFENSE POLICY

Chapter Goals and Learning Objectives

President George W. Bush in his 2005 inaugural address boldly stated to the world, "All who live in tyranny and hopelessness can know the United States will not ignore your oppression or excuse your oppressors. When you stand for your liberty, we will stand with you." This pledge made at the start of his second term as president indicated his willingness to further commit American strength across the planet. When he made this pledge in January of 2005, some 140,000 U.S. troops were stationed in Iraq. Over 3,000 U.S. military personnel—men and women—have been killed in Iraq since the U.S. invaded and occupied that Middle Eastern country in the spring of 2003, with over 23,000 wounded.

The Bush Doctrine of using America's preeminent military power in preemptive attack reflects this country's status as the sole world superpower. The United States, particularly under George W. Bush, has taken the position of using its power in directing and influencing political affairs across the globe, enforced by a military budget greater than all the major world powers combined. It is a post-Cold War policy that has developed for a number of reasons.

Americans who grew up during the height of the Cold War lived under the threat of nuclear annihilation every day. They understood that the Soviet Union had enough nuclear weapons to destroy the United States many times over. And Americans understood that we could destroy all life in the U.S.S.R. several times over as well. Americans lived "eyeball-to-eyeball" with the Soviets in a game of nuclear chicken for decades, holding each other's entire populations as hostages in a mad game called "mutually assured destruction" or MAD.

When the Cold War came to an end in 1991 after over four decades of constant, non-belligerent conflict between the U.S. and U.S.S.R., the foreign and military policy of the United States suddenly, stunningly, and completely changed. For years it was us vs. them, two gigantic titans in the ring struggling for world domination. Yet in a matter of weeks, only one titan remained standing. The United States found itself as the world's remaining superpower with a new and ill-defined mission in the world. Foreign and military policy had to undergo drastic introspection and changes. Many Americans put foreign and military affairs on a back-burner and turned to domestic matters—butter rather than guns.

Until September 11, 2001, when Americans found themselves confronting the rest of the world following the first attack on the American mainland by foreign forces since the War of 1812 (an important distinction from Pearl Harbor, which was U.S. territory, but effectively a colony). America took stock of its foreign and military policy in a new and chilling light. Afghanistan, international terrorism, Iraq, an "axis of evil" and a new concern for our place in the world became apparent to a new generation of Americans.

While most Americans pay scant attention to foreign policy except in times of crisis, our lives are intertwined as citizens of this nation with our policies in dealing with the world. We do a substantial amount of foreign trade, we have a substantial military force and substantial military commitments overseas, and we are interdependent on other economies in the world for our prosperity. Since the main purpose of government is to protect us and maintain our prosperity, it is incumbent upon Americans to understand and involve ourselves in our commitments and policies with the rest of the world.

This chapter is designed to give you a basic overview of U.S. foreign and military policy. The main topic headings of the chapter are:

- The Developments of U.S. Foreign and Defense Policy
- The United States as a World Power
- Foreign and Defense Policy Decision Making
- Twenty-First Century Challenges

In each section, there are certain facts and ideas that you should strive to understand. Many are in boldface type and appear in both the narrative and in the glossary at the end of the book. Other ideas, dates, facts, events, people, etc. are more difficult to pull out of the narrative. (Keep in mind that studying for objective tests [multiple choice, T/F] is different than studying for essay tests. See the Study Guide section on test taking for hints on study skills.)

In general, after you finish reading and studying this chapter, you should understand the following:

- the development of U.S. foreign and defense policy before the United States became a world power
- U.S. policy during and after the Cold War; and the United States as a world power
- foreign and defense policy decision making by the executive branch, Congress and other groups
- twenty-first century challenges in foreign and defense policy

Chapter Outline and Key Points

In this section, you are provided with a basic outline of the chapter and key words/points you should know. Use this outline to develop a complete outline of the material. Write the definitions or further explanations for the terms. Use the space provided in this workbook or rewrite that material in your notebook. This will help you study and remember the material in preparation for your tests, assignments, and papers.

The Development of U.S. Foreign and Defense Policy

isolationism—

unilateralism—

moralism—

pragmatism—

The Constitution

what the Framers' wanted as U.S. foreign relations—

the Framers divided authority for foreign and military policy—

constitutional role of president in foreign and military policy—

constitutional role of Congress in foreign and military policy—

how this division of responsibility in the U.S. Constitution for foreign and military powers differed from European foreign policy—

The Early History of U.S. Military and Foreign Policy

Washington's Farewell Address—

Washington's foreign policy—

Barbary Wars—

impressment—

Embargo Act—

Napoleonic Wars—

U.S.-British War of 1812—

1814 Treaty of Ghent—

Monroe Doctrine—

The United States as an Emerging Power

Trade Policy and Commerce

    Alexander Hamilton's *Report on Manufacturers*—

    reciprocity—

    MFN status—

    tariffs—

    "American system" of trade protection—

Continental Expansion and Manifest Destiny

    acquisition of land from Native Americans and Europeans—

    1846 Mexican War—

    manifest destiny—

    American colonialism—

Interests Beyond the Western Hemisphere

    U.S. trade with Asia and the Pacific—

    1898 Spanish American War and U.S. colonial acquisitions—

    1899 Filipino revolt against U.S. colonialism—

The Roosevelt Corollary

Panama Canal, 1914—

Roosevelt Corollary to the Monroe Doctrine—

the "Colossus of the North"—

World War I

World War I begins in Europe, 1914

"he kept us out of war"—

German unrestricted submarine warfare—

collective security—

U.S. enters "war to end all wars" in 1917—

Wilson's role in the League of Nations—

Senate rejects ratification of Treaty of Versailles—

The Interwar Years

isolationism and unilateralism—

1930 Smoot-Hawley Tariff—

effects of Great Depression—

Neutrality Acts—I

<u>**The United States as a World Power**</u>

Germany invades Poland, September 1, 1939, initiating World War II—

December 7, 1941 and Pearl Harbor—

U.S. declaration of war—

Axis powers—

Grand Alliance—

U.S. world role before and after World War II—

World War II and its Aftermath: 1941-1947

industrial and military mobilization—

the war transforms American society—

V-E Day—

Hiroshima, Nagasaki and birth of nuclear age—

V-J Day—=

United Nations—

international governmental organization (IGO)—

the "Big Three"—

Bretton Woods Agreement—

International Monetary Fund (IMF)—

World Bank—

General Agreement on Tariffs and Trade (GATT)—

multilateralism—

The Cold War and Containment: 1947-1960

relations between U.S. and Soviet Union during war and after—

Truman Doctrine—

Marshall Plan—

containment—

George Kennan—

North Atlantic Treaty Organization (NATO)—

Korean War—

deterrence—

mutual assured destruction (MAD)—

Americans reject isolationism—

Cold War Alliances in Europe (Figure 19.1)—

Containment, Cuba, and Vietnam: 1961-1969

John F. Kennedy's inaugural address—

Kennedy and Khrushchev in Vienna—

Cuban Missile Crisis—

hot line—

Vietnam War—

Lyndon Johnson and Vietnam War—

Détente and Human Rights: 1969-1981

détente—

Nixon Doctrine—

arms control agreements—

human rights—

Iranian hostage crisis—

Soviet Union invasion of Afghanistan—

Carter Doctrine—

Containment Revisited and Renewed: 1981-1989

Reagan arms build-up—

Reagan's activist foreign policy—

Reagan Doctrine—

Soviet President Mikhail Gorbachev—

Reagan-Gorbachev cooperation—

Gorbachev's "perestroika"—

Searching for a New International Order: 1989-2001

George Bush in 1989—

Eastern Europe in 1989—

Gorbachev response to revolts in Eastern Europe—

collapse of "Iron Curtain"—

1990 Iraq invasion of Kuwait—

Operation Desert Storm—

Powell Doctrine—

1991 attempted coup against Gorbachev—

collapse of Soviet Union—

end of Cold War—

post-Cold War questions—

Bill Clinton, 1993—

engagement—

enlargement—

no easy benchmark for intervention—

North American Free Trade Agreement (NAFTA)—

World Trade Organization (WTO)—

The War on Terrorism: 2001 to the Present:

George W. Bush, 2001—

September 11, 2001—

al-Qaeda—

war on terrorism—

Osama bin Laden—

Taliban—

war in Afghanistan—

Strategic Offensive Arms Reduction Treaty—

impact of 9/11/01 attacks on U.S. foreign policy—

Bush Doctrine—

weapons of mass destruction (WMDs)—

Saddam Hussein—

changing Bush administration justifications for invading Iraq—

dismal assessments of situation in Iraq—

disagreements and controversies over how to combat terrorism—

Foreign and Defense Policy Making

The Executive Branch

The President

preeminence of president in foreign and military policy—

presidential use of authority to order U.S. forces to battle without seeking approval from others—

exclusive sources of information for president—

president's foreign and military power not absolute—

The Departments of State and Defense

Department of State—

Department of Defense—

National Security Agency (NSA)—

Joint Chiefs of Staff—

Central Intelligence Agency (CIA)—

Director of Central Intelligence—

Director of National Intelligence—

CIA during Cold War—

CIA post-September 11—

National Security Council (NSC)—

members of the NSC—

special assistant to president for national security affairs—

The United States Intelligence Community (Figure 19.2)—

Department of Homeland Security (DHS)

Department of Homeland Security—

massive government reorganization under Department of Homeland Security—

Transportation Security Agency (TSA)—

Federal Emergency Management Agency (FEMA)—

Customs and Border Protection—

Coast Guard, Secret Service, immigration services and enforcement—

9/11 Commission—

criticisms of Homeland Security—

Michael Chertoff—

Congress

Congressional Leadership

Congress has power to develop and implement policy—

Sputnik—

NASA—

Congressional Oversight

oversight powers of Congress—

deference to president from World War II to late 1960s—

348

changes since Vietnam—

more vigorous oversight—

oversight by Senate Foreign Relations Committee in 2005 and 2006—

Treaties and Executive Agreements

Senate power to approve or reject treaties—

Senate has rejected treaties how many times?—

executive agreements—

Appointments

Senate advise and consent power on presidential appointments, including ambassadors—

1997 William Weld nomination—

John R. Bolton, 2005—

Appropriations

sole power to appropriate funds—

U.S. Defense Spending, 1940-2010 (Figure 19.3)—

Congress, Reagan and funding for Contras—

Congress, Clinton and funding for Kosovo—

War Powers Act of 1973

1964 Gulf of Tonkin Resolution—

support for Vietnam War—

elements of War Powers Act—

Nixon veto, Congress overrides—

unconstitutional?—

President Ford—

fundamental weakness of War Power Act—

The Military Industrial Complex

Eisenhower's farewell address of 1961—

military-industrial complex—

five ways military-industrial complex acquires power:

    1)

    2)

    3)

    4)

    5)

Representative Randy "Duke" Cunningham (R-Ca)—

The News Media

reporting and investigation—

the press in Vietnam and Watergate—

the press in Gulf War—

military uses news media for its own ends—

media broke story of Abu Ghraib—

Defense Department paid contractors planting favorable stories—

influencing public opinion—

The Public

militarism/nonmilitarism and isolationism/internationalism—

rise in presidential popularity in foreign/military crisis—

The Most Important Problem: Domestic or Foreign (Figure 19.4)—

Bush and "Mission Accomplished"

Bush and Hurricane Katrina—

Elections

citizens exercise of electoral control over presidential power—

1952, Eisenhower and Korea—

1968, Nixon and "secret plan to end the war" in Vietnam—

Public Action

protests and Vietnam—

opposition to the draft—

nongovernmental organizations (NGOs)—

activists influence on NGOs—

Twenty-First Century Challenges

Identifying Policies to Pursue in the National Interest

what policies to pursue?—

pre- and post-9/11—

North Korea—

Iran and uranium—

Israel and Palestine—

war on terrorism—

Israeli-Palestinian conflict—

Deciding When to Intervene Overseas

decision to intervene—

Richard Perle—

Muammar Qaddafi—

Critics of Bush Doctrine say—

1)

2)

3)

Promoting Democracy in the Middle East

Hamas—

National Assembly (Iraq)—

al-Maliki—

Afghanistan—

Transnational Threats to Peace

terrorists as nonstate actors—

information warfare—

Drug and Environmental Problems

Three tactics used by the United States against illegal drugs—

1)

2)

3)

opium and Afghanistan—

1987 Montreal Protocol—

UN Rio Earth Summit—

1997 Kyoto Conference on Global Climate Change—

Kyoto Protocol—

Choosing Between Unilateralism and Multilateralism

how should U.S. interact with the world—

problem for policy makers—

in the twenty-first century—

lessons learned in Iraq—

Multilateralism and Unilateralism in American Foreign Policy—

Research Ideas and Possible Paper Topics

1)   Choose a foreign policy crisis (either contemporary or historical). Conduct research to determine what issues were at hand, what actors were making the decisions, and what the outcome was. Did public opinion matter? Was the president the strongest actor in the crisis? How did the various interests play themselves out?

2)   American news, be it press or broadcast media, tends to skimp on international news. The argument is that Americans are not interested. Is that true? Interest increased after 9/11 but some say Americans have again lost interest in foreign news. Find public opinion polling data; ask friends and colleagues, etc. about their interest in international relations. Next, test the hypothesis that the media ignores foreign affairs. Watch several different types of media (network TV, newspapers, cable TV, news magazines) and determine if that is true. Now that you know more about U.S. foreign policy, are you more interested in such news? Discuss these issues or structure a debate about them.

3)   As a class, discuss what the grand strategy of the U.S. ought to be now that the Cold War is over. What are U.S. national interests? Should we intervene in other country's affairs as President Bush has suggested in his second inaugural, and why or why not? What about Iraq and the Middle East? What is our national interest in that region? Trade and aid policy—with whom should we trade and to whom should we give aid? Are there limits to U.S. generosity? What are they?

4)   Research the history and development of international terrorism. Has there been attacks on U.S. interests before the 9/11 attack on New York and Washington? What was U.S. policy toward international terrorism before 9/11 and after? What has happened since 9/11? Has there been any significant terrorist threats to the U.S. since 9/11? Why or why not? What is the future of U.S. anti-terrorism on the domestically and internationally?

5)   Do some research on businesses in your area that are involved in international trade. Use the Internet or library to find out what kinds of businesses are doing business where and why. Are there more international ties in your area than you thought? What kinds of impacts does this trade have on you, your town/city, the country?

Web sites

The **Council on Foreign Relations**, founded in 1921, is an independent, national membership organization and a nonpartisan center for scholars dedicated to producing and disseminating ideas on U.S. foreign relation. Its Web site offers a broad range of information, data, papers and links.
   www.cfr.org/index.php

Faces of the Fallen: U.S. Service Members Who Died in Operation Iraqi Freedom and Operation Enduring Freedom is a service of the **Washington Post**, honoring the sacrifice of American service members by posting small photographs of each American who died.
   http://projects.washingtonpost.com/fallen

Iraq Coalition Casualty Count is a private Web site sponsored by private donations that tabulates war dead and wounded in Iraq and offers links to information about the war not usually available from the government or mainstream media.
   http://www.icasualties.org/oif

Iraq Body Count provides much the same service as above but also provides names of American men and woman killed in Iraq.
   http://www.iraqbodycount.org

Official site of the United States **Department of State**
   http://www.state.gov

The **U.S. State Department** maintains an electronic archive of foreign policy history including documents and photographs that can be searched and accessed online.
   www.state.gov/www/about_state/history/frus.html

Official Web site of the **Department of Defense**
www.dod.gov

Official Web site of the **Department of Homeland Security**
www.dhs.gov

Official Web site of the **Central Intelligence Agency**
www.cia.gov

Official Web site of the **Senate Foreign Relations Committee**
http://foreign.senate.gov

Official site of the **Pentagon**
http://pentagon.afis.osd.mil

Official site of the **Air Force**
www.af.mil

Official site of the **Marine Corps**
www.hqmc.usmc.mil

Official site of the **Army**
www.army.mil

Official site of the **Navy**
www.navy.mil

Official site of the **Joint Chiefs of Staff**
www.dtic.mil/jcs

The **International Responsibilities Task Force** of the American Library Association's Social Responsibilities Round Table hosts a Web site titled **"Alternative Resources on the U.S. 'War Against Terrorism'"** which features numerous links to a wide variety of sources.
http://www.pitt.edu/~ttwiss/irtf/Alternative.html

National Center for Policy Analysis is a nonprofit public policy research institute from a conservative perspective.
www.ncpa.org

Center for Defense Information is a nonprofit public policy center with a moderate to liberal perspective. "Founded in 1972 as an independent monitor of the military, the Center for Defense Information is a private, nongovernmental, research organization. Its directors and staff believe that strong social, economic, political, and military components and a healthy environment contribute equally to the nation's security. CDI seeks realistic and cost-effective military spending without excess expenditures for weapons and policies that increase the danger of war. CDI supports adequate defense by evaluating our defense needs and how best to meet them without wasteful spending or compromising our national security."

www.cdi.org

Foreign Policy in Focus is a nonprofit foreign policy study group that examines such issues from a progressive perspective.

www.fpif.org

Foreign Affairs Magazine is a monthly journal published by the Council on Foreign Relations and has long been considered one of the most prestigious publications on the issue of foreign policy. A selection of articles is online from the current issue.

www.foreignaffairs.org

Cold War Hot Links is a Web site maintained by a professor at St. Martin's College in Washington State. This site offers links to a myriad of sites dealing with the Cold War and U.S. foreign and military policy during that period following the end of WWII until 1991.

http://homepages.stmartin.edu/fac_staff/dprice/cold.war.htm

The Web site for the **Technical Support Work Group**, a multi-agency federal study group, follows U.S. anti-terrorism developments.

http://www.tswg.gov/tswg/home/home.htm

The **Office of Trade and Economic Analysis** does research and analysis of international trade issues and publishes data and statistics, which are available at this site to the public.

www.ita.doc.gov/td/industry/otea

Practice Tests

MULTIPLE CHOICE QUESTIONS

1) What early president warned in his farewell address to the nation against entanglement in foreign alliances?
   a. George Washington
   b. Thomas Jefferson
   c. James Monroe
   d. Theodore Roosevelt

2) Under the leadership of this president, the United States sent a naval squadron to Panama to help it win independence from Colombia, intervened in the Caribbean and Latin America numerous times, and expanded on the Monroe Doctrine to include U.S. intervention as an international police power. Name the president.
   a. James Monroe
   b. Theodore Roosevelt
   c. Franklin Roosevelt
   d. George W. Bush

3) The "war to end all wars" was the
   a. War of 1812.
   b. Spanish-American War
   c. first world war.
   d. second world war.

4) A Republican-controlled Congress in 1930 dramatically raised tariffs as a response to European economic reconstruction with the passage of the
   a. Roosevelt Corollary.
   b. Treaty of Versailles.
   c. Taft-Hartley Act.
   d. Smoot-Hawley Act.

5) An isolationist Congress, seeking to keep the United States from becoming involved in foreign conflict in the 1930s passed a number of
   a. Interventionist Acts.
   b. collective security agreements.
   c. resolutions condemning Democratic President Franklin Roosevelt.
   d. Neutrality Acts.

6) A few days after a U.S. declaration of war against Japan on December 8, 1941, the United States, which countries declared war against the United States?
   a. Germany and the Soviet Union.
   b. Germany and China.
   c. Germany and Italy.
   d. Germany, Italy, and France.

7) The birth of the nuclear age occurred with
   a. the development of the atomic bomb by the Soviet Union.
   b. the American dropping of atomic bombs on Berlin and Hiroshima.
   c. the American dropping of atomic bombs on Hiroshima and Nagasaki.
   d. the American development of the hydrogen bomb.

8) The policy adopted in 1947 to contain Soviet expansion, initially in Greece and Turkey, was called the
   a. Roosevelt Doctrine.
   b. Truman Doctrine.
   c. Churchill Doctrine.
   d. Marshall Plan.

9) The first peacetime military alliance joined by the United States was
   a. NATO.
   b. ASEAN.
   c. the League of Nations.
   d. the Organization of American States.

10) During the late 1960s and 1970s, the relaxation of tensions between the Soviet Union and the United States was called
    a. a thaw.
    b. a respite.
    c. détente.
    d. containment.

11) The policy that the United States would provide arms and military equipment to countries but not do the fighting for them was called the _____ Doctrine.
    a. Carter
    b. Brezhnev
    c. Ford
    d. Nixon

12) The dramatic relaxation of tensions between the United States and the Soviet Union and the decision to not subdue rebellions in Eastern Europe in 1989 came under the leadership of
    a. Nikita Khrushchev.
    b. Mikhail Gorbachev.
    c. Boris Yeltsen.
    d. Vladimir Putin.

13) One of the greatest foreign policy advantages the president has over Congress is
    a. the power to declare war.
    b. greater access to and control over information.
    c. treaty power.
    d. All of the above.

14) The president has the power to make treaties
    a. unilaterally.
    b. with the consent of the House.
    c. with the consent of the Senate.
    d. with the consent of both houses of Congress.

15) A U.S. government-to-foreign government accord binding only the current administration and not requiring Senate approval is called a(n)
   a. executive order.
   b. treaty.
   c. tariff.
   d. executive agreement.

TRUE/FALSE QUESTIONS

1) Manifest Destiny was a declaration by the United States that European powers should not involve themselves in our sphere of influence in the Western Hemisphere.

2) The European Recovery Program, better known as the Marshall Plan, provided a massive transfer of aid to Western Europe after WWII in order to rebuild the basis for strong economies.

3) The doctrine of mutual assured destruction (MAD) deterred the United States and the Soviet Union from attacking one another with nuclear weapons during the Cold War.

4) The Cuban Missile Crisis of 1962 brought the world closer to nuclear war than at any time.

5) Jimmy Carter dramatically decreased military funding and enhanced relations with the Soviet Union as a result of the Soviet invasion of Afghanistan.

6) The president is preeminent in foreign and military policy making.

7) Congress rarely plays a significant role in foreign policy.

8) John F. Kennedy warned against a military-industrial complex in his 1961 inaugural address.

9) Public action can lead to a change in foreign policy.

10) Solid evidence of the presence of weapons of mass destruction was discovered prior to the U.S. invasion of Iraq.

COMPARE AND CONTRAST

treaty and executive agreement

Monroe Doctrine and Manifest Destiny

League of Nations and the United Nations

isolationism and interventionism

unilateralism and multilateralism

International Monetary Fund, World Bank, and the General Agreement on Tariffs and Trade

Cold War, Truman Doctrine, containment, NATO, and the Marshall Plan

National Security Council, National Economic Council, and the Central Intelligence Agency

Department of State and Defense and Homeland Defense

American interventionism and Bush policy of preventive war

presidential vs. congressional powers in foreign affairs

media and public role in foreign policy

ESSAY AND SHORT ANSWER QUESTIONS

1)   What were the views of the Framers on foreign affairs?

2)   What is an executive agreement, and why is it important?

3)   What is isolationism? When and why did the U.S. adopt this policy?

4)   Discuss the Truman Doctrine, the Marshall Plan, and NATO.

5)   What is MAD?

6)   Discuss the early history of U.S. military and foreign policy from the early days of the country through World War I.

7)   Explain how the U.S. became a world leader in WWII and the role it played in the Cold War. What was the Cold War, and why is it so significant historically and in our present development of foreign and military policy?

8)   Discuss the role of the executive branch in foreign policy making.

9)   Discuss executive-legislative conflict in the realm of foreign and defense policies.

What other actors also vie for influence in these decisions, and how effective are they?

10) Discuss President George W. Bush's initial rationale for the U.S. invasion of Iraq in 2003? What errors were made or falsehoods told to lead the U.S. into invading Iraq? What purpose has the war there served?

ANSWERS TO STUDY EXERCISES

Multiple Choice Answers

1) a
2) b
3) c
4) d
5) d
6) c
7) c
8) b
9) a
10) c
11) d
12) b
13) b
14) c
15) d

True/False Answers

1) F
2) T
3) T
4) T
5) F
6) T
7) F
8) F
9) T
10) F

CHAPTER 20
THE CONTEXT FOR TEXAS POLITICS AND GOVERNMENT

Texas history, geography, and mythology provide the social, cultural, ideological, and economic context for Texas politics and government. The Texas image competes with the reality of the Lone Star State. Texas has been an expansive land of opportunity and wealth for many. They possess a pride in their state unmatched by any other state in the nation. That pride over how earlier Texans carved a civilization out of a wilderness can, however, also create a culture of denial about the very real lack of civilization experienced by other Texans. The State of Texas can be a hostile, uncivilized environment for children, the elderly, the poor and the laborer. It is generally unpopular to point out the social, economic, and racial problems to the Texas media and political elite because they rely on the mythical image of Texas. Politicians and special interests who deny the problems facing modern Texas while paying homage to the historic and mythical Texas are rewarded. Yet the state is changing. The growth of minority populations in the state may yet force changes in the economic, social, and political character of Texas.

To gain a better understanding of the power of the mythical Texas, students may want to watch such motion pictures such as *Giant*, *The Alamo*, *The Searchers* or *The Last Picture Show* or such television programs as *Dallas*, *Lonesome Dove*, *The Lone Ranger* or *Walker, Texas Ranger*.

This chapter is designed to introduce you to the background, nature, and context of Texas politics and government. The main topic headings for this chapter are:

- The Origins of Texas Politics and Government
- The Ideological Context
- The Economy of Texas
- Wealth and Poverty in Texas

In each section, there are certain facts and ideas that you should strive to understand. Many are in boldface type and appear in both the narrative and in the glossary at the end of the book. Other ideas, dates, facts, events, people, etc. are more difficult to pull out of the narrative. (Keep in mind that studying for objective tests [multiple choice, T/F] is different than studying for essay tests. See the Study Guide section on test taking for hints on study skills.)

In general, after you finish reading and studying this chapter, you should understand the following:

- the origins of Texas government and politics, the land and people of Texas and how these people have historically influenced and continue to influence their government and politics
- the ideological context for Texas politics and government, and how ideas Texans share with other Americans have been modified by Texas's unique experience
- the Texas economy and its evolution from a colonial, land-based economy to a modern, information-based economy
- wealth and poverty in Texas and how those factors influence government and politics in the state

Chapter Outline and Key Points

In this section, you are provided with a basic outline of the chapter and key concepts and terms you should know. Use this outline to develop a complete study guide for the chapter. Use the space provided in this workbook to write notes from your reading, defining the terms and explaining the concepts listed below. You may wish to rewrite the material in your notebook or computer. However you work up this outline, the effort and information will help you study and remember the material in preparation for your tests, assignments, and papers.

The Origins of Texas Politics and Government

size of Texas—

variety of landforms in Texas—

Texas population in 2005—

U.S. and Texas ethnic percentages of population—

Native Americans

Native Americans in Texas today—

Native American legacy in Texas—

Tejas—

gambling on reservations in Texas—

Hispanics

   four institutions of Spanish colonization—

   Mexican independence from Spain—

   growth of Hispanic population in Texas history—

   Hispanics in Texas politics—

   party affiliation and Hispanic population—

African Americans

   African American population before 1836—

   bulk of African American settlement in Texas—

   sharecropper system—

   African American officer holders in Texas—

   Wallace B. Jefferson—

Asian Americans

   first permanent resident Asian Americans in Texas—

   growth of Asian population

   Vietnamese immigrants—

   Asian American population in Texas as of 2000—

   Asian American officer holders in Texas—

Anglos

   Anglos—

   empresario program—

   increase in Anglo immigration from Texas's independence to Civil War—

   post-Civil War Anglo immigration—

365

Anglo domination of Texas politics—

The Contemporary Population of Texas

patterns of settlement established by Texas's first residents—

2000 and 1990 Census reports on Texas population—

Texas population compared to other states—

urbanization of Texas—

metropolitan growth accounts for Texas's population growth in 1990s—

change in ethnic demographics in Texas in 1990s—

impact of Hispanic population growth in Texas—

issues important to Hispanics—

population trends in Texas—

relative decline of Anglo population—

policy changes anticipated because of Hispanic population growth—

<u>**The Ideological Context**</u>

The Texas Creed

Texas Creed—

the battle for Texas—

five ideas of the Texas Creed:

Individualism

individualism—

landowners' ethos—

frontier era—

Texas Rangers—

cowboy—

Liberty

    liberty—

    differences between Anglo settlers and their Mexican governors—

    Texas independence—

    Alamo—

    heroes of the Alamo—

    symbolic power of the Alamo—

    Tejanos—

Constitutionalism and Democracy

    constitutionalism—

    Texans' desire for democracy—

    Jeffersonian democracy—

Equality

    equality—

    Texas idea of equality—

    Texas Equal Rights Amendment—

    T. R. Fehrenbach description of African American slavery in Texas—

    Anglo response to Hispanics—

    American Creed—

Political Ideologies in Texas

    politics—

    the Texas Creed and ideas about government—

kinds of conflict in Texas over proper role of government (which determine a person's political ideology)—

The Four Ideologies (Figure 20.1)—

Libertarians

    libertarianism—

    Libertarian Party in Texas—

Populists

    populists—

    People's Party in Texas—

    Farmer's Alliance—

Conservatives

    American conservatism—

    conservatives in contemporary Texas—

Liberals

    liberalism—

    modern liberalism in Texas—

two reasons ideologies in Texas are important:

    1)

    2)

The Economy of Texas

Cotton

the money crop—

commercial center of Texas from 1840s to 1880s—

plantation system replaced, post-Civil War—

percentage of Texas's cotton production as part of total U.S. production—

total cotton production receipts in Texas in 2000—

Cattle

late-nineteenth century in Texas—

XIT Ranch—

Petroleum

influence for much of twentieth century—

Spindletop—

Santa Rita No. 1—

OPEC—

oil boom of 1970s—

oil bust of 1980s—

petroleum industry portion of state's gross state product in 1981 and 1999—

The Contemporary Economy

gross state product in 2008—

change in Texas economy since 1980s—

area in Texas currently with greatest economic growth—

service sector—

Texas and national economy—

growth in jobs—

unemployment—

globalization of Texas economy—

industries accounting for 66 percent of Texas's exports in 2000—

Texas exports revenue—

advanced technology—

How Should Texas Educate Students of Limited English Proficiency?—

<u>Wealth and Poverty in Texas</u>

distribution of income in Texas—

Texas Family Income by Decade, 1980s-2000s (Figure 20.2)—

factors contributing to income disparity—

Texas ranking in income inequality—

Texas ranking of high school graduates and the influence of that factor—

poverty more pronounced in Texas than in nation as a whole—

ethnic breakdown of poverty in Texas—

Texas in Comparison: The Socio-Economic Context in the States—

extreme poverty for young children in Texas significantly higher than U.S. average—

Houston's "8-F Crowd"—

George Brown—

George Bush—

Bill Clements—

Clayton Williams—

Ross Perot—

other wealthy Texas businessmen in politics—

Research Ideas and Possible Paper Topics

1) Select a state and compare Texas to that state according to economic structure, political ideologies, and population.

2) Discuss what you think might be important demographic and economic changes in Texas during the next 40 years. How might these changes affect partisan politics and public policy issues in Texas?

3) Select five major historical events in Texas history and explain how these events contributed to the development of the Texan Creed.

4) Do research into the history of the Texas Rangers examining the view of the heroic law enforcement cowboys in Texas Anglo mythology versus the view of vigilante justice in the eyes of many minority groups in Texas.

5) Examine the mythology of Texas and how it ignores the state's dismal record of poverty and treatment of minorities.

Web sites

Every ten years, the **U.S. Census** conducts a count and study of the U.S. population. The 2000 census contains a wealth of information about the nation's population as well as individual state population, including Texas.

> www.census.gov

Lone Star Junction is a nonprofit organization chartered by the state of Texas. The organization provides facts and details about Texas history, giving particular attention to Texas's early history.

> www.lsjunction.com

The Institute of Texan Cultures is an educational center established and maintained by the University of Texas at San Antonio. The center's primary objective is to provide the public with information about the history of the diverse cultures of Texas. The center's Web site includes photographs of Texas settlers, primary, and secondary documents on Texas history, and other material helpful to understanding Texas's diverse cultures.

> www.texancultures.utsa.edu/public/index.htm

Texas Historical Commission is a state agency, created by the Texas Legislature to preserve Texas's architectural, archaeological, and cultural landmarks and inform the public about Texas history.

> www.thc.state.tx.us/aboutus/abtdefault.html

The **Daughters of the Republic of Texas Library** is supported and maintained by the Daughters of the Republic of Texas. The library assists researchers interested in the history of the Alamo, San Antonio and Texas.

www.drtl.org

The **Center for Public Policy** is a Texas nonprofit, nonpartisan research organization studying policy issues involving low- and moderate-income Texas. Its Web site features a wide-range of information about poverty in Texas including **Texas Poverty: An Overview,** which examines the demographics and characteristics of poverty in the state.

http://www.cppp.org

Practice Tests

MULTIPLE CHOICE QUESTIONS

1) The largest minority ethnic group in Texas is
   a. African Americans.
   b. Asian Americans.
   c. Native Americans.
   d. Hispanics.

2) Texas politics and government have been dominated since independence from Mexico in 1836 by which ethnic population?
   a. African Americans
   b. Hispanics
   c. Anglos
   d. Native Americans

3) The majority of Texans have lived in urban areas since the
   a. 1890s.
   b. 1920s.
   c. 1940s.
   d. 1960s.

4) Which of the following historical events was important to the development of the Texan Creed concept of individualism?
   a. the American revolution
   b. World War II
   c. the frontier era
   d. the presidential election of Lyndon B. Johnson

5) The historical concept of equality, which developed in Texas in the nineteenth century, reflected a society based on land ownership and afforded equality to
   a. male and female Anglos only.
   b. all ethnic groups.
   c. Hispanics and Anglos.
   d. male Anglos only.

6) In contemporary Texas, conservatives are prominent in
   a. both of the major political parties.
   b. only the Democratic Party.
   c. the Republican Party.
   d. the Populist Party

7) Liberals favor a government that
   a. promotes an ordered liberty.
   b. regulates individual behavior.
   c. promotes extreme individualism.
   d. promotes equality.

8) Which of the following sectors of the Texas economy began a serious decline in the 1980s?
   a. cotton
   b. cattle
   c. computer
   d. petroleum

9) Between 1998 and 2000, Texas ranked _____ among the 50 states in income inequality between rich and poor families.
   a. third
   b. 15th
   c. 20th
   d. 31st

10) Which of the following is not an example of wealthy Texas businessmen who has taken the leap into electoral politics?
    a. David Dewhurst
    b. David Crockett
    c. George W. Bush
    d. Tony Sanchez

TRUE/FALSE QUESTIONS

1) Texas is the second-largest state in population and in territory.

2) By 2003, Hispanics had achieved considerable political clout in Texas.

3) Texas's minority populations have increased much less rapidly than the Anglo population.

4) The frontier era in Texas proved important to the development of equality.

5) Cotton, cattle, and petroleum were important sectors of Texas's early economy.

COMPARE AND CONTRAST

the Texan Creed and the American Creed

liberalism and conservatism

the early Texas economy and the contemporary Texas economy

wealth and poverty in Texas and wealth and poverty in the nation

Hispanics, African-Americans, and Anglos

ESSAY AND SHORT ANSWER QUESTIONS

1) What are the major landforms in Texas, and where are they found in Texas?

2) What important demographic changes have occurred in Texas between 1990 and 2000?

3) Why was the Alamo important to many Texans' concept of liberty?

4) How had the Texas economic history of dependence upon cattle, cotton and oil changed in the late twentieth century?

5) How are Texas's minority ethnic groups affected by poverty?

ANSWERS TO STUDY EXERCISES

Multiple Choice Answers

1) d
2) c
3) c
4) c
5) d
6) a
7) d
8) d
9) a
10) b

True/False Answers

1) T
2) T
3) F
4) F
5) T

CHAPTER 21
THE TEXAS CONSTITUTION

Chapter Goals and Learning Objectives

Like many states, particularly those in the South, Texas has drafted and adopted several constitutions. Constitutions are social contracts which create governments, outline civil rights and liberties as a means of protecting citizens from their governments, and institute procedures for peaceful change in the form of the process of constitutional amendments. Like all constitutions, Texas's constitutions reflect specific historical circumstances of the periods in which these documents were written. Texas's current constitution is a reaction to Reconstruction, yet the amendments to the Texas Constitution reflect the impact of modern living on a structural foundation laid in a post-Civil War political and social environment. As is the case with many state constitutions, particularly in the South and Southwest, Texas's current constitution, the Texas Constitution of 1876, is long, confusing, poorly structured and hindered by an over-reliance on amendments that undermine the very nature of a constitution—a set of basic laws for governing.

This chapter is designed to introduce you to the background, structure, and operation of the Texas Constitution. The main topic headings for this chapter are:

- The Development of the Texas Constitution
- The Current Texas Constitution
- Constitutional Revision

In each section, there are certain facts and ideas that you should strive to understand. Many are in boldface type and appear in both the narrative and in the glossary at the end of the book. Other ideas, dates, facts, events, people, etc. are more difficult to pull out of the narrative. (Keep in mind that studying for objective tests [multiple choice, T/F] is different than studying for essay tests. See the Study Guide section on test taking for hints on study skills.)

In general, after you finish reading and studying this chapter, you should understand the following:

- the development of the Texas Constitution and the legacies of Texas's first five constitutions
- the current Texas Constitution, the convention that framed it, its provisions, and criticisms of it
- constitutional revision in Texas, both piecemeal change through constitutional amendments and comprehensive revision efforts

In this section, you are provided with a basic outline of the chapter and key concepts and terms you should know. Use this outline to develop a complete study guide for the chapter. Use the space provided in this workbook to write notes from your reading, defining the terms and explaining the concepts listed below. You may wish to rewrite the material in your notebook or computer. However you work up this outline, the effort and information will help you study and remember the material in preparation for your tests, assignments, and papers.

The Development of the Texas Constitution

definition of a constitution—

The 1836 Constitution

Texas as a Mexican state—

Republic of Texas—

Texas Constitution of 1836—

Washington-on-the-Brazos—

typical American features of the Texas Constitution of 1836—

Spanish Mexican law influence on 1836 Constitution—

The 1845 Constitution

annexation—

Texas Constitution of 1845—

simple, straight-forward form of 1845 Constitution—

the government under the 1845 Constitution—

General Provisions—

The 1861 Constitution

secession—

Texas Constitution of 1861—

slavery and states' rights—

emancipation in 1861 Constitution—

The 1866 Constitution

presidential Reconstruction—

Texas Constitution of 1866—

restructure of executive branch—

legislative branch changes—

The 1869 Constitution

end of presidential Reconstruction—

additional requirements placed by Congress on Texas's readmission to the union—

constitutional convention of 1868—

Texas Constitution of 1869—

new constitution met requirements of congressional Reconstruction—

<u>The Current Texas Constitution</u>

effects of Reconstruction on current Texas Constitution—

Governor Richard Coke—

Texas Constitutional Convention of 1875—

delegates to the 1875 constitutional convention—

Reasons for 1876 Constitution

three factors which explain the adoption of the Texas Constitution of 1876:

       1)

       2)

       3)

"retrenchment and reform"—

motives of the convention delegates as to the way government should be active—

Provisions of the 1876 Constitution

liberal constitution—

statutory constitution—

Articles of the Texas Constitution (Table 21.1)—

Texas Bill of Rights (Article 1)—

separation of powers (Article 2)—

legislative branch (Article 3)—

executive branch (Article 4)—

judicial branch (Article 5)—

education (Article 7)—

constitutional provision on local government—

constitutional provision on fiscal policies—

dedicated funds—

amending the Texas Constitution (Article 17)—

by 2006, Texas Constitution amended how many times?—

Voter Turnout for Constitutional Amendments—

Criticisms of the 1876 Constitution

too many amendments—

Amendments to the Texas Constitution, 1877-2006 (Table 21.1)—

plural executive—

part-time legislature—

structure of judiciary and election of judges—

restrictions on local government—

Constitutional Revision

piecemeal revision—

comprehensive revision—

Piecemeal Revision Efforts

Piecemeal revision—

addition of amendments—

Citizens' Advisory Committee—

Angelo State University Students' Texas Constitution—

efforts by Governor John Connally—

Representative Anna Mowery—

2005 amendment on marriage—

The Texas Marriage Amendment—

Texas in Comparison: State Constitutions—

Comprehensive Revision Efforts

first attempt in 1877—

1917 legislative resolution and Governor Jim Ferguson—

efforts between 1919 and 1949—

efforts by Governor Beauford Jester—

1967-1968 Constitutional Revision Commission—

The 1974 Constitutional Convention—

Constitutional Revision Commission—

legislature meets as constitutional convention—

several reasons for failure of the constitutional revision effort—

1)

2)

3)

4)

Committees of the 1974 Constitutional Convention—

right-to-work—

Speaker Price Daniel, Jr.—

cockroach—

revisionist—

1975 Constitutional Amendments

eight proposed amendments—

Sharpstown scandal—

Governor Dolph Briscoe—

1999 Constitutional Revision Effort

Representatives Rob Junnell and Senator Bill Ratliff—

proposed changes in structure of Texas government—

Research Ideas and Possible Paper Topics

1) Scholarly dispute exists regarding the level of political experience and training of delegates to the Constitutional Convention of 1875. Research the lives of three of the delegates and evaluate whether they did or did not have the political experience and training necessary to draft an impressive constitution.

2) The current Texas Constitution has been criticized for its failure to provide an adequate foundation for governing in the twenty-first century. If you were a member of the Constitutional Revision Commission, which provisions of the Constitution would you change and why?

3) Imagine you have been elected governor of the state of Texas. Would you support a reform that would allow you to have appointment power over key offices in the executive branch? Is so, why? If not, why not?

4) Students in the Department of Government at Angelo State University developed a proposed new state constitution that was presented to the Texas Legislature for consideration in 1999. What were its provisions? Who carried the proposed constitution to the legislature and why? What were the results?

5) Examine the reactions of Texans to Reconstruction. Why did Texans react so vigorously against it, and what where the problems they had with the administration of Governor E.J. Davis? Were their objections sound in your opinion?

Web sites

The Web site maintained by the **Texas Legislature** offers a copy of the entire Texas Constitution and features that allow users to search the Constitution according to concept or exact wording.

http://tlo2.tlc.state.tx.us/txconst/toc.html

In 1969, the Texas legislature created **The Legislative Reference Library**. The Library's primary purpose is to serve as a research and reference center for the legislature and its staff. The library's Web site allows users to review past and current constitutional amendments by session/year, or by subject, by clicking on "Amendments to the Texas Constitution" and "Proposed Amendments to the Constitution."

www.lrl.state.tx.us

The Texas Constitutions' Digitization Project is presented by the Tarlton Law Library of the University of Texas at Austin. The project makes digital versions of Texas's constitutions available online and provides explanatory texts. The project also offers an excellent list of links to other Web sites related to Texas constitutional history.

http://tarlton.law.utexas.edu/constitutions

Texas Reform Net, which describes itself as "a gateway to reform efforts and groups throughout the State of Texas," hosts a Web site titled "A Revised Texas Constitution," featuring a proposed Texas reformed constitution, an annotated 1975 constitutional proposal, and other related links.

http://www.constitution.org/reform/us/tx/const/rev_con.htm

Practice Tests

MULTIPLE CHOICE QUESTIONS

1)   _____ led to the drafting of the 1861 constitution.
   a.   Secession
   b.   Presidential reconstruction
   c.   Congressional reconstruction
   d.   Independence

2)   The current Texas Constitution is described as
   a.   a liberal constitution.
   b.   an organic, restrictive constitution
   c.   a populist constitution.
   d.   an anti-populist constitution.

3)   Reconstruction is one of the reasons that the Texas Constitution is
   a.   similar to the U.S. Constitution.
   b.   different from previous Texas constitutions.
   c.   similar to previous Texas constitutions.
   d.   similar to the Confederate Constitution.

4)   Texas has the _____ constitution in the United States.
   a.   tenth longest
   b.   ninth longest
   c.   longest
   d.   second longest

384

5)	The Texas Constitution of 1876 was not only a reaction to Reconstruction but was also the product of
	a.	the governorship of E.J. Davis.
	b.	a national movement for a politics of substantive issues and restrictive constitutionalism.
	c.	a complex mix of motives among the delegates on the manner in which government should be active.
	d.	All of the above.

6)	By 2006, the Texas Constitution has been amended
	a.	439 times.
	b.	332 times.
	c.	128 times.
	d.	 27 times.

7)	Which of the following is not a criticism of the Texas Constitution of 1876?
	a.	it is one of the longest constitutions in the United States
	b.	it limits the executive power of the governor to implement public policy
	c.	it severely limits the efficiency of local government
	d.	it lacks a bill of rights

8)	One of the reasons the 1974 Constitutional Convention failed was because of
	a.	extreme partisan bickering.
	b.	the lack of legislators present at the Convention.
	c.	the presence of cockroaches and revisionists at the Convention.
	d.	All of the above.

9)	In November of 1975, voters rejected eight constitutional amendments in part because of the
	a.	Sharpstown scandal.
	b.	opposition of Lieutenant Bill Hobby to the amendments.
	c.	the decision of the Supreme Court on Texas's sodomy law.
	d.	the opposition of Governor John Connally to the amendments.

10)	Efforts to revise the current Texas Constitution by piecemeal and comprehensive methods have
	a.	dramatically changed the basic structure of Texas government
	b.	not fundamentally changed the basic structure of Texas government.
	c.	changed the basic structure of the judicial branch.
	d.	changed the basic structure of the executive branch.

TRUE/FALSE QUESTIONS

1) Immediately before its annexation by the United States, Texas was an official territory of the United States.

2) One reason the administration of Governor E.J. Davis was controversial was because he opposed universal public education.

3) The Texas Constitution of 1876 mandates a balanced state budget.

4) Under the Texas Constitution of 1876, all state court judges are elected to office by partisan ballot.

5) Governor Dolph Briscoe announced his support of constitution revision during the 1974 Texas Constitution Convention.

COMPARE AND CONTRAST:

the current Texas Constitution with the U.S. Constitution

the Texas Constitution with other state constitutions

the Texas Bill of Rights with the U.S. Bill of Rights

cockroaches and revisionists

liberal constitutions and restrictive constitutions

ESSAY AND SHORT ANSWER QUESTIONS

1) Select one of Texas's six constitutions and explain the historical circumstances that gave rise to and helped shape that constitution.

2) Why did Texans choose to adopt a restrictive constitution in 1876?

3) What are some of the weaknesses of the current Texas Constitution?

4) Discuss constitutional revision aimed at the executive branch.

5) Why did the 1974 Constitutional Convention fail?

ANSWERS TO STUDY QUESTIONS

Multiple Choice Answers

1) a
2) b
3) b
4) c
5) a
6) c
7) d
8) c
9) a
10) b

True/False Answers

1) F
2) F
3) T
4) T
5) F

CHAPTER 22
LOCAL GOVERNMENT AND POLITICS IN TEXAS

Chapter Goals and Learning Objectives

Most students who have grown up in this country have, no matter what level of previous governmental studies, some intrinsic understanding of national and state politics and the three branches of government. Watching TV, sitting through civics class, or going to movies, students hear about at least some aspects of the national and state governments. However, few students have a real sense of what local government is, how it works, and how it affects them (except, perhaps, when a student receives a ticket from a city police officer).

Local government is comprised of political subdivisions within state governments. There are three basic categories of political subdivisions that can be characterized as local governments: city governments, county governments, and special district governments.

City governments are chartered by the state and most of them can conduct their governmental affairs independently of state government as long as they are not in conflict with the state constitution. County governments are essentially branch offices of state government and act as the local entity that administers and executes state law. Special districts are the fastest-growing form of local governments in Texas, serving single government purposes for specific geographic areas, governmental purposes not available in the area from other levels of local government.

This chapter is designed to introduce you to local politics and government in Texas. The main topic headings for this chapter are:

- The Development of Local Government in Texas
- Counties
- Cities
- Special Districts

In each section, there are certain facts and ideas that you should strive to understand. Many are in boldface type and appear in both the narrative and in the glossary at the end of the book. Other ideas, dates, facts, events, people, etc. are more difficult to pull from the narrative. (Keep in mind that studying for objective tests is different than studying for essay tests. See the Study Guide section on test taking for hints on study skills.)

In general, after you finish reading and studying this chapter, you should understand the following:

- the development of Texas local government including historical and constitutional influences
- the structure, role and function of counties as local governments and administrative arms of the state
- city governance in Texas and how the forms, powers and politics of municipal government have changed
- the many and varied special district governments in Texas with an emphasis on water districts and school districts

Chapter Outline and Key Points

In this section, you are provided with a basic outline of the chapter and key concepts and terms you should know. Use this outline to develop a complete study guide for the chapter. Use the space provided in this workbook to write notes from your reading, defining the terms and explaining the concepts listed below. You may wish to rewrite the material in your notebook or computer. However you work up this outline, the effort and information will help you study and remember the material in preparation for your tests, assignments, and papers.

three basic categories of political subdivisions that can be categorized as local government (and their numbers):

1)

2)

3)

The Development of Local Government in Texas

local government in Texas under Spanish and Mexican rule—

municipal corporations—

counties in the Republic of Texas and when Texas joined the Union—

early public education concerns—

local government under the Texas Constitution of 1876—

home rule—

home rule comes to Texas cities—

<u>**Counties**</u>

number of Texas counties—

Brewster County—

Harris County—

Loving County—

Texas Association of Counties—

multiple functions of counties—

Texas Counties and Population—

Structure of Counties

fragmented power—

county offices—

four-year terms—

County Commissioners' Court

county judge—

commissioners' court—

county commissioners—

precincts—

roads and bridges—

redistricting county commissioners precincts—

Avery v. *Midland County* (1968)—

District Attorneys and County Attorneys

district attorney (DA)—

regulatory zoning authority—

Texas Association of Counties—

Elgin Bank v. *Travis County* (Tex.App.-Austin, 1995)—

platting—

administrative functions—

county responsibility for elections—

Help America Vote Act of 2002—

Finances of County Government

revenue for county services—

property tax—

fee revenue—

counties propose constitution amendment regarding state mandates—

Cities

number of Texas cities—

largest city—

size variation of Texas cities—

home rule cities—

home rule requirements—

powers of city government and Local Government code—

general-law cities—

flexibility—

city charter—

no neat categories—

tension between local and state authority—

Forms of City Governments

Organizational Chart: City of Waller (General Law) (Figure 22.1)—

Types of Government and Election Systems in Texas's Top Ten Cities (Table 22.1)—

four general types of city government:

1) Weak Mayor-Council—

Organizational Chart: City of White Oak (Weak Mayor) (Figure 22.2)—

2) Strong Mayor-Council—

Organizational Chart: City of Houston (Strong Mayor) (Figure 22.3)—

Strong Mayor, Weak Mayor—

3) Council-Manager—

Organizational Chart: City of Austin (Council-Manager) (Figure 22.4)—

4) City Commission—

Galveston—

city commission governments in Texas today—

Authority and Functions of City Governments

multiple functions of cities—

collision of public needs and private property rights—

Texas Municipal League—

Finances of City Governments

sources of city revenue—

bond sales—

effect on Texas cities of eliminating federal funding to local governments
by Reagan administration—

capital budgeting by Texas cities—

sewage and water treatment—

innovative policies involving tax incentives—

Municipal Annexation

annexation—

Municipal Annexation Act, 1963—

extraterritorial jurisdiction (ETJ)—

limited-purpose annexation—

strip annexation—

amendments to Municipal Annexation Act—

steps required of cities to annex after 1999 amendments—

writ of mandamus—

Politics and Representation in City Governments

nonpartisan elections—

municipal election dates—

at-large election—

at-large-by-place election—

single-member districts—

cumulative voting—

proportional representation—

effect of election changes on ethnic and racial make-up of city governments—

Special Districts

Special Districts in Texas (Table 22.2)—

reasons for special district governments—

Water Districts

Texas Constitution and water management—

Water Code—

water districts—

TCEQ—

School Districts

local school districts in Texas and comparison to other states—

elected school trustees—

division of state into school districts—

no uniformity in size—

local school districts—

State Board of Education—

Texas Education Agency—

home-rule school districts—

charter schools—

school district elections, legislation and litigation—

property taxes—

school-finance revisions and problems—

Research Ideas and Possible Paper Topics

1) Select two Texas cities that are demographically diverse and that hold two different types of elections, specifically at-large city council elections and single-member districts' council elections. Evaluate the policies supported by the councils according to whether or not the policies address the political interests of the minority ethnic groups in the two cities.

2) Annexation is a politically explosive issue of local government. To gain a better sense of the advantages and disadvantages of the annexation, select a city in Texas that has had direct experience with the issue. Interview city officials about their opinion of the annexation and interview residents who reside in a newly annexed area.

3) Attend an open city council meeting in your city. Identify the city officials who attended the meeting, explain the meeting's agenda, and describe the extent of public participation in the meeting. Then, based on your experience at the meeting, discuss whether or not you think local government is efficient and democratic.

4) Many Texans live in suburbs that use special district governments known as MUDs (municipal utility districts). What are MUDs? What are their function, how are they formed, how are they operated and how do they fund their services?

5) Public school financing in Texas remains a fluid and controversial issue for school districts and state government. What are some of the current problems surrounding public school financing in the state and in your local school district?

Web sites

Most **Texas cities** have Web sites. To access a city's Web site, click on the name of the city on this Web site by the **Texas State Library and Archive Commission**.
http://www.statelocalgov.net/state-tx.cfm#City

Most **Texas counties** have Web sites. To access a county's Web site simply click the link for the county as listed on this Web site provided by **Online Texas**.
http://www.state.tx.us/category.jsp?language=eng&categoryId=6.2.1

The Texas Association of Counties maintains a Web site that offers users information about the Association's membership, activities, publications, legislative bills related to counties, and more.
www.county.org

The Texas Municipal League is a private, non-profit association providing legislative, legal, and educational services to member cities in Texas.

http://www.tml.org

The **Texas Association of Regional Councils** serves as a coordinating entity for the local Councils of Government (COGs) in Texas. Texas COGs are regional planning boards in Texas to assist local governments in the given regions to coordinate local services. The TARC's Web site provides local government information, including information regarding special district governments.

www.txregionalcouncil.org/index.htm

The **Local Government Code** for the State of Texas is available online.

http://tlo2.tlc.state.tx.us/statutes/statutes.html

The **Special District Government Code** for the State of Texas is available online.

http://tlo2.tlc.state.tx.us/statutes/sd.toc.htm

The **Texas Education Agency** Web site provides information about Texas schools and links to all independent school districts in the state.

www.tea.state.tx.us

Practice Tests

MULTIPLE CHOICE QUESTIONS

1) In county government, which of the following is not a responsibility of the county commissioner's court?
   a. set the county budget
   b. set county tax rates
   c. general ordinance making
   d. redistrict county commissioners' precincts

2) The most common form of municipal government for home-rule cities in Texas is
   a. weak mayor-council.
   b. strong mayor-council.
   c. council-manager.
   d. city commission.

3) In the council-manager form of city government, who hires and directs most city employees?
   a. the city council
   b. the city manager
   c. the mayor
   d. All of the above.

4) A form of city government, no longer in use in Texas, in which elected members served on the governing body and also served as head administrators of city programs is called
   a. weak mayor-council.
   b. city commission.
   c. strong mayor-council.
   d. council-manager.

5) The highest priority for municipal capital budgeting is for
   a. police and fire protection.
   b. recreational services.
   c. health services.
   d. sewage and water treatment.

6) In Texas, _____ are granted the power of annexation.
   a. county governments
   b. city governments
   c. school districts
   d. water districts

7) Most large cities in Texas abandoned at-large elections in favor of either
   a. cumulative voting or proportional representation.
   b. proportional representation or a mixed system of single-member districts and cumulative voting.
   c. single-member districts or a mixed system of single-member districts and some at-large.
   d. cumulative voting or single-member districts.

8) What kind of city election system is likely to produce results that closely reflect a city's population?
   a. proportional representation
   b. at-large-by-place
   c. appointed
   d. recall

9) Special district governments are often used rather than multifunction governments such as counties and cities in Texas because
   a. some policy areas must be addressed on a larger basis than cities or counties.
   b. constitutional limits on counties make it difficult to take on new tasks.
   c. some functions are better served by a single-focus governmental entity.
   d. All of the above.

10) The most common type of special district government is a
   a. school district.
   b. municipal utility district.
   c. water district.
   d. metropolitan transit authority.

TRUE/FALSE QUESTIONS

1) The district attorney is an elected official who prosecutes criminal cases.

2) The county treasurer is an official appointed by a district judge to audit county finances.

3) Strong mayor-council city governments do not hire city managers.

4) In 1999, amendments adopted to the 1998 Texas Municipal Annexation Act granted county governments the power of annexation.

5) Special districts are usually unifunctional.

COMPARE AND CONTRAST

city governments and county governments

school districts and water districts

weak mayor-council and strong mayor-council

council-manager and city commission

home rule cities and general law cities

ESSAY AND SHORT ANSWER QUESTIONS

1) Discuss the political philosophy behind annexation and offer an argument opposing or supporting the political philosophy.

2) Discuss the reasons behind the adoption of home rule and explain how home rule cities differ from general law cities.

3) Discuss the authority and functions of county government.

4) How do special districts differ from county governments?

5)   In your opinion, which form of city government is more preferable: weak mayor-council or strong mayor-council?

ANSWERS TO STUDY EXERCISES

Multiple Choice Answers

1) c
2) c
3) b
4) b
5) d
6) b
7) c
8) a
9) d
10) a

True/False Answers

1) T
2) F
3) T
4) F
5) T

CHAPTER 23
THE TEXAS LEGISLATURE

Chapter Goals and Learning Objectives

Back in 1866 Mark Twain said, "No man's life, liberty, or property is safe while the legislature is in session." The same is often said every two years of the Texas legislature when it is gaveled into session in Austin in January of odd-numbered years for a 140-day regular session.

A part-time body whose members are paid $7,200 a year for their services, this so-called "citizens legislature" was conceived for a rural state in 1875 by Texans angry over heavy-handed Reconstruction rule by Carpetbagger Radical Republicans from the North. Those angry Texans eviscerated the governorship and met their desire for a weak legislature in the Constitution of 1876 so as never to suffer a powerful government over them again.

Some would say that their efforts were quite fruitful if, indeed, the goal was to create a government of inefficiency in general and control by the wealthy elite in particular. The Texas legislature reflects the Old South concept of protection of the wealthy landholder. Once controlled solely by conservative Democrats, the institution in now run by conservative Republicans, both groups often taking their direction from powerful special interest groups that serve as the institutional memory for the body every two years.

The dominance of the Republican Party in Texas from a minority party to the majority party is illustrated in changes in the Texas legislature. The legislature is not structured along minority/majority party lines because of the post-Reconstruction dominance of the Democratic Party. There was no need to organize the legislature by party membership because the vast majority of the membership was Democratic. Today, both the Texas House of Representatives and the Texas Senate are led and dominated by Republicans.

This chapter is designed to introduce you to understand the history, structure, purpose, activities and decision-making process of the Texas legislature. The main topic headings for this chapter are:

- The Origins of the Legislative Branch
- The State Constitution and the Legislative Branch of Government
- Legislative Membership: Representing the Public
- How the Texas Legislature is Organized
- The Law-making and Budgeting Function of the Legislature
- How Legislators Make Decisions
- The Legislature and the Governor

In each section, there are certain facts and ideas that you should strive to understand. Many are in boldface type and appear in both the narrative and in the glossary at the end of the book. Other ideas, dates, facts, events, people, etc. are more difficult to pull from the narrative. (Keep in mind that studying for objective tests is different than studying for essay tests. See the Study Guide section on test taking for hints on study skills.)

In general, after you finish reading and studying this chapter, you should understand the following:

- the historical and constitutional roots of the legislative branch, its evolution from its roots in Mexico to its contemporary structure
- the structure of legislative branch under the Texas Constitution and how legislators perform their duties under that constitution
- legislative membership: how members represent the people, how they are elected, and their personal and political characteristics
- how the Texas legislature is organized, including ways the leadership and opposition organize and operate
- the law-making and budgeting function of the legislature, including the stages of the legislative and budgeting process
- how Texas legislators make decisions and how their voting choices are influenced
- the relationship between the legislature and the governor and how the governor influences the legislature

Chapter Outline and Key Points

In this section, you are provided with a basic outline of the chapter and key concepts and terms you should know. Use this outline to develop a complete study guide for the chapter. Use the space provided in this workbook to write notes from your reading, defining the terms and explaining the concepts listed below. You may wish to rewrite the material in your notebook or computer. However you work up this outline, the effort and information will help you study and remember the material in preparation for your tests, assignments, and papers.

constitutional amendments—

redistrict—

impeach—

79th Legislature—

80th Legislature—

The Origins of the Legislative Branch

predecessors to the Texas legislature—

bicameral Congress under the Constitution of the Republic of Texas—

1st Legislature of the State of Texas—

first legislature to meet under the Texas Constitution of 1876—

Texas legislatures historically have governed a society of mixed populations—

African American representation during and after Reconstruction—

white supremacists regain power over the legislature after Reconstruction—

The State Constitution and the Legislative Branch of Government

bicameral legislature—

size of Texas Senate—

size of Texas House—

bill must pass both houses—

responsibility of initiating action to raise revenue—

responsibility of approving gubernatorial nominations—

impeachment process—

Article 3, Texas Constitution and rules governing the legislative process—

Constitutional Provisions Affecting Legislators

Constitutional Requirements Affecting Texas Legislators (Table 23.1)—

Length of Terms

length of terms for House—

length of terms for Senate—

staggered term—

term limits?—

Temporary Acting Legislators

Article 16, section 72 amended—

replacement for active military service—

Compensation

Texas legislative salaries compared to other states—

monthly salary—

1974 constitutional amendment regarding legislative pay—

per diem—

Sessions of the Legislature

biennial legislature—

regular session—

special (called) session—

Legislatures in the United States—

<u>Legislative Membership: Representing the Public</u>

Sam Rayburn—

other Texas leaders who served in the legislature—

Variables Affecting Members' Elections

Redistricting

single-member districts—

redistricting—

census—

approximate size of Senate district after 2000 census—

approximate size of House district after 2000 census—

gerrymander—

U.S. Voting Rights Act—

U.S. Supreme Court divided on racial gerrymandering issue—

1991 redistricting—

2001 redistricting—

Legislative Redistricting Board—

courts' influence on 2001 redistricting—

Republican controlled legislature changes congressional districts in 78th Legislature—

Dewhurst and two-thirds rule—

Texas Democrats battle against Republican effort to change redistricted lines—

2006 Supreme Court decision on the Republican revisions—

Reelection Rates and Turnover of Membership

incumbents—

reelection rates after redistricting—

average tenure of incumbents in Texas legislature in 2005—

term limits—

Personal and Political Characteristics of Members

Texas House Membership, 1977-2007 (Figure 23.1)—

Texas Senate Membership, 1977-2007 (Figure 23.2)—

Occupation, Education, and Religion

nineteenth and early twentieth centuries—

decline of on set of occupations and growth of another today—

2005, percentage of businesspersons and attorneys—

possible reasons for continued domination of businesspersons and lawyers—

results of increasing number of Republicans—

2005, education characteristics—

religion characteristics from 1970s to 1990s—

Gender, Race, and Age

historically male—

current trend—

percentage of women by 2005—

differences among the states—

2007 Texas House membership—

age characteristics—

2005 average age of House and Senate—

Political Party

past dominance of Democratic Party—

contemporary dominance of Republican Party—

Ideology

conservatives—

liberals—

populists—

libertarians—

Ideological Voting Patterns in the Texas House of Representatives—

distinct difference between legislative Democrats and legislative Republicans—

changes in party unity and diversification in Democrats and Republicans in legislature—

How the Texas Legislature is Organized

Leaders

president of the Texas Senate—

president pro-tempore (pro-tem)—

Speaker of the House—

critical factor in how the House operates—

evidence of majoritarian form of democracy in Texas legislature—

Committees

committee—

Types of Legislative Committees (Table 23.2)—

standing committees—

procedural committees—

substantive committees—

ad hoc and permanent subcommittees—

House and Senate membership on committees—

power of Lieutenant Governor and Speaker to appoint members to committees—

seniority—

committee work—

"dog and pony shows"—

Glossary of Legislative Lingo (Table 23.4)—

Organizing for Power and Influence in the Legislature

role of parties in the Congress, most legislatures and in the Texas legislature—

legislature party caucus—

in the absence of parties—

1980s and the first party caucuses—

strong party system antithetical to strong Speakers and Lieutenant Governors—

Leadership and Opposition in the House

Speaker—

custom in the 1800s—

Gus Mutscher—

1973 Dirty Thirty—

Bill Clayton—

Gib Lewis—

Pete Laney—

Tom Craddick—

the Speaker in 2007—

The Speaker's Race

Speaker's race—

pledge cards—

fundraising—

indictment of Tom DeLay—

Sharpstown scandal—

Speaker is a leader in recruiting and supporting other leaders but not in the partisan manner as in other states—

Speaker's lieutenants—

Speaker's team—

House Leadership and the Political Parties

Republican control of House before 2003—

Republican control—

House Democratic leaders supported bipartisanship and rejected attempts at party caucuses—

Speaker Laney—

Speaker Craddick—

in open balloting, both parties vote for the victor to avoid retaliation—

The Rise of Partisanship in the Texas House—

Speaker's Influence over Committees

Speakers' ability to stack important committees from controlling faction—

historically, norestraints on speaker's power to assign committee membership—
assignments as rewards and punishment—

1970s limited reform—

pledge card extortion—

1973 reform—

House Opposition and Political Parties

not along party lines traditionally—

party caucuses considered polarizing—

House Republican Caucus—

bipartisan committee leadership—

Organizing in the House Through Nonparty Caucuses

nonparty legislative caucus—

House Study Group—

House Research Organization—

Texas Conservative Coalition—

Texas Conservative Coalition Research Institute—

Legislative Study Group—

Leadership and Opposition in the Senate

constitution on the lieutenant governor—

1999 amendment requiring election of Lieutenant Governor from within Senate if vacancy in Senate Presidency—

Rick Perry and Bill Ratliff—

David Dewhurst—

Role of the Lieutenant Governor

stepping stone—

term of office—

change from two to four years—

pattern of long tenure—

Texas has one of the most powerful lieutenant governorships in the country—

powers of the Texas lieutenant governor—

Coalition Building in the Senate

Bill Hobby and Bob Bullock—

Rick Perry—

Bill Ratliff—

David Dewhurst—

Senate two-thirds rule—

The Law-making and Budgeting Function of the Legislature

legislative process—

What Is a Bill? What Is a Resolution?

resolutions—

bill—

joint resolution—

simple resolution—

concurrent resolution—

Rules, Procedures, and Internal Government

housekeeping resolutions—

How a Bill Becomes a Law

reading a bill—

filing and clerk assigning a number—

Basic Steps in the Texas Legislative Process (Figure 23.3)—

bills in committee—

committee chair decides—

public and formal hearings—

referral to subcommittee—

reported from subcommittee—

House and Senate diverge on what happens after committee—

The House Calendars Committee

Calendars Committee—

1993 changes in Calendar Committee's operation—

advance posting; public vote on placing on calendar—

circumventing this requirement—

The Senate Calendaring Function

Senate Administration Committee—

Local and Uncontested Calendar—

intent calendar—

bottleneck bill—

vote to suspend the rule on regular order of business—

two-thirds rule—

1979 Killer Bees—

414

2003 Ardmore 51—

Dewhurst, two-thirds rule "merely a Senate 'tradition'"—

"Bullock precedent"—

John Whitmire—

Bill Reaches the Floor

"floor"—

quorum—

first reading—

third reading—

second reading—

filibuster—

germane—

engrossed bill—

Two Bill Into One: The Final Stages

must be adopted by both houses in exactly the same form—

concur or not concur—

conference committees—

enrolled bill—

The Budgeting Process

states with annual budgets—

biennial budget—

1931, legislature designates Governor state's chief budget officer while giving State Board of Control responsibility to prepare the budget—

1951, Governor Shivers moves budget function into governor's office—

1951 Legislative Budget Board (LBB) implemented—

legislature ignores governor's proposed budget in favor of LBB's budget proposals—

balanced budget—

deficit spending—

debt—

growth of Texas economy for 2006-2007—

comptroller's revenue estimate—

budget execution authority—

How Legislators Make Decisions

back scratching and logrolling—

conflicting influences on legislators—

Growth of Legislative Staff

staff roles—

individual, institutional, and group staffing—

growth of staffing in Texas legislature—

Staffing for Technical Assistance, Specialized Information, and Political Assistance

Legislative Council—

Legislative Budget Board (LBB)—

committee staff—

2003, Speaker Craddick abolishes House Bill Analysis Office, returns to committee staff members job of analyzing bills—

typical legislative staff for House and Senate and their duties—

constituent services—

Relations With Lobbyists

open government measures—

2005, number of lobbyists registered with Texas Ethics Commission—

lobbyists role—

lobbyists as information source—

goals of lobbyists—

The Ethics of Lobbying

Frank Sharp—

Brilab—

Bo Pilgrim—

officeholder accounts—

lobbying activites and election and campaign activities—

symbiotic relationship of lobbyists-legislators in campaign finance—

questionable lobbying activity—

lobbyist and campaign finance—

<u>The Legislature and the Governor</u>

power in dealing with legislature—

emergency declaration—

governor and special sessions—

length and agenda of special sessions—

party loyalty—

veto—

Research Ideas and Possible Paper Topics

1) Select a bill and track its progress through the legislature. Explain why the bill was successful or unsuccessful. (Information regarding past and current bills can be accessed at the Senate's and the House of Representative's Web sites. For further information on these websites, see the websites section for this chapter.)

2) Although Anglos have dominated the membership of the Texas legislature, the legislature has become more ethnically and racially diverse and the trend is predicted to continue. Do you think this change in the demographics of the legislature's membership will affect the type of legislation produced by the legislature, especially around matters concerning minorities?

3) If you wanted to be elected Speaker of the House in the next legislative session, how would you run your "speaker's race"?

4) Examine the role of the lieutenant governor of Texas as president of the Texas Senate. Compare his powers as president of the Senate to the powers of the vice president of the United States as president of the U.S. Senate. Why are the lieutenant governor's powers over the Texas Senate so significantly greater than those of the vice president's over the U.S. Senate?

5) Examine the role of campaign finance as an influence over the decision-making process of Texas legislators. Why and how are lobbyists so powerful and influential over the legislative process in Texas that they are called often the "fourth branch" of Texas government? Who are some of the most significant lobbyists in Austin? Are they former members of the legislature or former key staff members?

Web sites

The Texas House of Representatives maintains a Web site that provides information about bills, committees, members, and more.
www.house.state.tx.us

The Texas Senate maintains a Web site that provides information about bills, committees, members, and more.
www.senate.state.tx.us

Texas Legislature Online is a Web site that provides users with legislative information and resources as well as links to the Web sites of agencies associated with the Texas legislature, such as the Texas Legislative Council and the Legislative Budget Board.
www.capitol.state.tx.us

Texas Legislative Council provides the Texas legislature and legislative agencies with bill drafting and research services. They also provide Texas's state agencies with information.

www.tlc.state.tx.us

Texas Legislative Reference Library provides research and reference assistance to the Texas legislature, other state agencies, and the public.

www.lrl.state.tx.us/library/about.html

A clip from the 1996 documentary "Vote for Me" shows how votes are won inside the Texas legislature by lobbyists. The four minute video clip introduces views to Texas lobbyists, many of them former Texas legislators who can use their political connections to influence and *practically write* bills for legislators. However, the lobbyists are paid a lot, a lot more than the legislators. Perhaps that is why many legislators become lobbyists after retiring or being defeated. The video clip is hosted on the Web site **Best Practices in Journalism** and is worth 8.48 minutes of your time to see how the Texas legislature *really* works.

http://www.bp2k.org

The **Texas Ethics Commission** hosts a searchable data base of lobbyists registered to work to influence the Texas legislature.

http://www.ethics.state.tx.us/dfs/loblists.htm

The **Texas Ethics Commission** also hosts a page on its Web site with information on lobbying in Texas and Texas law regarding lobbying.

http://www.ethics.state.tx.us/guides/LOBBY%20guide.htm

Texans for Public Justice has prepared a report entitled "Austin's Oldest Profession: Texas' Top Lobby Clients & Those Who Service Them," a scathing examination on the tremendous influence big-money lobbyists have over the Texas legislature.

http://www.tpj.org/reports/lobby02/index.html

Practice Tests

MULTIPLE CHOICE QUESTIONS

1) The Texas legislature consists of a
   a. 150-member House of Representatives and a 31-member Senate.
   b. 31-member House of Representatives and a 150-member Senate.
   c. 435-member House of Representatives and a 100-member Senate.
   d. a unicameral body with 181 members.

2) Which of the following is true concerning term limits for Texas legislatures?
   a. All legislators are subject to term limits.
   b. Only state senators are subject to term limits.
   c. Only state representatives are subject to term limits.
   d. No legislator is subject to term limits.

3) Historically, most legislators have been
   a. Anglo and Hispanic males.
   b. Anglo males and females.
   c. Hispanic males.
   d. Anglo males.

4) A _____ is formed if the Senate and the House of Representatives pass different versions of the same bill.
   a. standing committee
   b. interim committee
   c. special committee
   d. conference committee

5) An enrolled bill is a bill that has been
   a. rejected by the governor.
   b. approved by the Senate and the House of Representatives.
   c. rejected by the Senate and the House of Representatives.
   d. approved by the House of Representatives, but rejected by the Senate.

6) What must the Texas legislature consider in the budgetary process?
   a. a constitutional balanced budget requirement
   b. the proposed budget from the Legislative Budget Board
   c. constitutional spending limits
   d. All of the above.

7) Budget execution authority may be exercised during a(n)
   a. special session.
   b. regular session.
   c. biennial session.
   d. interim.

8) Which of the following is a joint legislative committee that provides legal advice, bill drafting, program evaluation and other services to members of the Texas legislature?
   a. Legislative Budget Board (LBB)
   b. Calendars Committee
   c. Legislative Council
   c. Office of the Lieutenant Governor

9) Which of the following is true regarding relations between lobbyists and Texas legislators?
   a.   lobbyists provide information that legislators need to evaluate
   b.   lobbyists are power players in the legislative process
   c.   lobbyists are heavily involved in raising and contributing money to legislators for campaigning
   d.   All of the above.

10) The Texas governor may influence the legislature through which of the following methods?
   a.   calling a special session
   b.   exercising the veto power
   c.   making an emergency declaration for their bills
   d.   All of the above.

TRUE/FALSE QUESTIONS

1) The length of term for a Texas Senator is six-years and for a Texas House member is two-years.

2) The Lieutenant Governor, who is the constitutional president of the Texas Senate, is a member of the Senate with full voting privileges.

3) A quorum is the minimum number of votes a bill needs to pass the Senate.

4) The Legislative Budget Board and the Governor's Budget Office prepare separate budget proposals.

5) The governor determines the agenda of a special session.

COMPARE AND CONTRAST

Rules in the House of Representatives and the Senate

Leaders in the House of Representatives and the Senate

A joint resolution, a simple resolution, and a concurrent resolution

First reading, second reading, and third reading

Special session and regular session

ESSAY AND SHORT ANSWER QUESTIONS

1) Discuss changes in the demographic profile of the legislature in the past 30 years.

2) Explain how term limitations and single member districts affect legislative members' elections.

3) Briefly identify the different types of legislative committees and their functions.

4) How does the Senate 2/3rds rule work to protect minority rights in the Senate?

5) Why are special sessions necessary, and what powers does the governor have over special sessions?

ANSWERS TO STUDY QUESTIONS

Multiple Choice Answers

1) a
2) d
3) d
4) d
5) b
6) d
7) d
8) c
9) d
10) d

True/False Answers

1) F
2) F
3) F
4) T
5) T

CHAPTER 24
THE GOVERNOR AND BUREACURACY AND TEXAS

Chapter Goals and Learning Objectives

When George W. Bush campaigned for the presidency in 2000, he often touted his record of executive leadership as Governor of Texas, laying claim to improving education, cutting taxes, and increasing important state services. To put it charitably, he was stretching the truth. Of course, politicians on the stump are want to stretch facts egregiously if not caught, and few caught Mr. Bush's big ones. He got away with the exaggerations because few folks understand that Texas's governor is not a true chief executive, responsible for managing the ship of state, but is instead, just one among many in the Texas plural executive model. And his actual powers over the legislature are weak as well. Too bad for Al Gore back in 2000 that he had not studied Texas government as you are now doing.

This chapter examines Texas's plural executive form of government. The strong executive or single-executive model exists on the federal level, while the Texas Constitution of 1876 constructs a plural or weak executive model. Power in the executive branch is divided among elected officials, appointed officials, and more than 100 executive boards and commissions. Texans, angered by the iron hand of the Republican Reconstruction administration of E.J. Davis, took the Texas governorship and placed it under the mallet of the Texas Constitution of 1876, smashing it as one might smash a ripe tomato, spreading its power about as far as fruit of the tomato would splatter.

While the Texas governorship is not without power and certainly not without prestige, it is, nevertheless one of the weakest governorships in the nation. Yet, candidates spend millions every four years to win the office. This chapter will examine why, and what the governor really can do, despite what the candidates are willing to tell you.

This chapter is designed to introduce you to the executive branch of Texas government. The main topic headings for this chapter are:

- The Development of the Executive in Texas
- The Constitutional Roles of the Governor
- The Development of Gubernatorial Power
- The Governor as Policy Maker and Political Leader
- The Plural Executive in Texas
- Modern Texas Bureaucracy
- Making Agencies Accountable

In each section, there are certain facts and ideas that you should strive to understand. Many are in boldface type and appear in both the narrative and in the glossary at the end of the book. Other ideas, dates, facts, events, people, etc. are more difficult to pull from the narrative. (Keep in mind that studying for objective tests is different than studying for essay tests. See the Study Guide section on test taking for hints on study skills.)

In general, after you finish reading and studying this chapter, you should understand the following:

- how the Texas governorship and division of executive authority developed
- the constitutional roles of the governor, particularly those of chief of state, chief executive, and commander in chief
- the development of gubernatorial power, the powers of the Texas governor in political roles, and the Texas governor's powers compared to the powers of other states' governors
- the role of governor of policy maker and political leader, and how Texas governors achieve policy goals through use of political and personal skills
- the plural executive, the elected officials of the plural executive, and their duties
- the structure of the modern Texas bureaucracy, its organization, and operations
- how state agencies are held accountable by the legislature and the governor

---

Chapter Outline and Key Points

In this section, you are provided with a basic outline of the chapter and key concepts and terms you should know. Use this outline to develop a complete study guide for the chapter. Use the space provided in this workbook to write notes from your reading, defining the terms and explaining the concepts listed below. You may wish to rewrite the material in your notebook or computer. However you work up this outline, the effort and information will help you study and remember the material in preparation for your tests, assignments, and papers.

plural executive—

The Development of the Executive in Texas

the emerging political systems of the United States and Mexico—

Governador de Tejas—

the governor and executive council of Coahuila y Tejas after the Mexican Revolution—

the governors of the early British and American colonies—

From President of the Lone Star Republic to Governor of Texas

Cabinet—

chief executive of the Republic of Texas—

Sam Houston—

governor after Texas joined the United States—

the governor under successive Texas constitutions—

effects of Constitution of 1876 on governor—

how many governors of Texas under this constitution?—

Texas Governors, 1876-2007 (Table 24.1)—

Terms of Office

Length and Number of Terms

established as two-year term in 1876, then four-year effective in 1974—

no term limit—

service of various governors—

Rick Perry's record—

Salary

set in constitution—

amended in 1954—

legislature sets governor's salary—

2007 salary—

Impeachment

Jim Ferguson—

Miriam Ferguson—

Succession

constitution provides for succession—

1999 constitutional amendment—

five lieutenant governors succeeded to governorship—

The Constitutional Roles of the Governor

chief of state—

chief executive officer—

commander in chief—

chief budget officer—

largely ceremonial powers of governor—

clemency—

Board of Pardons and Paroles—

governor's message to the legislature—

treat of veto—

The Development of Gubernatorial Power

Characteristics of Gubernatorial Power

scale to measure the power of governors—

four variables on the scale—

where strong governors are found in U.S.—

Restriction of Governor's Power

distrust of government and governors in the eighteenth and nineteenth centuries—

Jacksonian era—

reaction to Reconstruction—

E.J. Davis—

anti-administration legislature and new constitution—

desire to punish Davis and constrain future governors—

Comparing the Texas Governor with Other Governors

cabinet system—

plural executive in Texas—

Texas tied for the weakest state governors—

Powers of the Texas Governor Compared to Other Governors (Table 24.2)—

limited strengthening of Texas governor—

personal power of governors—

Texas in Comparison: Governors and the Executive Branch—

Should the Governor Have a Cabinet?—

The Governor's Power to Appoint Executive Officials

gubernatorial appointments—

appointment of agency heads—

State Agency Heads Appointed by the Governor (Table 24.3)—

appointments to boards, commissions and advisory panels—

Texas Senate approval of governor's appointments—

senatorial courtesy—

Bill Clements and lame-duck appointments—

constitutional amendment regarding lame-duck appointments—

overrepresentation—

under-representation—

governor appoints contributors and political allies—

Gender, Race and Money in Gubernatorial Appointment—

The Power of Staff and Budget

broad responsibility of governor's staff—

nineteenth-century governor's staff—

growth of Texas executive branch and governor's staff—

Office of the Governor—

budget for staff, housing, and other activities—

The Governor as Policy Maker and Political Leader

wielding political power—

"Chief Persuader of Texas"—

ideology and governors—

Public Opinion Leadership

media relations efforts—

news conferences—

Relationship with the Legislature

various tools used by the governor—

state of the state message—

working with the leadership in the legislature—

emergency proclamations—

special sessions of the legislature—

veto power—

pocket veto—

threat of veto—

override of veto—

"Father's Day Massacre"—

last ten days of the session—

line-item veto—

major appropriations bills passed at end of session—

riders—

Executive Orders

Texas governor uses executive orders for two purposes:

1)

2)

modern governors and executive orders—

Rick Perry's Executive Order RP-47—

The Plural Executive in Texas

many Texas state executive agency heads elected directly by the people of Texas—

other states—

Attorney General

attorney general—

chief civil council to state government—

little authority in criminal law—

Deceptive Trade Practices Act—

Hopwood v. *Texas* (5th Cir. 1996)—

advisory opinions—

Attorney General's Opinions—

Jim Mattox—

Dan Morales—

John Cornyn—

Greg Abbott—

Comptroller of Public Accounts

comptroller—

chief tax collector for Texas—

subsumed Texas Treasure's duties in 1996—

revenue-forecasting function—

Bullock's Raiders—

John Sharp—

Carole Keeton Strayhorn—

Susan Combs—

Land Commissioner

land commissioner—

oil leases and revenue—

fund for schools and universities—

Veterans Land Program—

Bob Armstrong—

Garry Mauro—

David Dewhurst—

Jerry Patterson—

Agriculture Commissioner

agriculture commissioner—

created by legislature—

Texas Department of Agriculture—

weights and measures—

pest-control regulations—

Jim Hightower—

Rick Perry—

Susan Combs—

Railroad Commissioners

three elected railroad commissioners—

staggered terms—

Texas Railroad Commission—

history of railroad commission—

oil and gas industry regulation—

regulation of trucking and mining—

captive of the industry—

State Board of Education

State Board of Education (SBOE)—

state education policy regulated by 15-member board—

Texas Education Agency—

religious conservatives and the State Board of Education—

Modern Texas Bureaucracy

implementation and execution—

legislatures make policy, bureaucracies implement it—

rule making—

regulation, and provision of services and products—

Administrative Procedures Act—

two basic patterns of how Texas executive agencies are organized—

Texas State Agencies Organizational Leadership (Figure 24.1)—

Top 15 State Agencies (Table 24.4)—

Secretary of State

Texas secretary of state—

keeper of state records—

Texas Register—

chief elections officer—

secretaries of state who have become governor—

Myra McDaniel—

Ron Kirk—

Tony Garza—

Alberto Gonzales—

Henry Cuellar—

Gwen Shea—

Geoffrey Connor—

Roger Williams—

Public Utility Commission

PUC—

quasi-judicial—

1995 changes to PUC—

1997 changes to PUC—

duties of PUC—

ERCOT—

Texas Commission on Environmental Quality

TNRCC—

TCEQ—

policy roles—

grandfathered status of polluters—

legislature reduction of TCEQ authority—

1995 "property rights" law—

agency must now consider environment impacts but cumulative impacts—

Insurance Commissioner

State Board of Insurance—

insurance commission—

Department of Insurance—

HMO regulation passed in 1995—

2003, insurance commissioner authorized to force insurance companies to lower homeowner's policy rates and insurance companies fought in court—

Commissioner of Health and Human Services

commissioner—

Health and Human Services Commission—

four departments of HHSC—

Public Counsels

captured agencies—

public counsels—

Boards and Commissions

boards and commissions system of government—

1999 constitutional amendment regarding boards—

Board of Criminal Justice—

six years, staggered—

governor may appoint but cannot independently remove appointments—

<u>**Making Agencies Accountable**</u>

legislatures may delegate authority—

oversight duty of legislature—

The Sunset Process

sunset law—

Texas Sunset Act—

good government—

Staff Size and Pay

growth of state and local governments—

Republican attempts to cut state workforce—

full-time equivalent workers—

number of Texas state workers in 2004—

pay scales—

top and bottom of pay scale—

Regulating the Revolving Door

revolving door—

regulators turned lobbyists—

Regulating the Relationship Between Agencies and Private Interests

executive agencies in policy-making roles—

final stage—

Texas Residential Construction Commission: Neutral Arbiter or Builder Protection Agency?—

iron triangle in Texas—

Research Ideas and Possible Paper Topics

1) Several of the constitutional revision efforts addressed in chapter 21 involved reforms aimed at the executive branch. How would you reform the Texas executive branch and why?

2) The first Sunset Commission strongly supported the idea of good government. Select two agencies and evaluate their performance according to the standards outlined by the first Sunset Commission.

3) Compare Governor Bill Clements and Governor Mark White in terms of their ability to exercise public-opinion leadership. Which governor do you think was more successful in his use of this power and why? How do they both compare to the effectiveness of Governor (now president) George W. Bush?

4) Article 4, section 9, of the Texas Constitution requires the governor to deliver governor's messages to the legislature. The messages emphasize policy goals, budget priorities, and more. Write the speech that you would deliver to the legislature if you were governor.

5) There are several elected offices in the executive branch. Select one of the offices (except that of governor) and explain why you would want to be elected to that office and what you would do if you were elected.

Web sites

The Web site of the **Texas Governor** offers users information about the governor's legislative priorities and information about divisions in the executive branch.
   www.governor.state.tx.us

The Web site for the office of **Lieutenant Governor David Dewhurst**.
   http://www.ltgov.state.tx.us

The Texas Library and Archives Commission Web site offers users a comprehensive list of links to Web sites for Texas agencies and commissions.
   http://www2.tsl.state.tx.us/trail/agencies.jsp

Texas Legislature Online provides a gateway to the executive, legislative, and judicial state agencies.
   http://www.capitol.state.tx.us/

The Texas Attorney General's Office online.
   http://www.oag.state.tx.us

Window on State Government is the Web site for the Texas Comptroller of Public Accounts, Susan Combs, and features state budget projects and other significant information about the Texas budget.
   http://www.window.state.tx.us

The *Texas Register,* the bulletin of Texas administrative rule making, is published and maintained online by the Texas Secretary of State.
   http://www.sos.state.tx.us/texreg/index.shtml

Practice Tests

MULTIPLE CHOICE QUESTIONS

1) The length and number of terms for the governor are
   a. two years with a two-term limit.
   b. four years with a two-term limit.
   c. four years with no term limit.
   d. two years with a four-term limit.

2)   Which one of the following Texas governors succeeded to the governorship from the office of Lieutenant Governor?
   a.   Sam Houston
   b.   John Connally
   c.   Mark White
   d.   Rick Perry

3)   In reaction to the Reconstruction-era governorship of E.J. Davis, delegates to the Texas constitutional convention in 1875 adopted which of the following provisions for the new constitution regarding the office of governor?
   a.   many of the key state administrative officials would be elected directly by the people of Texas, just as the governor
   b.   the governor's salary would be reduced
   c.   the governor's appointment and removal power would be restricted
   d.   All of the above.

4)   The practice of senatorial courtesy is associated with
   a.   the governor's power to appoint executive officials.
   b.   the governor's power to control the flow of legislation in the Senate.
   c.   the Senate's power to appoint the lieutenant governor.
   d.   the legislature's power to approve executive judicial appointments.

5)   Appointments by Texas governors tend to overrepresent
   a.   Hispanic males.
   b.   Anglo males and females.
   c.   African Americans.
   d.   Anglos and males.

6)   Which of the following is not a power the governor can use to influence the Texas legislature?
   a.   calling a special session and controlling its agenda
   b.   making emergency proclamations
   c.   appointing a political ally as lieutenant governor to control the Senate on the governor's behalf
   d.   threaten a veto

7)   The most significant elected state officials are the attorney general,
   a.   the governor, and the speaker of the Texas House of Representatives.
   b.   the lieutenant governor, and the comptroller of public accounts.
   c.   the governor, and the lieutenant governor.
   d.   the governor, and the chief justice of the Texas Supreme Court.

8) Elections for _____ are on a staggered basis.
   a. agricultural commissioner
   b. railroad commissioners
   c. land commissioners
   d. insurance commissioners

9) The state official appointed by the governor to be the keeper of the state's records and the state's chief elections officer is the
   a. secretary of state.
   b. comptroller.
   c. attorney general.
   d. land commissioner.

10) Captured agencies in the state resulted in the need for
    a. sunset laws.
    b. more elected offices in the executive branch.
    c. public counsels.
    d. more elected offices in the bureaucracy.

TRUE/FALSE QUESTIONS

1) The governor of Texas is, in terms of constitutional and structural power, one of the weakest governorships in the nation.

2) The land commissioner is more significant in Texas than in most states because the state owns so much land.

3) As the title implies, the principal function of the Texas Railroad Commission is to regulate railroad operations within the State of Texas.

4) The Texas legislature may not delegate decision-making authority to executive agencies.

5) Sunset is a concept of establishing a date at which agencies will cease to exist unless the legislature renews them.

COMPARE AND CONTRAST

The powers of the Texas governor with that of other governors

Underrepresentation and overrepresentation in governors' appointees

The governor as policy maker and political leader

Land Commissioner, agricultural commissioner, and railroad commissioner

Public counsels and executive agencies

ESSAY AND SHORT ANSWERS

1) Why were Sunset laws needed and have the laws been successful?

2) Describe the role and authority of the land commissioner, and explain why the land commissioner is so important in the state of Texas.

3) Discuss how the length of term, number of terms, and salary for the governor has changed during the 1900s.

4) Explain how the governor uses his or her constitutional powers and nonconstitutional powers when working with the legislature.

5) Discuss patterns of overrepresentation and under-representation in governors' appointees.

ANSWERS TO STUDY QUESTIONS

Multiple Choice Answers

1) c
2) d
3) d
4) a
5) d
6) c
7) c
8) b
9) a
10) c

True/False Answers

1) T
2) T
3) F
4) F
5) T

CHAPTER 25
THE TEXAS JUDICIARY

Chapter Goals and Learning Objectives

You may never meet the governor. You may never shake hands with the Texas attorney general. You might one day meet your state senator or representative. But it is probable, in fact, down right likely, that one day you will meet a state judge in a Texas courtroom. Maybe for a traffic ticket dismissal. Possibly for a child custody hearing or a divorce proceeding or a will contest. You could end up as a witness in a civil trial or sit on a jury in a capital murder trial. But it is likely that you will one day be in a Texas court. And if you watch local television news, you will far more often be exposed to the trials of murderers, robbers, and frauds in state courts (or even the will contests of former *Playboy* centerfolds, such as Anna Nicole Smith in a Harris County Court) covered by local reporters where you will hear about the trials and tribulations of your governor and state legislators.

The judicial is that branch of government that interprets the law and adjudicates disputes under the law between individuals and the community (the criminal law) and between private individuals or groups (the civil law). The Texas judicial system is divided into civil and criminal approaches to the law. It is also divided into trial and appellate courts. It is a complex and fascinating system for it reflects the passions and drives of human beings in conflict. Rather than take your disputes to the streets, you can take them to court where the weapons are facts in evidence as opposed to fists, guns, or knives.

This chapter is designed to introduce you to the legal system in the State of Texas. The main topic headings for this chapter are:

- The Development of the Texas Judiciary
- The Structure of the Texas Judiciary
- Judges and Judicial Selection
- Criticisms of the Texas Judicial Branch
- The Judicial Process in Texas

In each section, there are certain facts and ideas that you should strive to understand. Many are in boldface type and appear in both the narrative and in the glossary at the end of the book. Other ideas, dates, facts, events, people, etc. are more difficult to pull from the narrative. (Keep in mind that studying for objective tests is different than studying for essay tests. See the Study Guide section on test taking for hints on study skills.)

In general, after you finish reading and studying this chapter, you should understand the following:

- the development of the Texas judiciary, its structure and operation since the early 1800s
- the structure of the judiciary in modern Texas, including the various types of courts and their jurisdictions
- judges and judicial selection in Texas—how judges settle disputes in Texas and how they are chosen
- criticisms of the Texas judiciary, including persistent problems that affect the fairness and impartially of judges in Texas
- the judicial process in Texas and how criminal and civil cases are handled

---

Chapter Outline and Key Points

In this section, you are provided with a basic outline of the chapter and key concepts and terms you should know. Use this outline to develop a complete study guide for the chapter. Use the space provided in this workbook to write notes from your reading, defining the terms and explaining the concepts listed below. You may wish to rewrite the material in your notebook or computer. However you work up this outline, the effort and information will help you study and remember the material in preparation for your tests, assignments, and papers.

how the judicial branch differs from the other two branches of Texas government:

1)

2)

The Development of the Texas Judiciary

roots in English tradition with some features of Spanish law—

the judicial structure established in the 1836 Texas Constitution—

1891 constitutional amendment allowing an intermediate courts of appeal level in Texas—

other constitutional changes—

complicated and confusing nature of Texas judiciary—

The Structure of the Judiciary

The Court Structure of Texas (Figure 25.1)—

Local Trial Courts

municipal courts—

municipal court jurisdiction—

justice of the peace courts—

J.P. courts' jurisdiction—

County Courts

constitutional county courts—

jurisdiction of constitutional county court—

number of constitutional county courts in Texas—

probate cases—

trial *de novo*—

county courts at law (statutory county courts)—

jurisdiction of statutory county courts—

probate courts—

civil jurisdiction of county courts at law—

criminal jurisdiction of county courts at law—

bewildering array of county courts at law—

DWI in Texas—

District Courts

district courts—

civil jurisdiction—

felony criminal jurisdiction—

largest category of civil cases—

Intermediate Courts of Appeal

fourteen Texas Courts of Appeal—

1st and 14th Courts of Appeals—

cases usually heard by panel of how many judges?—

en banc—

jurisdiction of Texas Courts of Appeal—

The Supreme Courts

Texas Supreme Court—

Texas Court of Criminal Appeals—

jurisdiction of the two courts—

courts of last resort—

writ of *certiorari*—

how the two courts hear cases—

petition for review—

allowing lower court ruling to stand—

application for discretionary review—

per curiam—

administrative duties of Texas Supreme Court—

Judges and Judicial Selection

all but municipal judges are selected by partisan elections—

terms of office for various judges—

Judicial Qualifications and Personal Characteristics

judicial qualifications (Table 25.1)—

personal characteristics (Table 25.1)—

municipal judge—

justice of the peace—

constitutional county judges—

statutory county court judge—

district court judge—

all appellate judges—

Judicial Selection

partisan election process—

municipal judge selection—

vacancies from death or resignation filled by gubernatorial appointment—

Should Texas Elect Its Judges?—

Deceptive Trade Practices-Consumer Protection Act

plaintiffs' lawyers—

defense lawyers—

Texas Trial Lawyers Association—

State Commission on Judicial Conduct—

"Is Justice for Sale" on *60 Minutes* in 1986—

Texas Civil Justice League—

judicial campaign finance excesses—

business interest see opportunity—

costs of judicial elections rise in 1990s—

Republicans replace Democrats on Texas Supreme Court—

in Republican-controlled Texas Supreme Court, defendants overwhelmingly win over plaintiffs—

former Texas Chief Justice Thomas Phillips—

perceived effect on campaign contributions on judges decisions—

Stoking the Fires for Judicial Campaign Finance Reform—

Criticisms of the Texas Judicial Branch

Reforming the Court Structure

mixed and overlapping jurisdiction—

Texas Chief Justice's Task Force on Judicial Reform—

Proposal for a Unified, Simplified Texas Judiciary (Figure. 25.2)—

Reforming Judicial Selection

arguments for and against judicial elections—

1996 Texas Supreme Court task forces—

merit selection—

legislative efforts to change Texas judicial selection process—

The Battle Over Methods of Judicial Selection—

Reforming Campaign Finance

Texas Judicial Campaign Fairness Act of 1995—

limits on campaign contributions to judicial candidates—

loopholes in the act—

Texas Ethics Commission disclosure requirements—

no requirement for a judge to recuse herself in a case involving a large contributor to her campaign—

Increasing Minority Representation on the Bench

reasons why Hispanics and African Americans have never been represented on Texas courts in proportion to their percentages of the population—

selection of district court judges in countywide elections challenged by minorities as violating U.S. Voting Rights Act—

straight-ticket Republican voting in judicial elections has virtually eliminated minority judges—

2006 judicial elections—

The Judicial Process in Texas

The Criminal Justice Process

The Texas System of Graded Penalties (Table 25.2)—

Arrest and Searches

arrest and search warrants—

probable cause—

arrest without warrant based on what?—

warrantless searches—

consent—

Booking

booking—

station house bail—

Magistrate Appearance

examining trial—

Grand Jury Indictment

grand jury review (only for felonies)—

grand jury selection—

grand jury process—

true bill—

no bill—

indictment—

Arraignment

arraignment—

court appoints council for indigents (only 10 of 254 counties in Texas have a public defender program)—

plea is taken—

victim's impact statement—

Pretrial Motions

motion for jury or bench trial, continuance, competence, venue change, etc.—

Jury Selection

right to jury trial—

venire—

voir dire—

peremptory challenges—

12 jurors for felony; six for misdemeanor—

jury verdicts—guilty or not guilty—must be unanimous (in criminal trial)—

Trial

    guilt determination phase and punishment phase—

    seven stages in guilt determination phase:

        1)

        2)

        3)

        4)

        5)

        6)

        7)

    mistrial—

    sentencing stage—

    capital murder cases—

    Crime, Courts and Judges—

    Defending Actual Innocence—

Appeals

    death penalty verdicts automatically appealed directed by Texas Court of Criminal Appeals—

    appeals court reviews for reversible error—

    discretionary review—

The Civil Justice Process

Pretrial Procedures

    petition by plaintiff—

    remedy sought—

answer by defendant—

jury trial or bench trial—

Trial

steps in a civil trial—

charge to the jury—

district court, 10 of 12 jurors must agree—

in county court and justice of the peace court, five of six jurors must agree—

judge issues judgment—

Appeals

record from trial court and other steps—

court of appeals and possibly Texas Supreme Court—

Research Ideas and Possible Paper Topics

1) Judicial candidates must file disclosure reports with the Texas Ethics Commission. Select the reports of a judicial candidate who successfully ran for office. Examine the rulings the candidate made once he or she became a judge. On the basis of your research, do you think judges' rulings are affected by campaign contributions? Be sure to do research on the 1998 segment of *60 Minutes* on judicial campaigns and finances, which was a follow up to their 1987 investigative report on the subject.

2) The Texas Constitution guarantees defendants certain basic rights, such as the right to a fair and speedy trial and an individual's right to a court-appointed attorney if the individual is indigent. In your opinion, do the problems with the Texas courts (overlapping jurisdictions, lack of qualified court-appointed attorneys, etc.) affect a defendant's constitutional rights?

3) If you were appointed to a judicial reform commission, what reforms would you advocate and why? Talk to a local lawyer to see, from his or her experience in court, if he/she agrees with your assessments.

4) Examine the claims of "tort reform" advocates who wish to restrict citizens' rights to civil courts. What are the bases of their claims? Are the cases claimed to be

"frivolous" actually unjustified? What procedures do Texas judges use to eliminate frivolous lawsuits before they ever go to trial? What groups are behind the "tort reform" movement in Texas? Who is paying the bill for the movement, and who benefits?

5) The death penalty has come under criticism from many citizens and groups recently. Texas is one of the leaders in the nation in putting prisoners to death. What are some of the arguments against the death penalty and some of the arguments for? George W. Bush, when Governor of Texas, commuted the death sentence of only one individual on death row to a life sentence. Who was the inmate, and why did Bush do this?

Web sites

Texas Judiciary Online is a state judicial system Web site that offers information on a variety of topics: the structure of the judiciary, judicial agencies and groups, judicial records, resource materials, and much more.

www.courts.state.tx.us

The **Texas State Government** home page offers a list of links to the Web sites of various courts, state laws, court rulings, and much more.

www.state.tx.us/category.jsp?language=eng&categoryId=8

The **Texas Supreme Court** home pages provide attorneys and the public with information about Justices, opinions and orders, and information about cases before the court.

www.supreme.courts.state.tx.us

The **Texas Court of Criminal Appeals** maintains a Web site that provides information regarding opinions and rules of procedure and practice for attorneys and court reporters.

www.cca.courts.state.tx.us

The **State Bar of Texas** is an administrative agency of the judicial branch in Texas. Every licensed attorney is a member of the State Bar, which provides a wide array of services to its members and the public.

www.texasbar.com

The **Texas Trial Lawyers Association** is the professional organization for civil trial lawyers in Texas and works to keep the civil courts open to citizens in the face of the "tort reform" onslaught by business and corporate interests.

www.ttla.com

The **Center for Economic Justice** is a nonprofit organization that works to increase the availability, affordability, and accessibility of insurance, credit, utilities, and other economic goods and services for low-income and minority consumers. Its Web site includes a page debunking the arguments of "tort reform" advocates.

www.cej-online.org/tortrefo.php

Texans for Lawsuit Reform is an organization created and funded by big business and corporate interests promoting the tort reform agenda in Texas.

www.tortreform.com

Texas Watch is a nonpartisan advocacy organization working to improve consumer and insurance protections for Texas families. This consumer watchdog group works in opposition to tort reform activities backed by big insurance and corporate interests in Texas.

http://www.texaswatch.org/index.html

The **Texas Criminal Defense Lawyers' Association** is the professional organization for criminal defense lawyers. Its Web site provides a great deal of information about the criminal justice system in Texas and governmental threats to civil liberties.

www.tcdla.com

The **Texas District and County Attorneys Association** a nonprofit organization for Texas prosecutors and attorneys providing government representation and other services and information for district and county attorneys offices across the state.

www.tdcaa.com

Practice Tests

MULTIPLE CHOICE QUESTIONS

1) Why are there 254 constitutional county courts in the State of Texas?
   a. because under the law establishing these courts, the Texas Legislature set a cap of 254 statewide for the courts in 1929, a number which was reached just after the start of the Korean War
   b. because there are 254 counties in the State of Texas
   c. because the Texas Supreme Court, acting as the chief administrative body of the Texas judicial system, authorized the creation of 254 of these courts, as authorized by the Texas Constitution
   d. because under the state constitution, counties are given, under their home-rule authority, the power to create a constitutional county court when needed and as of 2007, some 209 counties have created a total of 254 constitutional county courts throughout the state

2)   If you have to probate a will in Texas and the will is uncontested, to which
      court would you go?
      a.   a municipal court or justice of the peace court
      b.   a county court
      c.   a district court
      d.   any one of the 14 regional courts of appeals

3)   How many courts of last resort does Texas have?
      a.   zero
      b.   one
      c.   two
      d.   fourteen

4)   The Texas Supreme Court has appellate jurisdiction over
      a.   civil cases only.
      b.   civil and criminal cases.
      c.   civil cases and criminal cases only when the docket for the Texas Court of
            Criminal Appeals is overloaded.
      d.   civil cases and criminal cases involving fines of over $1,000,000.

5)   How many judges on the Court of Criminal Appeals must agree to review a case
      before it will be accepted for review?
      a.   six
      b.   five
      c.   four
      d.   all—a unanimous vote

6)   Except for municipal judges, Texas judges are
      a.   appointed by the governor and approved by the Senate.
      b.   appointed by the governor and approved by the legislature.
      c.   elected in partisan elections.
      d.   elected in nonpartisan elections.

7)   Faced with the cost of judicial campaigns and the effect on the judiciary's
      imputed fairness, the Texas legislature
      a.   enacted the Judicial Campaign Fairness Act of 1995.
      b.   barred judicial candidates from receiving campaign contributions.
      c.   required judges to run in nonpartisan elections under the merit system.
      d.   All of the above.

8)   In a criminal trial in state district court, in order to find a defendant guilty or not
      guilty, what type of jury verdict is required?
      a.   10 out of 12 in agreement
      b.   5 out of 6 in agreement
      c.   a simple majority
      d.   unanimous verdict

9) In the sentencing phase of a capital murder trial in Texas, the jury considers which of the following?
    a. whether the defendant is likely to commit further violent crimes and is a threat to society
    b. whether the defendant actually caused, intended to cause, or anticipated that a human life would be taken
    c. whether mitigating circumstances warrant a sentence of life imprisonment rather than death
    d. All of the above

10) In a civil trial in district court, what decision is required of the jury to find for the plaintiff or defendant?
    a. 10 out of 12 in agreement
    b. 5 out of 6 in agreement
    c. a simple majority
    d. unanimous vote for either the plaintiff or defendant

TRUE/FALSE QUESTIONS

1) Texas judiciary has its roots in both English tradition and Spanish law.

2) Municipal courts may have jurisdiction over all three classes of misdemeanors.

3) Courts of Appeal never hear testimony or seat juries.

4) A petition for review is a request for Court of Criminal Appeals review.

5) All district court judges in large urban counties are elected on an at-large, countywide partisan basis in Texas.

COMPARE AND CONTRAST

the Supreme Court and the Court of Criminal Appeals

justice of the peace courts and municipal courts

Texas's highest appellate courts and intermediate appellate courts

judicial qualifications and the selection process for municipal judges and justices of the peace

the criminal justice process and civil justice process

ESSAY AND SHORT ANSWER QUESTIONS

1) Why do supporters of judicial reform want to make district courts the state's only trial courts?

2) What are the differences between constitutional county courts and statutory county courts?

3) Should qualifications for municipal judges and justices of the peace be increased and rendered more consistent across courts?

4) How does a case move from a county court to the Supreme Court?

5) Address the arguments for and against Texas judges being selected according to merit.

ANSWERS TO STUDY QUESTIONS

Multiple Choice Answers

1) b
2) b
3) c
4) a
5) c
6) c
7) a
8) d
9) d
10) a

True/False Answers

1) T
2) F
3) T
4) F
5) T

CHAPTER 26
POLITICAL PARTIES, INTEREST GROUPS, ELECTIONS, AND CAMPAIGNS IN TEXAS

Chapter Goals and Learning Objectives

Political parties and interest groups link citizens to government; however, the goals of the two entities differ. Political parties seek to control government, and interest groups seek to influence government. Elections are the mechanism through which political parties gain control of government and campaigns bind together political parties, interest groups, candidates, and the public.

This chapter is designed to introduce you to political parties, campaigns, elections and interest groups in Texas. The main topic headings for this chapter are:

- The Development of Political Parties, Interest Groups, Elections, and Campaigns in Texas
- Political Parties in Texas
- Interest Groups in Texas
- Elections and Political Campaigns in Texas

In each section, there are certain facts and ideas that you should strive to understand. Many are in boldface type and appear in both the narrative and in the glossary at the end of the book. Other ideas, dates, facts, events, people, etc., are more difficult to pull from the narrative. (Keep in mind that studying for objective tests is different than studying for essay tests. See the Study Guide section on test taking for hints on study skills.)

In general, after you finish reading and studying this chapter, you should understand the following:

- the development of political parties, interest groups, elections, and campaigns in Texas, and how these institutions and processes developed and evolved
- political parties in Texas including party organization, parties in the electorate, and parties in government
- interest groups in Texas and how the various types work to influence public policy in the state
- elections and political campaigns in Texas including types of elections; electoral participation; campaigns and voting behavior; the influence of money, media, and marketing in campaigns; and factors influencing voter turnout and choice

In this section, you are provided with a basic outline of the chapter and key concepts and terms you should know. Use this outline to develop a complete study guide for the chapter. Use the space provided in this workbook to write notes from your reading, defining the terms and explaining the concepts listed below. You may wish to rewrite the material in your notebook or computer. However you work up this outline, the effort and information will help you study and remember the material in preparation for your tests, assignments, and papers.

> focus of interest groups—
>
> focus of political parties—
>
> what elections provide—
>
> what campaigns create—

The Development of Political Parties, Interest Groups, Elections, and Campaigns in Texas

> the slow development of political parties and interest groups in Texas—
>
> era of one-party Democratic dominance in Texas (1874-1986)—
>
> populist challenge to Democratic Party dominance—
>
> split that developed liberal and conservative factions in Democratic Party during its era of one-party dominance—
>
> the Grange and interest group development—
>
> preeminence of business interest groups—
>
> importance solely of Democratic primaries until early 1960s—

Political Parties in Texas

Party Organization

> Formal Organization
>
>> role of Texas state law—
>>
>> temporary party organization—

precinct convention—

county convention—

state senatorial district convention—

party platform—

principal purpose of county or senatorial district conventions—

state convention—

state convention in presidential election years—

delegate allocation to national convention by Republicans—

delegate allocation to national convention by Democrats—

permanent party organization—

precinct chairperson—

county chairperson—

county executive committee—

state executive committee—

state party chairperson—

The Republican and Democratic Party Platforms—

Party Organization in Texas (Figure 26.1)—

Functional Organization

real story of how organization functions and where decisions made—

Democratic Party Unity

liberal influence since 1976—

Ralph Yarborough—

459

Jim Mattox, Jim Hightower, Garry Mauro, Ann Richards—

conservative Democrats becoming Republicans—

Republican Party Unity

greater ideological cohesiveness—

intraparty conflicts—

percentage of conservatives, moderates, and liberals—

pragmatists or economic conservatives—

ideologues or social conservatives—

Christian Coalition—

Kay Bailey Hutchinson—

Susan Weddington and David Barton—

"partial birth abortion" ban—

2004 Republican platform—

Party Effectiveness: What's at Stake

two ways state party's performance measured—

Republican Party's advantage in party building—

party organization activities at local level—

difference between Republican and Democratic chairpersons—

organizational challenges for Republicans and Democrats—

Party in the Electorate

most important function for the party organization—

Texans don't register by political party—

opinion polls for party identification in Texas—

party identification—

Distribution of Party Attachments

change in party affiliation from 1952 to 1991 to 1999, and in 2006—

increase in independents—

significance of increase in independents—

Party Identification in Texas: Republican Rise and Democratic Decline (Figure 26.2)—

Party Realignment in Texas

party realignment in Texas—

evidence of "attenuated" or "secular" realignment—

young voters—

some Democrats go over the Republican Party—

new residents of Texas—

party identification important in determining vote choices—

Republicans won more counties—

Republican and Democratic Strength in Texas by County (1970s) (Figure 26.3)—

Republican and Democratic Strength in Texas by County (1990s) (Figure 26.4)—

party dealignment in Texas—

Contemporary Party Coalitions

contemporary party coalitions—

Republican coalitions—

Democratic coalitions—

The Party in Government

> party in government—

> the theory of party in government—

In the Executive Branch

> impediments to cooperation created by Texas Constitution—

> independent election of most important executive officers in Texas—

> little incentive to campaign together or coordinate campaigns among executive office candidates—

In the Legislative Branch—

> partisan considerations minimized—

> party caucuses—

> party leaders—

> party organization in House after 1989—

> Texas legislature continues to work under strong institutional leaders—

In the Judicial Branch

> partisan election of all but what type judge?—

> judicial elections usually conducted independently—

> role of party in appointment of judges when a vacancy occurs—

> difference in how Democrats and Republicans interpret the law and decide civil cases—

Interest Groups in Texas

Types of Interest Groups

> Business Groups and Trade Associations—

general purpose—

business interest groups—

trade associations—

examples of both—

Professional Associations

examples—

what they try to influence—

Labor Groups

where they have any strength in Texas—

examples—

Racial and Ethnic Groups

what they promote—

examples—

Public Interest Groups

what they advocate—

examples—

what public policies they seek—

Political Activities of Interest Groups

Lobbying

growth of registered lobbyists from 1987 to 2005—

lobbying definition—

lobbyists' pay—

what is required in lobbying registration in Texas—

limits on money used in lobbying—

two trends in late 1980s which characterized lobbyists—

hired guns—

greater ethnic and gender diversity among lobbyists—

principal job of lobbyists, according to lobbyists—

personal friendships with legislators—

many former public officials—

relying on information and integrity—

lobbying legislative staff—

technical information from lobbyists—

expert testimony—

top-down strategy—

lobbying agencies and departments—

grassroots lobbying—

activating members of interest group—

Astroturf lobbying—

The Effects of Limiting Medical Liability—

Electioneering

prices of access—

PACs in Texas—

preference for incumbents—

study of campaign to limit patients' right to sue, 1995-1996—

Top General Purpose PACs, 2004 (Table 26.1)—

Litigation

>new judicial federalism—

>purpose of litigation by interest groups—

Elections and Political Campaigns in Texas

Types of Elections

>ballot tends to be long—

>uniform dates for general and special elections—

>elections can also occur at other times—

>Primary Elections

>>which parties, by Texas law, must hold primaries?—

>>primary elections—

>>Terrell Election Law—

>>supposed closed, function like open—

>>must win primary by majority—

>>run-off elections—

>>participation low in primaries—

>>2006 participation in party primaries—

>>parties responsible for run administering primaries—

>Special Elections

>>special elections—

>>participation in—

>>bond elections—

>General Elections

general elections—

Tuesday after the first Monday in November of even-numbered years—

governor and other statewide official elected when?—

nonpresidential year elections—

win general elections by plurality—

general elections funded and administered by the state—

Texas secretary of state—

Local Elections

local elections—

municipal elections and special district elections are nonpartisan—

when held?—

Political Campaigns in Texas

ideally, what do campaigns do?—

the "three M's—

Money: The Mother's Milk of Politics

money in elections—

in 2002 what do Perry and Sanchez spend?—

importance and high cost of television—

individual and group contributions to campaigns—

few restriction in Texas—

"Bo" Pilgrim—

Ethics Commission—

no limit on what contributions in Texas?—

466

Media: Linking the Candidates and the Voters

    importance of TV in Texas campaigns—

    size of Texas and number of media markets—

    political consultants—

Marketing: Selling the Candidates

    transition from party-centered to candidate-centered campaigns—

    effect of candidates' dependence on media and commercial advertising techniques—

    benchmark poll—

    tracking polls—

    focus groups—

    campaign consultants role—

The Voters' Decisions

    two decisions potential voter faces—

    low voter turnout in Texas—

Voter Turnout

    cost of voting—

    legal requirements for voting in Texas—

    motor voting—

    early voting—

    effect of early voting and 2006 gubernatorial election—

    lower Texas voter turnout—

    electronic voting and controversy—

Are Electronic Voting Systems Better than Paper Ballots?—

benefits of voting—

selective benefits of voting—

connection to politics—

trends in nonpresidential year gubernatorial election voter turnout—

factors contributing to variation in Texas voter turnout—

changing composition of electorate and voter turnout—

voting in 1890s—

Texas turnout for presidential vote in 2004 presidential election—

The Vote Choice: Parties, Issues and Candidates

vote choice during entire nineteenth and first part of twentieth century—

psychological factors influencing vote choice:

1)

2)

3)

comparison of 1986 and 2002 gubernatorial elections—

Research Ideas and Possible Paper Topics

1)   Select two different types of interest groups operating in Texas and compare the type of activities in which they engage. How are the activities different and why are they different? Compare the Texas interest groups you selected to their national counterparts. What differences or similarities in organization and purpose do you note?

2)   Voter turnout in Texas is quite low. If you were a member of the legislature, what type of legislation would you support to increase voter turnout in Texas?

3)   In 2006, Republican candidates won every statewide election. What forces contributed to that sweeping victory?

4)   Media is as significant a factor in elections as anything in modern politics. What factors come into play with regard to media campaigns? What role does television play in statewide and local campaigns? Is radio useful to a candidate? What about newspapers and direct mail? Does the Internet play a role in Texas campaigns?

5)   What are some of the factors in the growth of the Republican Party in Texas over the past 30 years? What happened to the Democratic Party, once dominant in Texas, in terms of elected officials and voter identification? What can the Democratic Party in Texas do to regain parity with the Republicans?

Web sites

The Secretary of State's Elections Division Web site offers voter information, election returns and forms, election law information, and election reports.
www.sos.state.tx.us/elections/index.shtml

Texas Democratic Party maintains a Web site at
www.txdemocrats.org

The **Republican Party of Texas** maintains a Web site at
www.texasgop.org

The **Texas Libertarian Party** maintains a Web site at
www.tx.lp.org

The **Reform Party of Texas** maintains a Web site at
http://www.texasreformparty.org

Based in Houston, the **Texas Politics Resource Page** is hosted by Texas political consultant George Strong, and presents facts and gossip about Texas elections and politics. An outstanding links page for current political candidates across the state. (Portions of the Web site are for paid subscribers.)
www.political.com

The **Texas Community College Teachers Association**, an interest group representing educators in Texas community colleges, provides its members with a guide on how to help the association lobby members of the Texas Legislature.
http://tccta.org/publications/TCCTA-Guide-04-05v4.pdf

The **Texas Ethics Commission** maintains an online list of registered lobbyists in Texas.
http://www.ethics.state.tx.us/dfs/loblists.htm

The **College of Liberal Arts at the University of Texas at Austin** maintains a Texas Politics Web site. This page features the cost of local television time space across Texas.
http://texaspolitics.laits.utexas.edu/html/vce/features/0701_01/slide2.html

Texans for Public Justice is a nonprofit organization working to research and reform campaign financing and lobbying practices in Texas.
http://www.tpj.org/index.jsp

Practice Tests

MULTIPLE CHOICE QUESTIONS

1) The temporary party organization consists of
   a. standing chairpersons and committees.
   b. conventions.
   c. permanent chairpersons.
   d. committees.

2) The principal purpose of a precinct convention is to
   a. select delegates to the party's county or state senatorial convention.
   b. increase voter turnout in local precinct elections.
   c. select delegates to the state convention and reform platform measures.
   d. elect state party chairpersons.

3) The permanent party organization consists of
   a. chairpersons and committees.
   b. precinct and county conventions.
   c. national conventions.
   d. delegates and committee members.

4) The most important function for the party organization is
   a. gaining the support of interest groups.
   b. winning elections.
   c. making sure conventions run smoothly.
   d. finding delegates for conventions.

5) Evidence for realignment in Texas is derived from the following indication(s):
   a. young voters are more likely to identify with the Republican Party than the Democratic Party.
   b. some Democrats are switching to the Republican Party.
   c. in 2002, Republican candidates won every statewide election.
   d. All of the above.

6) The party in government includes the party in the
   a. judicial branch.
   b. executive branch.
   c. legislative branch.
   d. All of the above.

7) Litigation was practiced extensively by _____ and _____ interest groups in the 1950s and 1960s.
   a. professional, labor
   b. business, professional
   c. civil rights, environmental
   d. professional, environmental

8) In order to win a primary in Texas, a candidate must win
   a. by a plurality.
   b. by a majority.
   c. by consensus of the party leaders.
   d. All of the above.

9) Special elections are held in Texas to
   a. fill vacancies in state legislative offices.
   b. approve local bond proposals.
   c. fill vacancies in U.S. congressional offices.
   d. All of the above.

10) The effect of the motor-voter-registration system has been to
   a. increase the voter turnout.
   b. increase the number of individuals registered to vote.
   c. increase the number of individuals registered to vote and increase the voter turnout.
   d. None of the above.

TRUE/FALSE QUESTIONS

1) In Texas, political parties and interest groups developed early and quickly.

2) Interest groups participate in lobbying, electioneering, and litigation.

3) Voter turnout is especially low in run-off primaries.

4) Some local elections generate high voter interest, but most do not.

5) The ultimate goal in a political campaign is exposing important public policy issues to debate, not winning.

COMPARE AND CONTRAST

interest groups and political parties

primary elections, special elections, and general elections

dealignment and realignment

permanent party organization and temporary party organization

party-in-the-electorate and party in the government

ESSAY AND SHORT ANSWER QUESTIONS

1) Do you think Texas has undergone a realignment or dealignment?

2) Explain the roots of intraparty conflict in the Republican Party.

3) Describe the different political activities performed by interest groups.

4) Describe the three types of elections.

5) How does money affect political campaigns in Texas?

ANSWERS TO STUDY QUESTIONS

Multiple Choice Answers

1) b
2) a
3) a
4) b
5) d
5) d
7) c
8) b
6) d
10) b

True/False Answers

1) F
2) T
3) T
4) T
5) F